The Shield of

PSALMIC PRAYER

Donald Sheehan at Giromeri Monastery, outside the town of Paramythia in Epirus, Greece, where his name-saint Dona-tos lived in the fourth century, and where the saint's relics now reside. Photo 2004: Benedict Sheehan/Miriam Warren. Used by permission.

The Shield of

PSALMIC
PRAYER

REFLECTIONS ON
Translating, Interpreting, and Praying
THE PSALTER

DONALD SHEEHAN

Compiled and Edited by Xenia Sheehan
Foreword by Sydney Lea

ANCIENT FAITH PUBLISHING   CHESTERTON, INDIANA

Published by:
  Ancient Faith Publishing
  A Division of Ancient Faith Ministries
  P.O. Box 748
  Chesterton, IN 46304

The Septuagint (LXX) psalms translations quoted in this volume were first published in *The Psalms of David, Translated from the Septuagint Greek by Donald Sheehan*, ed. Xenia Sheehan and Hierodeacon Herman Majkrzak (Eugene, OR: Wipf & Stock, 2013). Copyright © 2013 Carol (Xenia) Sheehan.

Quotations and citations from *The Ascetical Homilies of Saint Isaac the Syrian*: Copyright © Holy Transfiguration Monastery, Brookline, MA, used by permission. All rights reserved.

ISBN: 978-1-944967-68-0

Printed in the United States of America

Library of Congress Control Number: 2020937788

I dedicate this book to its author, my husband—God rest his soul!—who was, and in so many ways still is, my eyes, my heart, my very life. Our long marriage was certainly not perfect but it was entirely good, it went very deep, and it keeps on getting better as, through his words, I continue to see and understand, and to love. I am so grateful, Don, for all you gave to me, to your family, and to so many others. With this intimate sharing of your mind, your heart, and your profound love affair with Psalms—by the grace of the Lord whom you led me to know and love—may the gift go on giving! Memory eternal!

XENIA SHEEHAN, *editor*

We are always free to deny renewal. We can always refuse to move our current versions of unity—our fixed and arranged and composed lives—out into the shock of renewal. We can always cling to some version of verticality, refusing to risk it in the terrible disaster of actual history. Most of our "counsels of ungodliness," our scorn and twisting, lie in this refusal. Blessedness is risking the encounter, leaving the Egypt of our settled, enslaved lives, at every moment choosing to maintain as direct a contact as we can stand with the growling, the weeping, the thunderous shock. For this howling and thunder are our God and our history.

Psalmic meditation is direct contact with our God and our history, standing open before these charged and sacred words, these words that shock and growl and grieve.

DONALD SHEEHAN, *JOURNAL*, 1990, PSALM 1

CONTENTS

FOREWORD

The following essays were composed by a man I loved, and one I thought I knew well. Yet having read the following pages more than merely once, I feel I have come to know him at a level that even our most intimate conversations could scarcely have reached. If ever a writer laid bare his soul, Donald Sheehan does so here, and we are the better for prolonged exposure to that soul.

I begin thus in part because, whenever I spoke of Don to third parties—both men and women who knew him and those who did not during his too-brief lifetime—and when I recall him now for those who are curious about the legendary longtime director of the Robert Frost Place in Franconia, New Hampshire; when I do this, I always offer some version of a simple observation: "Don Sheehan was one of those rare individuals who, when he entered a room, made everyone in it a better person."

I scarcely mean to lapse into some New Age babble when I say that the man had an aura; you could feel the gentle energy of his being all but physically.

To know now that much of Don's extraordinary presence owed itself to his total and continuous immersion in the Psalter is both a revelation and not. I was fully aware of his devotion to the Psalms, and of course of his epic efforts at translating them anew; the revelation is that, without this posthumous collection of essays, I'd not have known how *profound* his commitment was.

Nor how ordinary. Indeed, that seemingly dismissive adjective is one of four he uses himself at a crucial early stage in these reflections. (The others are *actual*, *mysterious*, and *boundless*, but for the moment I refer the reader to the book at large for their implications.) There is a characteristically lyrical ring to the following passage, in which he hints at what ordinariness means by his lights:

> [P]raying Psalms is never a *drama*. There are no crashing cymbals; no drum rolls; no sobbing violins or shrieking brasses nor throaty cellos—all of that is banished away, set aside, forgotten utterly. It is the *plainest* of experiences; it is a cat washing herself in the sunlit window; it is doing the dishes late at night in a guest house; buttoning a shirt or tying a shoe, your mind miles away, and racing.

Such writing is, of course, gorgeous simply *qua* writing; and yet the reader who takes up this volume hoping for "poetic" evocation of life's daily flow will be disappointed. Or rather, the reader who seeks that *alone* will be.

Consider this passage from early in this volume:

> The pathway of psalmic prayer: the "letting-all-the-way-into-you" of the actual words of Psalms, so that every word touches every aspect (past, present, future) of your life. This is an actual, literal practice along salvation's pathway. Plainly, it is not the sole pathway; but it is a real one: a way (*hodos*) and a path (*tribos*) by which God makes Himself known to and teaches the one praying His holy Psalms (LXX Ps. 24:4: "Make known thy ways to me, O Lord, and teach me thy paths").

Such an utterance indicates the availability to our writer of experiences transcending most of our own. But lest we feel daunted, we can look at the very next paragraph:

> Carol and I were riding to an errand, talking about our currently deeply uncertain economic arrangements, and I asked her how she felt, and she said, "Tangled." I looked up at the hillside we were passing, and mid-October rain on the autumn trees now half or more winter-bare was a steady and cold rain; yet, nevertheless, it was a very beautiful hillside, the wet trees and dark earth and last yellow leaves giving—somehow—a strong sense of holy presence, of the God who always IS, a presence made more plain by the absence of prettiness and spectacle (that breathtaking riot of high-autumn color)—the very dreariness the strength of the beauty. And the hillside, the moment, the word "tangled," the disarray of our financial orders: all this seemed a psalm. That is, the way the hillside was, the way the beauty shone plainly in the bareness, is the way a psalm works and is in us.

The rhythms of this book, in short, involve a back-and-forth between the quotidian and the mystical, though not because the author's aims are desultory. Hardly. Indeed, my term *back-and-forth* feels instantly cumbersome, since it may very wrongly imply vacillation on the writer's part. What Sheehan truly means to indicate, I am certain, is that the psalmic presence is implicit *both* in the mysterious and in the seemingly banal. Or more accurately, like the poet he is at heart, Sheehan wants to indicate the *simultaneity* of both realms, to show that any distinction between them is an impoverished one indeed, though he makes that point without the least hint of arrogance.

Truth is (ask anyone who ever encountered the man even briefly), arrogance was utterly alien to Don Sheehan. His humility was more than genuine, even reaching at times to something like *humiliation*. And yet that condition is repeatedly presented in the pages as a starting point for the author's or anyone's spiritual journey. (I once heard Sheehan present a reading of Frost's "An Old Man's Winter Night" that relied on this premise. It was brilliant.)

~~~

In her heartfelt introduction, Don's widow refers to a journal entry of 2007, three years after his mother's death, the year of his brother's, and of the first diagnosis of his own progressive, terminal sickness. He asks,

> Will I ever have *life* again? . . . I don't know where all progress in Psalms has gone—but gone it has, completely gone. . . . This is where I start: my life is broken in the present; hence, my past swims up in its catastrophic vileness: my broken home of childhood claims me all over again. Way out? I don't know—but I *must* find it; and soon, soon, soon, before I lose all my present life in the swamps of a deathly past.

Elsewhere, Sheehan describes "the sword of depression" as "the single most devastating weapon the enemy possesses." It is "the despondency that cuts off prayer—and this cuts off our living connection to the Creator."

To read this was to recall a conversation he and I had, perhaps thirty years ago, in Don's Dartmouth office. On that gray winter day, I confessed that I was in that very same state, seemingly robbed of prayer as a shield and comfort. Though our respective Christian traditions were widely different, I was all but instantly rallied when, for the first time in my presence, he acknowledged his own lapses into depression—and announced his growing conviction that to be thus reduced was, yes, a place to start. In these reflections, he writes:

> That we must engage in spiritual (and *not* psychological) warfare means that we must meet the sword of depression with the shield of psalmic prayer: and must do so with such strength that the enemy's sword breaks against our shield.

He goes on to remember and approvingly to quote a passage from Orthodox Father Pavel Florensky, in which the priest describes a chilling nightmare and cites Psalm 129 (Ps. 130 in King James), *O Lord, hear my voice. . . .*

> My whole soul was in those words. Someone's hands gripped me, a drowning man, powerfully and threw me somewhere, far from the abyss. The jolt was sudden and powerful. Suddenly I found myself in my usual surroundings, my room. From mystical non-being I was thrown back into *ordinary, everyday life.* (Emphasis mine.)

And in a passing reference to Psalm 101 (102 AV), Don writes:

> The title's "poor man" is (say the Fathers) the one named most blessed by Christ in the Beatitudes (Mt 5:3): for such complete poverty of spirit signifies the complete absence of any arrogance before God the Father. In other words, the poor man of the psalm—like the guerilla warrior in the Davidic narratives—knows that strength is never his own but is *only* God's strength.

I said early on that in reading these essays, I came to know Donald Sheehan more profoundly than I think I or anyone could have known him via conversation, however conspiratorial. For these "reflections" are in fact *meditations*, and they deal with subjects that the great Wordsworth described as lying "too deep for tears." Yes, I knew that like me he could lapse into what might be described by medical people as clinical depression; no, I did not know how he understood "the shield of psalmic prayer."

How does that shield function? I cannot say. Even Sheehan's eloquence fell and still falls short of rendering the process exactly, because inexactitude is ineluctably a part of the human condition. Again like the poet he was and remains, and again by fusing mystic and quotidian in what I deem one of the most moving sectors of the book, the author leads us at least partway toward recognition. In quoting it, I come nearly full circle in this inadequate foreword:

> My immersion in Psalms has undoubtedly had decisive consequences in my life. But I have no real understanding—not even the merest *inkling*—of what these consequences might be.
>
> In other words, my experience of praying the Psalms is an experience of *loving*, and *being loved*. Hence, the experience is (and I use these four words with care): *actual*; *boundless*; *ordinary*; and *mysterious*.
>
> *Actual.* By this I mean that the reality of Christ's Personhood in the Psalms is, for me, neither a mental abstraction nor an emotional drama. Beyond any *idea* I might devise or any *feeling* I might undergo, Christ is *present* in the whole of Psalms in the same way that my wife is present in the whole of my life. And Christ's reality is so *fully* actual that I can say that, rather than experiencing Psalms by means of my marriage, I experience my marriage by means of the Psalms. In this sense, then, I use the word *boundless*.

There is no apt "ending" to my own reflections here. So I'll say only that I am boundlessly grateful that I knew the great Donald Sheehan; that I am equally grateful to his wife Carol/Xenia for the effort that went into redacting and preserving this collection. I spoke right off of how Don's presence exerted a positive spiritual effect on any company he kept. Thankfully, that presence lives on in this extraordinary book.

Sydney Lea
Newbury, Vermont
December 2019

ACKNOWLEDGMENTS

It is with great gratitude that I acknowledge a number of people who have helped me in producing this book. I stand in particular awe of the contributions made by two behind-the-scenes heroes: an old friend, John Taylor Carr, and a new one, Dr. John Wayne Coatney (now doctoring camels, teaching veterinarians and theology students, and raising a growing family in Ethiopia). Both of these inordinately busy men overcame demanding pressures at critical junctures in their own lives to help me over the daunting roadblock of deciphering the many handwritten Hebrew and Greek words, long-distance (by means of texted iPhone photos), converting them into a form and font I could enter into my digital document, and making consistent the transliterations that Don had written over a period of twenty years. In several cases, I have added their notes concerning various usages, tagged *JTC* or *JWC*. Occasionally, they offered corrections, which I have used. I know that Don, an energetic and persistent, even brilliant, student but not a pedigreed scholar of Greek or Hebrew, would have been very grateful for these thoughtful emendations of his errors. Thanks to you both!

I want also to acknowledge Jon Sweeney, who first set me on the course of organizing the book into themed chapters, which has given the wealth of journaled material I began with the exact shape it needed. I can't overstate my gratitude for the support and advice of my dear friend for over a quarter-century, Ann Brash, editor *par excellence,* who helped and supported me substantially at both ends of the project. I am grateful for the long friendship and support, to both Don and me, of Sydney Lea, who loved the book, read it twice, and wrote the beautiful Foreword to it; and of Baron Wormser, who contributed at my request the thoughtful and instructive paragraph in chapter 2 on the importance and nature of poetry, offering a perspective that I think is often ignored for lack of understanding in considerations of Psalms and their translation.

I am grateful also to our son Benedict Sheehan and daughter-in-law Maria for their contributions to the Epilogue; to Fr. John Konkle of Dormition Monastery, Don's godson Hieromonk Herman Majkrzak, Matthew Brown, and Arlyn Kantz for their help and advice at various points; to Dn. Justin Jackson for advice and some crucial last-minute research on linguistic matters; to the Holy Dormition Monastery of Rives Junction, Michigan, for a place to live and work in peace during the last year of the book's preparation (and for their patience with my delaying a project I had promised them I would do); to Katherine Hyde for her salutary recommendations and patience in regard to the final manuscript and willingness to put up with all my last-minute doubts, additions, and deletions; and to Stephen Ullstrom for stepping in to do the index. Finally, I again thank Mark Montague and Fr. Moses Hibbard for the foundation they provided for the glossary we together prepared for *The Grace of Incorruption*, numerous selections from which have turned out to be relevant here as well.

Xenia Sheehan

A LIFE IN PSALMS

Editor's Introduction

A life in Psalms, for me, includes this experience: the "non-tiring tiredness" I experienced in the months of translating nonstop the whole LXX Psalter. In those long hours of every long day, I was deeply tired—but, strangely, I was not at all tired: result: a kind of tiny-ness of spirit, a smallness of selfhood, that is, a poverty of spirit. Here is the key to a life, a whole life, in Psalms.

DONALD SHEEHAN

Don Sheehan devoted much of his life and work to what the great seventh-century Orthodox bishop, ascetic, and theologian Saint Isaac the Syrian called "noetic rays running between the lines."[1] In this book, a posthumous collection of his reflections on Psalms and psalmic prayer from his journals and teaching notes, you will find two quite different kinds of writing working in tandem: poetic and personal journaling by a man of faith, a scholar, a linguist, and, in the deepest sense, a teacher; alongside scholarly linguistic and poetic analysis by a man steeped in poetry who thought like a poet. It moves about freely within and between these ranges, changing in a moment from the sublime to a close examination of linguistic subtleties in two or three languages, and asking from the reader a commensurate effort of the heart's intelligence—the nous[2]—preferably in prayer.

Some of you will be challenged in these essays to think in a new way about *time*—that vast, highly specific (and not necessarily straightforward) pathway along which "history" unfolds. On one occasion he wrote of "cosmic time vs. abstract temporality," following Fr. Pavel Florensky.[3] Though Don admired and often studied those who followed intelligently a linear historical pathway, he was more often inclined to think of time in its aspect of being God's creature, made for us, in God's love for us, that we might move, though seldom straightforwardly, closer to Him. For Don its linearity was seldom the point, but rather an aspect, one avenue to the main point, which is God, and our God-becoming, without which history is an avenue to nowhere.

Following Saint Gregory of Nyssa, for instance, he believed that the order in which God forged the tools for the production of virtue in David's life is not the order in which the tools must be used on us, the readers; thus the sequence of psalms will differ from the historical sequence of the narratives. In chapter 3, he says, "we do not have the category of prophecy." In chapter 9, he writes of two dimensions of earthly time: "earthly time as seen from the divine perspective," in which illumined men "are gods" (Ps. 81:6); and that dimension of time "wherein such knowledge is entirely darkened and the earthly foundations disastrously shaken, with the result that a poisonous delusion is thereby produced: the delusion of self-glorification"— disastrous and delusional because, by making ourselves gods, "we enter into a history in which God no longer acts." In chapter 10 he speaks of "the deep structure of history as divine Presence," which he finds to be the subject of the center of the entire Psalter (in Psalm 77). And in chapter 12 he writes that "the pressures of historical actualities give concrete form to the statutes. For history (as *martyria*) is the dimension where death/resurrection occurs: the sole and full and salvific dimension." While the prophets and saints and certain poets may move about in the arena of divine Presence and fruitful divine/human interaction with greater freedom and ease than the rest of us—taking in more of the surrounding glory (and disaster) of the whole picture—on their journey toward the Holy, we are all called to take the way of the Cross, wherein the sacred and historical intersect and Love occurs, no matter how difficult we may find it.

Don frequently turns his attention (and ours) in this book toward God's *statutes*: the "divinely generative" and "foundational patterns of the created world, the patterns with which God first created and still sustains the entire creation. Therefore the statutes are the patterns that we cannot fully comprehend with our minds." They "contain (among other things) (1) linear human history; (2) angelic interventions in that linearity; and (3) the shaping hand of God Himself." This is what he asks us to seek and follow and understand in Psalms. He is always, with the psalmist, asking:

Make me comprehend the way of thy statutes,
I shall ponder thy wondrous works. (118:27)

What binds this book together is the author's own love of Psalms and his deep discernment, on many levels, of what they are saying to us and how they can act in—can even save—our lives; because, as he shows us so eloquently, the Lord is in them, always moving toward us, and moving us toward Him. A humble man, an intelligent lover and student of poems, neither prophet nor saint nor poet himself, Don, like so many before him, truly heard something—perhaps even a great deal—of what the Psalms are saying. By immersing himself in them, he became able in some measure to discern—often by the light offered by the great ones of the past—such things as the presence of Christ in the Hebrew Psalms, even Christ Himself noetically composing Psalm 118 on Holy Saturday, in His tomb, to open for us a pathway to resurrection that He had given us long before but had not yet opened.

A dear friend, once a student of Don's, recently recalled his "replying to someone who asked him how to know the truth, how to know the value of someone's essays. He said, in essence, that we cannot—that we must ask, *What if* this were true? That we should listen and read and live and go forward with what our heart, our *nous*, recognizes as true and good."

In sharing with you the personal insights and reflections of this excellent man—into which he invested so much of his time and intelligence—of course I feel some compunction. He never shared this writing as far as I know, most of it not even with me—though I think that was from a modest undervaluing of its worth. A great reviser in his lifetime, he is no longer present to censor an entry or correct his mistakes or develop an idea. But I believe he would not mind what I have done, and I invite you to take this journey with him in just such a *What if?* manner; for he finds his way in these pages to a great deal that is true and good.

Donald Sheehan was born a twin on April 2, 1940, in Kingston, New York. At a critical time in his troubled youth, he began reading poetry, which was to become his lodestar. Everywhere he went, even (hidden out of sight) through "the sustained fury of Army bootcamp," he carried with him the Untermeyer paperback anthology, *A Concise Treasury of Great Poems*, finding that "the nearly incomprehensible sonorities [of Milton, for instance] . . . held and focused me on things far beyond the painfulness of my life, on things whose vastness and stability and truth made what was little, false, and broken in my life lose its fierce grip on me." He wrote that he "understood almost none of it: not the poems, not my life. And so therefore I started to write poems; and they were about peace we cannot understand."

In college, he became aware of what he considered to be his "real work: to turn the full light of sympathetic intelligence into the depths of hope and terror and beauty that was—and is—true art." And it led him next to graduate study in English at the University of Wisconsin, Madison, from which, in 1969, he earned a Ph.D. with a dissertation on T. S. Eliot and Dante.

His first teaching position was at the University of Chicago (1967–72). But after five years, having grown uncomfortable with the spiritual shape he believed his life would take if he continued through the tenure process, he left university teaching and the three of us (he, our three-year-old David, and I) went West (with so many of our generation), only to discover that we were Easterners after all. In 1973, he found a second teaching home at Franconia College, a small alternative college in the New Hampshire mountains with no tenure system. When that worthy experiment ended in 1978, he soon found employment that led to his appointment as director of the newly founded Robert Frost Place—a farmhouse acquired by the Town of Franconia, New Hampshire, in which the Frost family had lived and summered during the poet's early years as a writer. Under Dr. Sheehan's direction, the museum the town had created there soon expanded to become a Center for Poetry and the Arts, offering a summer home for a resident poet, along with a now internationally acclaimed program of poetry writing workshops. Don Sheehan's unvarying message to the Frost Place poets (and the model he gave to all his students) was this:

> If you must make a flash choice between sympathy and intelligence, choose sympathy. Usually these fall apart— sympathy becoming a mindless "being nice" to everyone, while intelligence becomes an exercise in contempt. But here's the great fact of this Festival of Poetry: as you come to care about another person's art (and not your own), then your own art becomes mysteriously better.[4]

He held this position until his retirement in 2005. Concurrently, he taught Latin at a nearby state college and, in 1989, moved to Vermont to become a Senior Lecturer in English for freshmen and graduate students, and Latin for undergraduates, at Dartmouth College, moonlighting in the University of New Hampshire's adult degree program. By this time he had acquired a reading knowledge of two modern languages besides English (French and Italian) and four ancient ones (Old English, Middle English, Classical Greek, and Latin); Septuagint Greek and Hebrew were yet to come.

The next critical turning point in Don Sheehan's life—his conversion to Eastern Orthodox Christianity in 1983–84—is described in the opening chapter of *The Grace of Incorruption*.[5] In brief, following a 1983 visit to his father's grave in Tennessee, he was awakened at five a.m. by a prayer: "Lord Jesus Christ, son of God, have mercy on me a sinner." It quietly filled his whole being and remained with him in this way for most of a year, fading slowly over time, until it had led him to the Orthodox Church.[6] Soon after the prayer's arrival, he began to establish a rule of prayer focusing on Psalms—a rule that gradually came to occupy two to three hours of each long day.

Over time, as he became aware of the numerous deficiencies of Western scriptural texts based on the Masoretic Hebrew, his prayer Psalter changed, from the King James or Authorized Version (AV) to the Septuagint (LXX).[7] For the Septuagint, he learned, represents a closer historical link and more accurate witness to the original Hebrew Scriptures than any other translation that exists today and is preferred in the Orthodox Church, being the language of Scripture known and used by Christ Himself. Moreover, Dr. Sheehan has observed, "in the LXX one can sense everywhere an openness—in ways one cannot similarly sense it in the Masoretic Hebrew, to Jesus as Messiah." "By 1990," he wrote, "I'd become fully persuaded that my psalms for prayer were simply *not* saying what the older Hebrew text known to early Christianity had said and that the LXX Greek translation of the Hebrew contained a far deeper and truer Psalter."

When in 2001 he was asked to undertake his own English translation of the Septuagint Greek, based on the New King James English, he approached this in deep consultation with the language and poetics of the older Hebrew—inferred and intuited through his study and understanding of the work of the LXX translators and possibly with some advice from a Hebrew teacher with whom he studied for a time at Dartmouth. He then began, first, to correct his King James (which he loved for its beauty) by the Septuagint, and finally to use the Septuagint alone in his own prayer.[8]

After his conversion, Dr. Sheehan's writing and teaching turned to recasting his life and understanding, both personal and academic, in the light of Orthodox Christianity. Most of his public lectures reflecting this transition have already been published, posthumously, in *The Grace of Incorruption* (Paraclete, 2015). The present volume is based largely on his journals—whose constant and dominant theme was understanding and delighting in Psalms, psalmic poetics, and psalmic life and prayer—along with a number of hand-written presentations to Psalms study groups and notes for uniden-tified talks or classes, or just for himself. Many brief journal entries are gathered together herein as reflections on psalms (chapter 1) and the practice of a prayer rule (chapter 4). Some entries, at times interleaved with others in the journals, actually did form continu-ous essays; these have been culled from the surrounding text and are presented here in their intended essay format. In the end, nearly all of his significant writing concerning Psalms is represented here, though not in the sequence in which it was written (which may lead to some inconsistencies as his focus and understanding and psalmic text changed over time).

The reader will find in this volume the seeds and soil from which his earlier books grew, especially *The Psalms of David*, to which this may be considered a helpful companion, and vice versa. It offers significant commentary and insight on Psalms in general, on many individual psalms, and on a life given to and shaped by the prayer of Psalms.

⟋

Dr. Sheehan wrote at one point, "I do not really understand my devotion to the Psalms; it seems far stronger than anything I can understand. Something in the textures of the words that carries the enormous Presence of God; something, too, in the ease with which I open wholly to God in them. I hope devoutly I am not fooling myself; that I can, in fact, live wholly into God's holy word in the Psalms." In reading through his journals and papers seven years after his repose, I once again felt the pleasure of being in conversa-tion with him—a kind of conversation that was at the heart of our forty-seven years together. What I've come to understand from this distance is that Don's life did indeed become psalmic, even itself a psalm; and as I immerse my life so deeply in care for this art of his, my own becomes mysteriously better.

The Field of Blood

When in 1986 Don Sheehan was tonsured a reader in the Orthodox Church (a minor clerical order), he was given to read aloud, by *sortes*, Acts 1:12–22—a shocking text—where the eleven remaining disciples return to Jerusalem following Christ's Ascension. Peter speaks of the necessity of the Scriptures having been fulfilled with regard to Judas. We learn that Judas had purchased a field with the "wages of iniquity" and had "burst open in the middle and all his entrails gushed out"; that the field is to be called Akel Dama, the Field of Blood; and that this field will be a desolate place where none may live. Led by Peter, the disciples prepare to draw lots for a replacement to restore their number, choosing from among those who had, in Saint Peter's words, "accompanied us all the time that the Lord Jesus went in and out among us, beginning from the baptism of John to that day when He was taken up from us, one of these must become a witness with us of His resurrection" (Acts 1:20–22).

In January 1987, on retreat at Saint Tikhon's Monastery, Don was for the first time able to give his full attention to this reading, asking in his journal, "What is it saying, and especially to me?" He is first of all concerned for the Lord's Mother: "O Blessed Theotokos," he writes, "how Thy world has now been so changed; at this instant in the upper room, all that Thou hast pondered in Thy heart has become immense actuality: the prophetic life."

He sees in the selection process the need for the disciples to be able to "bear witness—*martyria*—to the resurrection: here is the great call to Christ. The death of Judas: that Akel Daman field is the place of our rending, our final scattering of ourselves in our own achievements, our own rewards." Asking himself—"*Why* was the Akel Daman field so necessary to the psalmic fulfillment? Why was Judas so necessary to the Psalms' action in our Lord's life?"—he answers:

> Because Judas as Enemy bore the full prophetic weight of the destruction of Jerusalem—the rending that would *in time* be the healing and making whole. That psalmic killer is the one who stands *deliberately* outside God's work of making whole in love. No one can dwell in the Field of Blood, for it is the cessation of all dwelling in the destruction of all wholeness. He, the Enemy, was once *within*; now he is wholly outside: by his own choice. For what he did was to pull all choosing *into himself*, to see himself as author of his acts, sole and perfect.
>
> Note, too, the gushing out of the bowels (*viscera* in Jerome): that is, this scattering of inwardness. All through the Psalms there is this rending, this scattering of inwardness into the billion fragments we call the world.
>
> To replace Judas is what our Lord did: He replaced Adam's curse; He reversed the Fall. Why? So that He could plunge into the field of death and rise again: showing us the true way, the way of baptism into the water and resurrection from the Tomb.
>
> Thus, the arc Peter actually describes here is that from Johannine baptism to heavenly Ascension. The baptism is the ἀρχή (*archē*), the beginning; and the Ascension is the τέλος (*telos*), the end or fulfillment. Together, they make one unified and permanently occurring Event. By sketching this arc in this way, Peter is revealing the *shape* of this Event. He does this in order to create the context within which the choosing of Judas' successor will occur; he is creating the

Judas chose to take "too much" into himself and was turned inside-out

field of the choosing—that is, it will be all those who were with us *within* this arc in time. . . .

The calling forth from the historic field of those who were *in* this arc with our Lord and His companions: this shows us that *inwardness*—that is, actually being present with—is the crucial criterion of participation in Christ. For all of those (the Greek says) were the συνελθόντες (*synelthontes*), "the going-with-ones.". . .

The Petrine criterion: going with Christ, *being in* His going in such a way that one is *with* Him in His going.

Some years later, he wrote of Psalms:

Because our Lord made His whole life in and through these poems, and thereby made manifest what always was potentially in them (i.e., God's power to make whole the earth), we participate, we are with Him—that is, we are in the intense circle of His praying—when we chant these holy poems. And as we read—and pray deeply—the Psalms, we are becoming ourselves psalmic.

Thus did Don Sheehan live his life and fulfill his ministry.

~⸺

The reader will find in this volume much about violence, depression, and the rending of inwardness—both because much is in Psalms, and because the author had himself, in his own words, "involuntarily researched" the subject in his own life. As we see in this passage from Acts, however, all of this is held within the larger arc of steady prayer and faithfulness, of "going-with" our Lord into the resurrection that He won and keeps on winning for those who walk with Him.

Don Sheehan deeply understood God's Psalms, went with them

into dark places, and, like the psalmist, prayed them, *kept the conversation going*—and this made all the difference. In this book he passes on to us something of the art of that conversation and how to keep it going. His whole life bears witness, μαρτυρία (*martyria*).

A final point about conversation. Conversation was Don's gift. He listened, he responded with care, deep meaning happened and thrived. This is at times a difficult book. Much of it was private writing, his mind moving quickly over terrain where many of us need clearly defined paths. None of it is "finished." And in many cases there was no person present to whom he was listening and responding. I call you, his reader, to *be* that person, to scratch your head and interrogate him, even to stamp the ground in frustration, and then to open your heart to him and listen *from your heart*, waiting for his words to open to you. I don't believe you will be disappointed. The heart is the key.

The End-Point

At the end of 2007—the year of his twin brother's passing, three years after his mother's passing, and the year his own terminal illness began to show itself—he wrote in one of his last journal entries, "The year comes to an end; so does my life in active love. Grief overwhelms me." And again, a few days later: "Will I ever have *life* again? . . . I don't know where all progress in Psalms has gone—but gone it has, completely gone. . . . This is where I start: my life is broken in the present; hence, my past swims up in its catastrophic vileness: my broken home of childhood claims me all over again. Way out? I don't know—but I *must* find it; and soon, soon, soon, before I lose all my present life in the swamps of a deathly past."

Reading this years afterward, I was struck most by his identifying this darkness as a starting point, not an end. A few days later, at the beginning of the following year, January 2, 2008, he jotted down this brief verse:

> This: my father sees my pain,
> Agonizes with me in my suffering.
> But he is helpless to ease my agony.
> Except this: he always and always loves me.
>
> The hour I walked with my father and mother
> Into their afflictions and agonies
> Is the hour I broke my heart:
> This, this is where I start.

I am not aware that he had written any poetry for a long time, and I nearly overlooked it, scribbled, with crossings-out, on a torn scrap of paper. But *watch!* It has a chiastic[9] a-b-c-d-d'-c'-b'-a' structure, made more obvious by the line lengths once it is typed out. I am seeing it now as the chiastic heart of his own psalm—his whole life—its turning point: starting again where he began, beginning again where he has appeared to come to an end, passing in both directions through and then beyond the agonies, the breaking of his heart, to the center where he walks with his father and mother in their pain and knows that he is always and always—that is, eternally—loved by his father. The father of his childhood—who in so many ways failed him, at the same time loved him, and then posthumously (so he believed) showed him the Way—has become the Father whom he passed through the doorway of Psalms to meet. Whatever his intent, he has left us a potent clue for navigating his landscape, revealing that his rule of psalmic prayer had in no way failed him.

On the contrary, it was drawing him now toward the End-Point—that point wherein you are stripped of absolutely all you possess—"except," in Mother Maria's words, "your sins, and the cry for mercy"; that point where all our imperfection "lies prostrate, before Christ," while we are free to engage what the next instant of time is already bringing us.[10] Don knew and wrote of this. And even when he lost his voice entirely, even when, as far as anyone who was with him knows, his long rule of prayer had come to an end, he never ceased bearing witness to Christ in his unassuming way. He never ceased being, as a student and friend once described him, a man "so immersed in soul-work that he threw off a little light. And he was always casting that light toward you."[11] Thus is a life in Psalms.

Don died at home in Charleston, South Carolina, on May 26, 2010, surrounded by friends, young and old, most of whom had known him, ill, for fewer than two years but found themselves drawn to him and wanting to join his family in praying Psalms and anointing and preparing his body for funeral and burial. He is buried at Panagia Prousiotissa Orthodox Monastery in Troy, North Carolina, where his grave is tended and honored, and his lamp kept burning, by faithful Orthodox nuns who pray for his soul.

HELPFUL INFORMATION

Psalm Numbers

Psalm numbers throughout this volume indicate, unless specified otherwise, the LXX (Septuagint) Greek number. Sometimes, in brackets, the Hebrew Masoretic text (MT) or AV (Authorized Version) number that is more familiar to many readers has been added for clarity. See the appendix on numbering of psalms as well as the glossary concerning the LXX and Masoretic texts. Unless otherwise noted, quotations of psalms herein are from the author's *Psalms of David: Translated from the Septuagint Greek by Donald Sheehan*, ed. Xenia Sheehan and Hieromonk Herman Majkrzak (Wipf & Stock, 2013).

Sources

Don was remarkably meticulous about citing his sources, but he missed a few that could not be tracked down, mostly in the older journal entries.

Dating of Chapters

On the dating of the material included in the book: Chapters 1, 3, and 4 are an assemblage of journaled material of varying lengths and dates written between 1987 and 2007. The material in chapter 2, on the poetry and translation of Psalms, is a composite drawn from variously dated essays or journal entries from 1990 on; it also includes a portion of an unfinished handwritten essay entitled "Being and Thinking: Notes on Translation," written in 2001 as the author was beginning the Psalms translation project. Most of the material in chapters 5–9 is from essays he wrote in 2005 for a Psalms study group he led at Saint Basil's Orthodox Church in Simpson, Pennsylvania; and, a year or two later, for a group he led for parishioners of Saint Jacob of Alaska Orthodox Church in Northfield, Vermont. Chapter 10 is dated Thanksgiving day, 2006. The material on Psalm 118 (chapters 11 and 12) is dated in his journal as beginning on June 30, 2005, and certainly continued for some time after that, segueing into (or more likely concurrent with) the book he was writing on psalmic poetics (the final draft of which, unfinished, is published as the second part of *The Grace of Incorruption*). Throughout the book, passages from the journals (usually brief) that appeared to fit within a particular essay have been woven into the essay without regard for their date of composition.

The book, therefore, is not about the author's intellectual development but rather his love-inspired, scholarly, poetic, and very personal engagement with Psalms. Though the date of his "Notes Toward an Orthodox Poetics" in the Epilogue is uncertain, it is almost surely late and may possibly be taken as his last word, revealing, in summary style, how all of his previous thought and writing on psalmic poetics fits together and where he was thinking it might productively lead any who choose to follow it further.

Transliterations of Greek and Hebrew

Although the author himself favored the modern Greek pronunciation of biblical and patristic texts, nevertheless in transliterating Greek words in this volume we have followed the guidelines of the Society for Biblical Literature, which are based on the reconstructed classical pronunciation. We have done this merely because their transliteration system distinguishes Greek vowels, and not in an attempt to endorse the reconstructed pronunciation of biblical and patristic texts. Similarly, in transliterating Hebrew text, we have largely followed the SBL's "General with Glottal Stops" system; however, there are some instances where a Hebrew word is familiar enough that the more familiar transliteration has been used instead (as with *Aleph* for *Alef*). —*JTS and JWC.*

Chapter Introductory Text

Finally, as editor, I have taken the liberty of introducing most of the chapters with a summary explanation of what I see as the chapter's overall arc. You might find these helpful. Don seldom allowed himself to stick to one angle or follow a straight line in looking at a thing and instead, kaleidoscopically, found his mind turning here and there to gather together many elements of all sizes and shapes and colors into his picture to disclose new glories. Some of his chapters can therefore seem like wandering into a foreign country with winding byways, lovely bits of scenery, and road signs in various languages that you may not know but wish you did, telling you, with passion, things that you really need to know in order to find your way. So, not wanting you to give up at the start on this marvelous journey through Psalms, I've done my best to make you some maps. —*Ed.*

The Shield of

PSALMIC PRAYER

1

Reflections on Psalms
and Psalmic Prayer

The psalmic reflections in this chapter are from the author's journals, written at various times over the two decades spanning 1987 to 2007. —*Ed.*

> Psalmic prayer can part the very veil of the
> high holy place to call down God's mercy.
>
> DONALD SHEEHAN

The key to the Psalms, to all sacred text, is this: the holy WORD is our food, is God incarnated; hence, *is* Christ. We know this is so by how our hearts respond to the WORD: with abundant life. This is what our Lord promised us, abundant—super-abundant—life, life unceasing, life eternal. And He gave this life as Himself, as and in the WORD. And He is everywhere in Scripture; not a sentence passes that He is not everywhere the inner life, the mainspring, of its rhythm and idea and image and urgency.[1]

The Actual, Boundless, Ordinary
Mystery of Psalms

1

My wife and I were riding to an errand, talking about our currently deeply uncertain economic arrangements. I asked her how she felt, and she said, "tangled." I looked up at the hillside we were passing. Mid-October rain on the autumn trees now half or more winter-bare was steady and cold; yet, nevertheless, it was a very beautiful hillside, the wet trees and dark earth and last yellow leaves giving—*somehow*—a strong sense of holy presence, of the God who always IS, a presence made more plain by the absence of prettiness and spectacle (that breathtaking riot of high-autumn color)—the very dreariness the strength of the beauty. And the hillside, the moment, the word "tangled," the disarray of our financial orders: all this seemed a psalm. That is, the way the hillside was, the way the beauty shone plainly in the bareness, is the way a psalm works and *is* in us.

2

The Psalms: the torment and beauty and God-hungering and God-knowing—*everything* is in them; absolutely nothing whatever has been excluded, even the tiniest detail. Without the Gospels, of course, and the great teachings of Saint Paul, we couldn't finally know the Psalms in their true nature: as the perfect *prayer-system*. Our Lord knew this; He made His own life whole in and through the Psalms. The Gospels reflect His practice in this perfect system—for He alone brought it into perfection by the *practice of it on the level of personhood*.

As He accomplished this great work of *making inward* the Psalms, He made them into one unified and complete work. For prior to His accomplishment, the poems were spiritually scattered (though gathered into one text)—that is, they were "used" at certain liturgies of the Temple, but they were not experienced as *one experience of personhood*. Our Lord prayed them all, and so He made them all אֶחָד (*'ehad*): one, coherent.   *recapitulation*

Note well: He did not "personalize" the Psalms; rather, He made them responsive to His Personhood—that is: who He was (and is) in (and as) God. He accomplished the great work of *making inward* the Psalms. He made them into one unified and complete work; and in doing so He made comparably whole the entire course of Israelite history.

In AD 70, when the Temple was destroyed, our Lord had already said this was coming; He foretold it. His resurrection is the recreation of the true Temple: His Body. Psalms—especially 73 and 78, which experience the first destruction of 587 BC—give the central terms: the Jerusalem of pure, devotional consciousness is overwhelmed by the dark forces that scatter and dissipate and destroy the sacred אוּר (*ur*), that most holy light of God.[2] To the AD 70 nonbelieving Jew, the destruction of the Temple was a cessation of historic actuality. To cease history is to experience the end of God's active presence in time. To the Christian Jew, the holy figure on the Cross was defeat-become-triumph: a break with the literalized deathtrap of history into the spiritual freedom of true history: the ceaseless Presence that is never lost. The holy *ur* of Psalms becomes vast spiritual suggestion: the Jerusalem of Presence is never lost, even in physical wreckage.

3

I think we do not know—cannot truly these days even glimpse fleetingly—the mysteries of the Psalms. To turn from the dark confusions of our lives to the endless harmonics of these most sacred poems is to turn from death to life: not from the death that leads us to resurrection but rather the death that is our absolute and final wasting; and not to the life that is swirling with vivid ambiguities but the life that is ceaselessly illumined in depths of brightness both in and beyond us.

4

No one who has not submersed himself for a long time (say, two years minimum) in the Psalms can understand truly their primary quality: strength. They can bear the whole weight of one's life in the same instant they can go on carrying the weight of the countless millions in all ages of earth who have before prayed them: for once you pray them you enter into them forever; and there, in them, you find living all those who have also always entered so.

This is why our Lord entered. It is also where He can be found now, always.

5

Can I write about my own experience of psalmic prayer in any way like the experience itself? Abba Philemon[3] comes closest; but centuries of devotional history separate me from the Desert in which he prayed—as the weakness and dryness and shallowness and "mechanistic-ness" of my pitiable prayer separate me from his richly splendid practice of psalmic humility. I can only say: something in Psalm-prayer touches me always with an undying freshness of heart.

6

Can anyone ever tell truly and well the sweet freshness of psalmic prayer: tell of the lightheartedness, the inner spaciousness of its Grace, its melodic aliveness?

7

This *sweetness* of psalmic prayer, of which Saint Theophan[4] also speaks—a sweetness almost indistinguishable from soreness—that is, an aching beauty—: this sweetness occurs in psalmic prayer solely because our Lord chanted Psalms so perfectly in His life. His chanting of the Psalms was perfect in that He found in them the secret binding power they'd always possessed but never manifested: the power to make whole in God all of human historic experience. His chanting manifested this power because, in doing so, He began to live solely from the consciousness they formed in Him: and so He repeated, cohered, transfigured the whole of Israelite historic/sacred experience in His own life—a repetition, coherence, and transfiguration made possible in and through the direct experience of the whole of the Psalms as God-consciousness.

(I wish I could say this plainly—with all the heartbreaking, simple beauty and reality of it: it's so clear, so pure!)

8

Only the Psalms stay, day after day, bright with meanings (some of them quite dark). "Do not turn thy countenance from me; in the day I am afflicted incline thine ear to me; in the day I call out to thee, hear me speedily" (102:1). This nearness is always true to all days.

9

The Psalms embed all ranges of knowledge and experience: from the tiny "comfort" knowledges of kitchen and table to the vast comprehensions of God powerfully active in a limitless universe: from teacup to tempest. The way these ranges are embedded—are inwoven and interlocked—is the key to the syntax of the Psalms. Note well: the grammar of Psalms is first of all a spiritual patterning.

10

My own immersion in Psalms has undoubtedly had decisive consequences in my life. But I have no real understanding—not even the merest inkling—of what these consequences might be. I don't know the Psalms by heart—that is, I can't recite them aloud without the text before me. Also, I don't have very many ideas about the Psalms; and when I sometimes look into scholarly works, I always feel fairly dumb. These great and modest scholars are learned in ways, and into depths, I shall probably never know anything about.

And so I can say little about what the Psalms have meant to me. The reason why this is so is, I think, the same reason that I can say nothing at all about my thirty-five-year marriage to my wife, Carol.[5] That is, like my relation to her, my relation to the Psalms is something I am entirely *in*. In both cases, what I am aware of is— not myself—but the other person; and this *other* is, in both cases, mysteriously substantial and real. In other words, my experience of praying the Psalms is an experience of loving, and being loved. Hence, the experience is (and I use these four words with care): *actual*; *boundless*; *ordinary*; and *mysterious*.

Let me explain these four words.

Actual. By this I mean that the reality of Christ's Personhood in the Psalms is, for me, neither a mental abstraction nor an emotional drama. Beyond any idea I might devise or any feeling I might undergo, Christ is *present* in the whole of Psalms in the same way that my wife is present in the whole of my life. And Christ's reality is so fully actual that I can say that, rather than experiencing Psalms by means of my marriage, I experience my marriage by means of the Psalms.

In this sense, then, I use the word *boundless*. Now, a marriage cannot, I think, be based upon an ideology, a theory of relationship, no matter how good or true or persuasive the ideas may be. Nor can a marriage run for long on how one or both persons feel toward the other. Ideas and feelings are surely present, even abundantly so, in a marriage. But they have only the humblest of roles to play. For personhood exceeds ideology and even emotion so completely that personhood in the other can only be experienced as boundless. Just so are the Psalms in my experience of prayer.

My third word for this experience is *ordinary*. I mean, first of all, that praying Psalms is for me never a drama. There are no crashing cymbals; no drum rolls; no sobbing violins or shrieking brasses or throaty cellos—all of that is banished away, set aside, forgotten utterly. It is the plainest of experiences; it is a cat washing herself in the sunlit window; it is doing the dishes late at night in a guest house; buttoning a shirt or tying a shoe, your mind miles away, and racing. It is difficult to think about the ordinary, for our ideas slide away from it at the slightest touch. It is also assuredly difficult to emote about the ordinary, for nearly all our feelings seem to evaporate in its presence. Yet my deepest experience of praying the Psalms is precisely ordinary; and therefore my constant spiritual task is simply to be as present as I can manage to this essential ordinariness of the experience. For when I can (and this is the point), the ordinary becomes the very *way*, or *mode*, wherein Christ's actuality and boundlessness are made manifest in the Psalms.

Thus, my fourth word for my experience of praying the Psalms is *mysterious*. Let me express what I mean in this way (I take this understanding directly from my friend Prof. John Konkle[6]): I can know a great deal about my wife, and the years can keep on increasing my store of knowledge about her. But *who* she is in the fullness of her personhood in God—this is, and will remain, a mystery to me. And yet: the boundless mystery of her personhood is made manifest in her very ordinariness and actuality.

Just so: Christ is in the Psalms actually, boundlessly, ordinarily, and mysteriously.

Psalmic Prayer Is Spiritual Warfare

1

When we pray the Psalms, we are engaged in spiritual warfare against real enemies who really seek our actual destruction, both spiritual and physical. Hence, meditation in the Psalms is conceived as direct engagement with these enemies. We may reflect for a moment on the predominant word used in Psalms for meditation. In the LXX Psalter, there are ten occurrences of the noun μελέτη (*meletē*, meditation) and fifteen of the verb μελετάω (*meletaō*, to meditate). In Hebrew, the word is הָגָה, *hagah*. Brown-Driver-Briggs begins its presentation of this verb by noting that later Hebrew poets considered it *onomatopoeic*: that is, the word sounds to the ear very like the meaning it carries to the mind.[7] Its primary meaning is to *growl*, like a lion growling over its prey.[8] In this Hebrew verb, then, we can see the primary significance of psalmic meditation as spiritual warfare: it is an action wherein you overcome the enemy the way a lion brings down its prey. In the Great Psalm, 118, line

92—the line immediately *preceding* the psalm's chiastic heart[9]—carries vivid light; it reads: "If thy law had not been my meditation, I would have perished in my affliction." To meditate in God's Law (*torah* in Hebrew; *nomos* in Greek) is to seize hold of the Law the way the lion seizes its prey: in such devouring, one finds nurture, sustenance, life instead of death. Significantly, the Hebrew noun here used for "my meditation" is שַׁעֲשֻׁעָי (*sha'ashu'ay*), a plural noun meaning "intense delight."[10] Here, then, is the lion's deep pleasure; here, then, is the end and whole purpose of psalmic delight: to devour one's passions so as to experience the deepest nourishment in God.

2

The Protestant writer Eugene Peterson has noted that in our culture there is "a pseudo-prayer that promises its practitioners entrance into the subliminal harmonies of the way-things-are, putting them in tune with the general hum of the universe. . . . This so-called prayer reduces tension, lowers stress, and extends longevity. The people who get good at it *are* calm, their voices soothing, and their actions poised. They meditate beautiful thoughts and sleep well." He goes on to say that "Psalm-prayer also enters into the way-things-are, but finds that the way things are is pretty bad. Evil is encountered. Wickedness is confronted. . . . They are engaged, or soon to be engaged, in an act of war. Prayer is combat. Prayer brings us before God—and there, before God, we ourselves are grappling with 'The spiritual hosts of wickedness in the heavenly places' (Eph. 6:12)."[11] And the end of all our quickenings and grapplings is direct participation in the resurrection of Christ.

3

Father Sophrony, writing about Saint Silouan, echoes precisely Saint Paul's sentence from Ephesians when he says: "The world is plunged deep in the darkness of spiritual ignorance." He continues: "The way to life eternal is preached unceasingly in all languages but in each generation those who really find it may be counted on one hand."[12] The beautiful response of Saint Silouan to this darkness is: "Keep thy mind in hell, and despair not." "Everyone who would follow our Lord Jesus Christ," says Silouan, "is engaged in spiritual warfare." "Our battle rages every day, every hour."[13]

4

The psalmic way of Prayer is the way of affliction. The first fruits of psalmic prayer are—in the words of Abba St. Isaac the Syrian— "despondency [i.e., depression], hardship, painful limbs [from long standing in prayer], cutting off of friendships, and separation from acquaintances."[14] In this first season of bitter fruits, the work is plain: do not eat, do not touch; simply endure them patiently.

5

Stillness is the patient endurance of these bitter first fruits of psalmic prayer. Stillness is not an "experience" we might have. It is, instead, the enduring of all our experiences until they all pass over into being present with God. Abba Isaac tells us: "Let us see, my beloved, whether in our soul at the time of prayer we possess divine vision into the verses of psalmody and prayer. For this is born of true stillness."[15]

6

One's (my own) darkness and depravity and selfishness cannot be set aside by inventing some image of holiness; to do so is to invent an idol and worship it (the worst kind: self-idol). The darkness will not go away; it will clamor and clamor to get in. The idol of "holiness" will be smashed; for God wants no such idol.

7

History is a process of idolatry: the making by us of self-idols and the smashing of them by God. So in one's own life, as historical process. The Psalms, only (and Scripture as a whole), know this; and they alone show the whole process. For God is in our darkness, that is, in what we are withholding from Him of ourselves in our (violent, crazed) attempt to make ourselves holy *in our own eyes*, not in His.

The Psalms know this: the violent men who roam the city are simultaneously our own darkness seeking admission into the light and the punishment God inflicts on us for making and worshiping the idols of ourselves. "What does all this *mean?*" the Psalms are saying.

8

The words of Psalms are not provisional; not relative guideposts to the Absolute; not aids to enlightenment (all of which are true of Buddhist texts): rather, they are the exact, illumined, and vividly essential Word of God: hence, they heal the sick, support the active, deepen the contemplative, rebuke the unrepentant, forgive the sinful—: where contemplative technique aided by texts may do these things in Buddhism, the Psalms in and of themselves accomplish all of them (and much more) for the Orthodox Christian who chants them in daily prayer. For in them lives the mind of Christ, *nous Christou* (νοῦς Χριστοῦ).

9

In Psalm 16 we find this: "To keep my mouth from the talk of men's deeds, through the words of thy lips I held to hard ways" (16:4).

To hold to hard ways of psalmic prayer is the one and only way to free one's mouth from the endless, dark swirl of words that arise from human violence. This swirl is like water running fast down a drain, it is always flowing away from us. Psalmic words flow forever *into* us, straight to our own heart, because they are the words from God's Psalm.

10

The *ruggedness* of the Psalms—their tough, grainy, flinty *singularity*—is salvific: for only in their sharpness are our eyes and hearts opened: "The Lord is my strength, my refuge, my deliverer, my God is my helper, on him I will hope, my shield, the horn of my salvation, and my protector" (Ps. 17:2).

"Blessed the people who know the joyful sound"

1

Just as Christ infused into Psalms His own presence, so they formed in Him the consciousness that was always latent in them. And just as He brought forth the consciousness and the Personhood latent in Psalms, so our own personhood. By this I do *not* mean who we individually and accidentally are and experience: our own personhood is *who we are in God*. He, in our encounter with Him in Psalms, brings that forth in us. One's personhood may feel a tiny bit impersonal at first; but the fire of prayer quickly burns away those attachments to our individualisms which are making it seem thin. And then we *are* in Christ; we are Where we have always been but did not recognize and affirm as so.

2

The pathway of psalmic prayer: the "letting-all-the-way-into-you" of the actual words of Psalms, so that every word touches every aspect (past, present, future) of your life. This is an actual, literal practice along salvation's pathway. Plainly, it is not the sole pathway; but it is a real one: a way (ὁδός, *hodos*) and a path (τρίβος, *tribos*) by which God makes Himself known to and teaches the one praying His holy Psalms (Ps. 24:4: "Make known thy ways to me, O Lord, and teach me thy paths").

3

The existence of the Psalms—in their endless praise of God's presence and inventiveness in the earth and its peoples and histories— the existence of this psalmic praise is the instantaneity of the eternity of God in the temporality of (and in) ourselves. Psalms are purely so, wholly so.

4

The ways, in each instance, psalmic prayer takes shape—that is, the particularity of rhythmic texture, the depths and *horizontality* in the heart's being held and opened in the rhythm and the phrase and syllable and word and sentence and whole poem: the ways this all occurs in a given instance of psalmic prayer are as various in their livingness, and as intense in the exactness of their tenderness, as the sacred poems themselves: hence, as God Himself.

5

What does it mean to pray the Psalms ceaselessly? To understand in the experience of one's heart the full reality of ὁ ὤν (*ho ōn*, I AM)[16] would be to pray the Psalms ceaselessly. *To pray the Psalms ceaselessly*—this is to fulfill the Law, to manifest חֶסֶד (*hesed*, mercy; ἔλεος, *eleos*, in Gk.) in and as the whole of one's life.[17] Ceaseless psalmic prayer would be to compose them anew at every reading; that is, to write them anew in every contact. That is, to read in such a way that we experience them as if we were writing *at that very moment*.

But praying the Psalms unceasingly is much more than all I've said.

6

In Homily 54 of Saint Isaac the Syrian's *Ascetical Homilies*, we read this: "Understand this also with discernment: in the verses of our psalmody do not be like a man who borrows words from another, lest you imagine that you are diligently increasing your work of meditation, while in fact you are left utterly devoid of the compunction and joy to be found in psalmody. Rather, recite the words of psalmody as your very own, that you may utter the words of your supplication with insight and with discriminating compunction, like a man who truly understands his work."[18]

The action whereby we make psalmic words our "very own" is the twofold action wherein we first *see* the noetic ray that Saint Isaac speaks of in Homily 1 as running between the lines of Scripture and along the pathways of syntax; and because of this clear seeing, we can then receive the ray into our hearts. You receptively "fit" the ray into your heart as you actively "fit" your heart into the ray: where fitting actively means deliberately reconfiguring your heart's syntax to mesh with the psalm's syntax.

For "He has made a memorial of his works" (Ps. 110:4): That is, God our heavenly Father has in our Lord Jesus so fashioned the creation (and all in it) that every least and single work—as well as the whole of everything at once—*fits* into our memory because of convergence of the three orders of syntax: the syntax of creation, the syntax of Psalms, and the syntax of our heart.

To make "the words of psalmody as your very own" is therefore to approach these words of our Lord in the Great Priestly Prayer (John 17): "as thou, Father, art in me, and I in thee, that they also may be one in us" (l. 21).

The mystery: just as I am *always*—that is, have always been and always will be—*who I am*, so, too, the psalm antinomically coheres across every abyss of every shocking encounter. And the whole of the Psalter—like the whole of each week (that is, like the whole of the seven-day creation)—exhibits this antinomic coherence.

7
שׁמר

The keyword of the Psalms is: *Watch*! It means (a) look at the world, wake up, open your eyes, let in the vivid beauty—and evil—of the world and *act* on what you behold; and (b) attend closely to the movements within your own heart, asking also: where are they going—to God or away from Him? The combination of (a) and

(b) produces in us what the *Philokalia* calls νῆψις (*nēpsis*); "atten-tiveness" is a good translation.[19] All through the holy Psalms this attentiveness is both urged on us and manifested by the poets.

In Psalm 120[121], says Robert Alter, "The point of the poem is that the Lord is quite literally a guardian or watchman who never sleeps, who always has his eyes open to keep you from harm."[20]

Axiom: in a lifetime of praying the Psalms, we undergo, in and through the acts of sacred time, *theosis* (θέωσις): that is, we become "in-Godded." Thus, we see in Psalm 120 what we are to strive to develop in ourselves: unsleeping watchfulness.

8

The poet Kathleen Norris writes in an essay about the time when she found herself in O'Hare Airport in Chicago having to walk between the two huge terminals. She was in the last corridor of glass and steel when she suddenly found in her mind the first words of Psalm 122 (AV): "I was glad when they said unto me, Let us go into the house of the Lord." And all at once this exhausting world became a spiritual exercise: she was entering Jerusalem with these words: "Pray for the peace of Jerusalem. . . . For my brethren and companions' sake, I will now say: Peace be within thee." She says, "The newspapers that week were full of stories of car bombings in Israel, deadly assaults, and a fragile thing called a 'peace process,' making clear the importance of continuing to pray for the peace of Jerusalem."

The Psalms are boundlessly filled with such ordinary actual-ity of Christ's mysterious presence—in the Psalms themselves and therefore in all our lives.

Norris goes on: "As I recited the psalm in that empty airport corridor, I no longer felt alone. Those I love were thousands of miles away, going about their daily business. Other people, strangers in churches and monasteries all around the world, were praying this psalm. I marveled at the ordinary human means—good architecture, insane airline scheduling—that had conspired to bring me together with them."[21]

And here is my one real point: this experience of being brought together in God with the endless reality of actual persons is what the Psalms mean in Eastern Orthodox Christendom.

9

In Psalm 147 we read:

4   He sends his teaching to earth where his word shall
      run very swiftly . . .
7   He shall send his word and melt them, he shall breathe
      out his breath and the waters shall flow,
8   Declaring his word unto Jacob, his statutes and
      judgments to Israel.

Two motions here converge: the motion of water flowing, and the motion of the Word being shown to Israel. Israel is the body of Christ; and in the same way that our bodies will beguile and mislead us, so Israel betrays Our Lord. But: Christ never casts off Israel, He never discards her, never sets her aside—even as He knows she will finally crucify Him. Yet He is never overcome by her because He always beholds the way wherein the Law (God's "statutes and judgments") is what animates—quickens, gives life to—Israel, just as it is always the wind that moves the waters into flowing.

10

Nothing in all spiritual life equals the *tremendous* pull of these poems: no, not poems merely, but sacred sounds taking (for our joy) the outward shape of poems.

"Blessed the people who know the joyful sound" (Ps. 88:15)— and this is the stream of sacred sound that is the sonic life of the Psalms, a stream into which "torrents of . . . delights" our Lord immersed His holy mind (Ps. 35:8).

2

Translated to Life

In the beginning was the Word. All history is a translation of that Word, as our Lord first creates and then shepherds His creation toward receiving Him into it so that we may freely enter into union with Him. This chapter sees poetry as human words capable of moving our hearts and minds to open to "the goodness of what is" and to shape words of praise for it; it is words in search of their roots in the Word. Poetry, and especially Psalms, push back against the pressures of our material lives and call us to remain fast in their Creator. We possess a faculty, the nous, residing in the depths of our heart, that enables us to see, without mediation, the reality of God and the created world, and to translate that from one language to another in such a way that the life in things is increased rather than diminished by the particularities of culture and language that appear to define us. And it is by this means that God moves more fully into His creation, in self-emptying obedience to it, until we, mirroring that obedience, come to see His face in it, feel His rhythms in it, love Him in it, and receive the rushing wind of His Spirit at Pentecost. —*Ed.*

> The truest recreation of the psalmic "measure"—its char-
> acteristic rhythm and drive—is the holy life of our Lord.
>
> DONALD SHEEHAN

The Orthodox ground of all biblical translation is formed by two phenomena: the disintegration of the Ur-Edenic language registered in the Babel narrative from Genesis; and the Descent of the Holy Spirit at Pentecost, when each person hears the divine voice "in his own language" (Acts 2:6). This latter phenomenon overcomes the former in the sense that the *disintegration* into linguistic babble is fully matched by the linguistic *integration* of the Holy Spirit—matched—indeed, so *over*-matched that the spiritual integration may be seen as radically asymmetrical to the disintegrative babble. In this light, the meaning of all translation is best expressed by the Orthodox Troparion of the Dormition[1]:

> In giving birth you preserved your virginity,
> In falling asleep you did not forsake the world,
>   O Theotokos.
> You were translated to life, O Mother of Life,
> And by your prayers, you deliver our souls from death.

At her death, the Mother of God is "translated to life." She dies fully in the sense that her life is completely over; yet her life becomes in that moment forever perfectly incomplete by being translated into divinely ongoing life. This is the holy work of translation.

In translating Psalms—even in this, the translation to life of our Holy Mother may serve as our Great Example,[2] as the Orthodox Church considers her. For poetry is itself a living entity with a body and soul.[3] Poet Baron Wormser offers us this about poetry:

When we say "poetry" we are talking about the ancient mystery of words communicating through the concise medium of braided language and all the physicality that resides in language—sound and rhythm—something that cannot be said otherwise. Poetry was here, so to speak, before prose, because poetry is rooted in praise of being, the goodness of what is, just as language is so rooted. Poetry has moved people for millennia because it can express the inexpressible. It can go to that place where there is no paraphrase: this is it. Poetry, accordingly, cannot be split into molecules any more than spirit can be split into molecules. The poem is indivisible yet the choices that face the poet are something like infinite. Yet the poet seeks to find the right word, right sounds, right rhythm to create that whole. Poetry creates something indefinable out of its many precisions. The movement a poem makes is thus felt in our bodies. We are pulsating creatures and poetry gives us that feeling back in moving language: language that moves forward in time from word to word and line to line and language that moves our hearts and minds. Poetry has been esteemed and cherished for this ability to go to the eloquent essence of the matter. Poetry has mattered so hugely and continues to matter because this ability is deeply human. As we are creatures of the word, we use poetry to refine words to their utmost. In that light, people all over the world have agreed on the stature of poetry.[4]

Poetry is "rooted in praise of being, the goodness of what is." Here is our starting point. How is this done? And, achieved in one language, how can it be translated into another?

Let me put before you an example within English that may serve to suggest the scope of such a challenge. It's one of my family's favorite poems, written in the nineteenth century by Gerard Manley Hopkins and titled "The Grandeur of God":

The world is charged with the grandeur of God.
    It will flame out, like shining from shook foil;
    It gathers to a greatness, like the ooze of oil
Crushed. Why do men then now not reck his rod?

Generations have trod, have trod, have trod;
    And all is seared with trade; bleared, smeared with toil;
    And wears man's smudge and shares man's smell: the soil
Is bare now, nor can foot feel, being shod.

And for all this, nature is never spent;
    There lives the dearest freshness deep down things;
And though the last lights off the black West went
    Oh, morning, at the brown brink eastward, springs—
Because the Holy Ghost over the bent
    World broods with warm breast and with ah! bright
    wings.

Translating Psalms

The Greek of Psalms, known as the Septuagint (abbreviated LXX), is itself a translation of a lost Hebrew original—according to one tradition, a translation done in the second century BC by seventy-two Jewish scholars living in Alexandria, Egypt. Briefly, the textual history is this. When the seventy-two scholars (six each from the twelve ancestral tribes of ancient Israel) completed their work, the Greek text passed immediately into widespread use among the countless Jewish communities who no longer could read the original Hebrew. When Jerusalem was destroyed in AD 70 by Roman armies, the original Hebrew manuscripts were also destroyed.

But the Greek version remained. By the fourth century AD, when Hebrew manuscript tradition began again, the Hebrew text showed—and continues to show—differences from the Greek text of six centuries earlier. Thus, the circumstance has arisen wherein the older Greek translation has suggested ways to emend the (now lost) Hebrew original. My Hebrew teacher at Dartmouth College— herself a biblical scholar from Jerusalem—said once to me in passing, "Oh, of course, we use the Greek text to correct the Hebrew."

When I got the assignment in April 2001 to translate the LXX Psalms from Greek to English, I had been praying Psalms morning and evening for seventeen years. I was, I felt, maybe ready. But then this happened: When I got to Psalm 1:1, I was suddenly not at all sure. I said to my wife later that day, "Can I really do this: I mean, why did they ask me?" She looked at me and said, "Because you're the right person."

What I found, that first line, was this: there is no good starting point. I'm always pressed, rushed, stressed, and pushed by the various things I have to do to make the money come out right for my family. Evening and morning prayer in the Psalms is always—without fail—a deliberate practice in staying at least awake, if not actually alert enough to understand the words of the psalms.

Not having ever a good, open, clear place to begin meant, and continues to mean, that translating the psalms is always resisting the pressures. And this resistance is, I came to suspect, both the very subject and the actual form of the Psalms themselves.[5] For in the Psalms, the psalmist continuously searches for strength, from God, to resist the distress and violence coming to him from everything around him. Just so, in Psalms, the chiastic form—in which first and final lines, second and penultimate lines (and so on) echo and speak across a center point to one another—is the form wherein the experience of stress is most perfectly, most fully, most exactly registered.[6]

My question "Why me?" brought into focus for me two simultaneous things: (1) not being prepared meant I'd offer no agenda of my own to replace God's purposes; (2) praying the whole Psalter each week straight through for so long meant I had few other words than psalmic ones in my heart. That is, my mind was empty of any purpose of my own; my heart was filled with the English words of Psalms. Thus, when my wife answered me, "Because you're the right person," she was registering two things: (1) my mind was ready to let God speak; and (2) my heart was prepared to speak His Psalms. I knew very clearly, however, that my translation would succeed only if I sustained the practice of praying the whole of the Psalter each week in my morning and evening prayer.

The Noetic Action of Translation

A unique collection of poems, the Psalms' rage and their sweetness constitute a way of loving God and all created persons and creatures that is inescapably *noetic*. That is, the way you *think* and the way you *are* become one and the same solely in the light of a sustained relationship to the Psalms. I knew from my years-long study of Plotinus—which I set aside to translate Psalms—that were I to betray this relationship I could not translate them.

Thinking and Being

The fifth-century BC pre-Socratic philosopher Parmenides of Elea has a striking sentence that can be approximately translated as "Thinking and being are one and the same." I say approximately translated because Parmenides' verb here—*noein*, "thinking"—possesses no real equivalent to anything whatever in modern English. Whenever we directly face this verb in any Greek with modern

English equipment, we become aware of a radical emptiness in our verbal networks, a hole in the system that runs nearly to the very bottom. The result in us is a kind of conceptual stutter, an expressive interruption we never welcome because we never choose it, an interruption we can end only when we substitute—loosely—the English verb that means "to think." But Parmenides' verb does not mean anything whatever of what we mean by thinking.

What, then, does this Greek verb *noein* mean? To approach it, let me begin with an experience ordinary enough to be familiar yet unusual enough to carry significance. The experience is simply that of looking at someone's face and all at once seeing that face as very much older or very much younger. You see in the three-year-old girl's face a woman of sixty; you see in the elderly man's face a boy of seven; you see in the face of a newborn child a wise old person you seem to have known from before time. Such "seeings" cannot exactly be *willed* by us; we're always in some way surprised by them. And this element of surprise is, in fact, crucial for two reasons. First, our surprise reveals the way in which *noetic seeing* (for "noetic" is the English adjective formed from the Greek verb) is always triggered in us by something *outside* ourselves. Second, our surprise at noetic seeing shows us that we are seeing something being *disclosed* to us, being unveiled and revealed to us. That is, our noetic seeing is primarily a fact about the thing, or the face, we are beholding— rather than about ourselves. And we are always being surprised by the reality of others: such is noetic seeing.

When this verb from Greek philosophy entered into early Christian theology, an extraordinary thing happened. The verb was understood to be, first, an essential attribute of God and, second, a divinely given attribute in us. In this new context, the verb and its noun (*nous*) came to be defined as that supreme faculty in us by which we know directly, *without any mediation*, both the reality of

God and the reality of the created world. The primary characteristics of this knowing are therefore swiftness and completeness: all in an instant, we see fully and we comprehend entirely. This supreme faculty was, in turn, distinguished from that other inward faculty in us which reasons sequentially and results in statements. This other faculty, called *dianoia* in the early Greek Christian texts, was understood to have limited powers, useful for looking out of a window and seeing that rain was imminent or for deriving a conclusion from a given set of data. *Dianoia* served useful purposes; but it was decidedly not the main event. The *nous* was the main inward event, for it alone connected us to both the Creator and the creation. In this sense, our noetic faculty revealed us to be creatures possessing a power that joined us to the very Creator; that is, *nous* manifested *who we are* as persons made in the image and likeness of God. Thus, thinking and being became one and the same.

From this understanding, we can see something of what the seventh-century AD Greek text called the Akathist to the Mother of God means when it addresses Mary as the Guide or Leader of Noetic Remaking or Refashioning. This highly shaped poetic text is a sequence of 24-line stanzas of praise to Mary as the Mother of God, with brief prose pieces connecting them, stanzas so intricately patterned as to defy—if not defeat—any real translation. Why is Mary called the Guide or Leader of Noetic Remaking? The Akathist is very clear. As the one who carries in her womb the God who created everything, and as the one who then gives birth to this very God who reshapes and re-illumines everything that has been twisted and darkened in us and by us, Mary is the one who reshapes our noetic faculty. She does this by—and this is the phrase used two lines later—*en-noeticizing our nous*. That is, her childbearing and birthgiving cause us to *see*—to behold fully—the God of all creation. And in this beholding of God in her child and simultaneously in the Person her child becomes and is, our noetic power is fully awakened, fully healed, fully restored.

The Way the Heart Sees

One further significance of the noetic faculty also derives from early Christian texts. The *nous* is understood to reside in the depths of the heart and to be, in effect, *the way the heart sees.* Here is where modern English translations of *nous* as "mind" are especially unhelpful, for whereas we conceive mind as located in the head, the *nous* is understood as dwelling in the heart. The contemporary translators of the eighteenth-century work called *The Philokalia*—that anthology of Greek texts on prayer drawn from Christian writings of the fourth to the fifteenth centuries—append a very useful definition of the heart as "the spiritual center of man's being, man as made in the image of God, his deepest and truest self. . . . 'I called with my whole heart,' says the psalmist. . . . 'Heart' has thus an all-embracing significance: 'prayer of the heart' means prayer not just of the emotions and affections, but of the whole person, including the body."[7]

Heart, in other words, is the *ontological* center of our being; our heart is *who we are*, integrated and actual persons who physically sense, psychologically feel, and discursively think.[8] The *nous* is the way our heart sees, and as such, it is that which we most abundantly *are.* The *nous* is the directly ontological organ of our personhood, disclosing who we are in and through the actions wherein we comprehend—swiftly and completely—the divinely given reality of someone other than ourselves.

"Noetic Action" in MacKenna's Plotinus

Early in 1917, as the United States entered into that inferno called
the First World War, Stephen MacKenna—an impoverished Irish-
man—published in Dublin the first of what were to be five volumes
of his astonishing translation of the third-century AD Greek philosopher Plotinus. The conditions in which this translation appeared
are, now, almost inconceivable. In April of 1916, Ireland had under-
gone that violent political trauma called the Easter Uprising, ending
in mass executions and the installation of a police state. Meanwhile,
the war in Europe had, by late 1916 and early 1917, reached levels
of wholesale destruction unmatched in ferocity by anything before
or—until the atomic holocausts in Japan in 1945—since.

At age forty-five in 1917, Stephen MacKenna had had some
moderate success as a European newspaperman. But he had deliberately abandoned every form of success some years earlier when in
1905—after finding the Greek text of Plotinus in a Moscow book-
stall—he was all at once seized with the desire to translate him.
MacKenna carried his Plotinus with him wherever he went, and, as
he wrote in his journal in December of 1907: "Whenever I look . . .
into Plotinus I feel always all the old trembling fevered longing: it
seems to me that I must be born for him, and that somehow someday I must have nobly translated him: my heart, untraveled, still to
Plotinus turns and drags at each remove a lengthening chain."[9]

A few days after writing this, MacKenna made an entry in his
journal: "Found myself, surprised myself, with a prayer on my lips, a
prayer to Plotinus that I might translate him. . . ." And early in 1916,
he had referred in a letter to his lifelong work on translating Plotinus: "This is a long wildness I've indulged in—I don't know why."[10]

My thesis is this. The only way even to begin to comprehend the
conditions and consequences of MacKenna's Plotinus is to understand them as *noetic action*. That is, MacKenna approaches Plotinus

in such a way that thinking and being become one: both in Plotinus's Greek and in MacKenna's English. In so doing, the violence of MacKenna's early twentieth-century world becomes enfolded in the cadences of Plotinus's strangely lyric Greek prose, and the result discloses what I am calling the *noetic action* of translation: in the same way you can see the girl's face in the woman of sixty, so you can see in MacKenna's elegance and strength of prose something of Plotinus's strangely compelling Greek. Here is his version of the passage near the end of Ennead III:

> The Universal circuit is like a breeze, and the voyager, still or stirring, is carried forward by it. He has a hundred varied experiences, fresh sights, changing circumstances, all sorts of events. The vessel itself furnishes incident, tossing as it drives on. And the voyager also acts of himself in virtue of that individuality which he retains because he is on the vessel in his own person and character.

These four lovely sentences of MacKenna's are, in Plotinus, a single Greek sentence. Here is the Loeb version, which maps something of the way the Greek sentence is arranged:

> And as the circuit of heaven, like a wind, courses round the man sitting, or even moving about, on the ship, there occur many and various sights and changes and incidents, and, just as in the actual ship [they occur because] he is moved either by the tossing of the ship or by himself, of his own impulse, whatever it may be, which he has because he is on the ship precisely in his own way.[11]

What MacKenna accomplishes here—and what the Loeb does not even attempt—is to register in English the *lyric movement* of Plotinus's Greek: to get the way Plotinus's phrases rise and fall in movements at once strange and clear. In registering this essential movement, MacKenna rephrases the Greek and creates English effects (e.g., "voyager, still or stirring") that possess no purely lexical basis in Plotinus—but which are effects decidedly furthering the accurate English registering of the Greek sentence's essential movement. In a letter from 1919, MacKenna says this:

> I constantly find myself unable to read, unable to understand, translations which would appear to satisfy the accepted ideas of "literalness": give me a free translation by a man of first-rate knowledge, and I'm quite often amused to find that out of the freedom I can reconstruct the Greek original almost verbatim. In other words, a good free translation can I think be proven to be much nearer to the original than most literal translation. . . .[12]

In this example, we can easily see the freedoms MacKenna employs. As the single Greek sentence becomes in his hands four English sentences, MacKenna alters the voice and mood of verbs, the subjects of sentences, the patterns of phrases as well as some actual vocabulary (both adding and deleting words). The net result of these freedoms in English is—as MacKenna says—"much nearer to the original than most literal translation" in that his four English sentences *move forward* in the way Plotinus's Greek sentence does. And in so moving MacKenna registers the mind of Plotinus—and not simply his words—the act of making significance (not merely sentences) occur. Toward the end of his work on Plotinus, MacKenna came to recognize what he had achieved: "What I have done with Plotinus is a miracle of persistent resteadying of a mind that dips and tosses and disappears like a cork on the waves of your Bay of Islands."[13] As we look into the freshness and grace of MacKenna's English, we actually draw near to the vivid beauty of Plotinus, such is the miracle.

In all of this endeavor, MacKenna is performing what I am calling the *noetic action* of translation. That is, in the contemporary face of MacKenna we see the ancient eyes and mind of Plotinus clearly and comprehensively. In this sense, then, the noetic translator is very like the voyager in Plotinus's ship: he is at once being carried forward by winds beyond his ken and control and yet he "also acts of himself, in virtue of that individuality which he retains because he is on the vessel in his own person and character." Each action MacKenna initiates—reconfiguring a phrase, adding a word—occurs wholly within the Plotinian ongoing current; and the "miracle of persistent resteadying" is the action of a noetic disclosure wherein Plotinus's mind is revealed to us. The old, bad dilemma of translation—literal vs. free—is here perfectly solved in MacKenna's noetic practice.

The relationship between a translator and a "translated" therefore consists of reciprocal obedience and mutual ascesis. The obedience of the translator is, of course, obedience to the mind and will and heart of the other author; the obedience of the translated lies in the gracefulness wherewith the original words and phrases and sentences accept the translator's "persistent resteadying." Thus, the fruitful translator and translated will find, in their relationship, the action of mutual ascesis. In this light, then, the noetic significance of MacKenna's Plotinus is plain: thinking and being are one and the same. That is, translation requires that you give your life so that another might live.

Let me end with an example I have created within English to reinforce MacKenna's point. George Herbert's beautiful lyric "Vertue" begins this way:

Sweet day, so cool, so calm, so bright,
The bridall of the earth and skie:
The dew shall weep thy fall tonight;
    For thou must die.

It is not only the rhyme and meter, so skillfully and intricately made, that creates the deep pattern here; it is also the many tiny patterns of syllable and shape (e.g., *bright–bridall*; The brid*all*–The dew sh*all*) that concentrate the energy so deeply and satisfyingly. All, all is unmade when we "translate" it literally:

> The day is so sweet, so cool and calm, and so bright:
> The earth and the sky are wedded.
> Tonight, when you are fallen, the dew will weep for you.

The big patterns are here gone; and, with them, the dozen or so tiny patterns—like the countless sparks of heaven's sun—are all gone out. And it is these thousand brightnesses that are the great loss, are the damage we cannot repair, when we move from the Hebrew Psalms . . . to any English version whatever.

The Answer Lies in the Gospels

Mother Maria (Gysi) leads us to the crux of the matter, offering this concerning the dilemma of the Hebrew Psalms' translatability:

> . . . and the distant, unhalting psalmody in the Orthodox Church had often carried me to the shores of eternity. . . . But, one day, I was aroused as out of a slumber, and with sudden, violent clarity I knew that I did not know the Psalms; that, what I knew, was but a surface, or what I myself projected into the Psalms; it was not the life of the Psalm. And I was ashamed.
>
> Could it not be that each Psalm had a *face*, a personal face, a particular, unique life, which had remained hidden from me within the eternity flow of liturgical prayer?[14]

And so she sought in the act of direct translation to find this "particular, unique life" in each Psalm: to let the sacred Hebrew— "word by word, listening, delicately, with held breath"—*breathe* in her English. She called her version *An Exploratory Translation*— signaling the tentative nature of the whole attempt: "So I set out as an explorer, with joy and trembling, on to the vast sea of the Hebrew Psalms. As I proceeded, I halted at every word, attentive and alert to its living nerve."[15] Her results are deeply moving and highly instructive. As in her essays, so here, she illumines, refines, deepens, and clarifies us. Yet her versions fail to resolve a primary problem, a problem she is very acutely aware she cannot resolve:

> The Hebrew Psalm is in a *rhythmic measure.* The beat of the rhythm carries the life of the Psalm. With the beat the Psalm moves swiftly forward, and, with the beat, it is austerely held, still, within its eternity life. But the beat is inseparably linked to the Hebrew language, inimitable. How could I learn to be vitally anchored in that beat, and how to comprehend its significance? Could that which is strange ever become familiar, my own, or, rather I His?

This could not be better put. The Psalms' "particular, unique life" is indeed linked to sacred Hebrew in a way that *cannot be imitated in another language.* The Judaic conclusion is, in this sense, the right one: Psalmic revelation either is directly in Hebrew, or it doesn't exist.

This, in turn, forces the central issue of all Christianity: How is Psalmic consciousness translatable? The answer lies in the Gospels, where every word of every event is alert to this issue of translatability. Put it this way: at what moment, exactly, is Jesus of Nazareth no longer a Jew? At Cana, when He first affronts custom? At the well, where He disregards old wounds? In the sharp exchanges with the

Pharisaical scholars? On the cross? In the resurrection? There is no one moment. *There is, instead, an unceasing process, wherein Messianic Judaism is steadily and wholly translated into the actual Person of Jesus.* In this "translation" He does not alter or change sacred Hebrew; rather, He fulfills the potential that was always in it from the start.

What this process of translation possesses in the Gospels is a characteristic rhythm: a *"rhythmic measure"* (to use Mother Maria's term) whose shape, strength, and character are—in and through the mind of Christ—determined by the psalmic measure. Understood otherwise, the problem of translation is insoluble. So comprehended, it becomes not simply soluble but actually *permeable*: that is, all languages begin to open to all others. Such is the meaning of Acts 2, when, on the day of Pentecost, the "rushing, mighty wind" of the Holy Spirit reverses the curse of Babel: "The multitude came together, and were confounded, because that every man heard them speak in his own language" (Acts 2:6 AV). These are the "Jews, devout men, out of every nation under heaven" (Acts 2:5). And they are amazed at what they hear—and in their amazement they at first deny what they hear and accuse the speakers of being drunk. But, rather, they are *acting noetically*: their ears are opened to hear the Holy Spirit of God Himself, who finds His voice in them through the words of their own languages.

The moment is charged with meaning, with a superabundance of charged meanings. Peter responds, "For these are not drunken, as ye suppose. . . . But this is that which was spoken by the prophet Joel" (Acts 2:15–16). The prophecies Peter points to are prophecies of *translatability*, of events in which opposites fuse, contraries exchange places, and everything feels the flood of the Holy Spirit.

Peter also quotes the final four lines of the eleven-line Psalm 15[16], the last of which is: "Thou makest known to me life's ways, thou wilt fill me in joy with thy countenance, at thy right hand are pleasures forevermore." Beyond death and its corruptions, the psalm says, lies "the path of life" (in the AV translation)—a path, Peter says, now open for us by the resurrection of Christ, a path of *translation into joy*. Joy in Lucan Greek is εὐφροσύνη (*euphrosynē*); in Psalmic Hebrew, it is החמש (*simhah*[16]), a regnant word. For the joy David sings in Psalm 15[16] is now (Peter says) actually here.

The spark leaps from Hebrew to Greek and both blaze up: and *euphrosynē* begins to burn with the intensities of *simhah*. This fire is in turn lit by the great Fire that Moses sees in Exodus 3, the Fire that burns with every conceivable intensity but without even the slightest destruction: the Fire of Permanent Livingness.

The Mosaic moment connects. What is your name? asks Moses of this Fire. My Name? says the Fire: it is *'eheyeh 'asher 'eheyeh* (אֶהְיֶה אֲשֶׁר אֶהְיֶה, I am that I am). I AM (*'eheyeh*) is a tiny syllabic step from both the Name of God and the verb *to be*. That is, these three words are deeply connected:[17]

אֶהְיֶה (*'eheyeh*) = I am
יהוה (*YHWH*) = God
הָיָה (*hayah*) = to be

The boundaries of each may be said to be permeable to the energies of the other two. "Thou wilt show me the *path of life*," says Psalm 16 in the AV translation: אֹרַח חַיִּים (*'orah hayyim*). The path of life, the Psalm says, *is* God—and (Peter says) God *is* the resurrected Christ. The spark leaps.

3

Five Conundrums
of Translatability

In this chapter the author focuses on the relationship between the original (or "Ur") Hebrew text of Psalms, the second-century BC Septuagint Greek (LXX) translation, and the much later reconstructed Masoretic Hebrew text upon which most subsequent Western translations have been based. He focuses first on four key points that point to the LXX text as a truer guide for Christians: (1) LXX grammatical "miracles of reconfiguration" allow for "living divine unity" to be incarnated within "living earthly diversity"; (2) the human "I" is established as distinct from the commonality of persons and therefore capable of entering into direct communion with the singular divine Thou; (3) the tiny ascetic practices of our personal and family lives are understood in the LXX to be one with the divinely shaped statutes that govern all of God's creation; and (4) the earth and its time are shown to "endure" in the same way the Holy Mother's life endures: through translation to life, direct participation in God. The author goes on to examine some apparently untranslatable aspects of the Hebrew psalms: Hebrew's compactness, its understanding of the very alphabetic letters as having the shape of God; the dense and tightly woven sounds of the language; and the mysterious biblical future tense for which English has no equivalent, and which allows one to "stay in the historically present and real until the truly Real," the actual God, "is met finally and fully." Nonetheless, the author concludes that, following a noetic process of study and prayer, all of this can be translated into any language as long as we remain steeped in the reality of the incarnate Christ. —*Ed.*

Greek or Hebrew?

In translating Psalms, the first perplexity one encounters is the text itself: that is, whether we are to give more weight to the Masoretic Hebrew or to the Septuagint (LXX) Greek. Yet, if we approach the matter as a place where God's judgment is occurring, then we can see that there exists a point where Masoretic Hebrew and LXX Greek are *together* pointing toward the vanished Ur-Hebrew text. This point is irrevocably lost to Hebrew except insofar as it gives itself, in kenotic love, to LXX Greek; and it is comparably lost to the Greek except insofar as it gives itself in love to the Hebrew. For in this reciprocal action of kenotic loving, the two (conflicting) texts together point to the vanished—but still active—Ur-Hebrew prototype, and therefore God's judgment is enacted.

Almost from the start in the second century BC the Greek of the Septuagint has been viewed in terms of condemnation. Learned Jews fluent in Hebrew have, in every age, seen any translation whatever of biblical Hebrew as at least degradation, if not outright blasphemy; and the appearance of the LXX Greek version caused the world (the Jewish legends say) to fall into three days of continuous darkness. Equally, Western Christendom, since the Renaissance period of vernacular translations of the Bible, has viewed the LXX translation as a clumsy deflection from the shining glory of the original Hebrew: that is, as bad in itself for being a deflection, and doubly bad for being so graceless and so labored and so—well—persistently *odd* in gait and whole spirit.

I want to make the claim that LXX Greek is, in essence, very beautiful in three distinct ways, and spiritually necessary to us in a fourth. First, it possesses beauty in relation to biblical Hebrew; second, it is beautiful in relation to classical Greek poetry; and third, it is beautiful in itself, as a sacred Christian language. But, perhaps most crucially, it is more open than the Hebrew to the Incarnation. And here we may return to Baron Wormser's point in chapter 2 that poetry is "rooted in praise of being, the goodness of what is." For the Hebrew Psalms, into which Christ infused His Presence, both prophetically through the poets of Psalms and in His own earthly life and prayer, are wholly filled with the *goodness of what is*: that is, with Christ Himself. And the LXX translators—learned Jews of Alexandria in the second century BC, highly alert to the Messiah's imminent arrival on earth—at some point in or before their work on Psalms left off their "Jewishness" to become open *in their work* to Jesus as Messiah. One can indeed *sense* this openness everywhere— in ways one cannot similarly sense it in Masoretic Hebrew.

I put before you four highly significant examples of this openness.

A Theological Grammar of the Incarnation

LXX verbs exhibit sharp and sudden changes in *tense*—often in exactly successive lines, and sometimes in the very same line. I would suggest that the LXX poet/translator of Psalms was using Greek verb tenses as a grammatical "commentary" on Hebrew verbal modes (as, for example, the Greek imperfect tense for the Hebrew iterative mode)—a commentary that is, at every point, theologically charged with the highest spiritual significance.

One can glimpse something of this significance in the relation between the LXX Greek participle and the Hebrew participle. In classical Greek—evidently everywhere familiar to the LXX poet/ translator—the use of the participle was wide, exact, and deeply far-reaching. The Homeric poems already exhibited the full range of such usage; and the fifth-century BC classical poets—such as Pindar and Sophocles—brought Homeric usage to its highest pinnacle. The tenses of the Greek participle, however, "express only continuance, simple occurrence, and completion with permanent result"— and are therefore "timeless."[1] Similarly, says Gesenius, the Hebrew "participle of all conjugations can apply to every tense."[2]

This similarity meant, then, that the LXX poet of the Psalter faced a difficult decision at every moment about how to adapt classical Greek usage to biblical Hebrew. For although both languages implied a kind of eternality in the participle, classical Greek tended always toward a prolongation of a *diversified earthly aliveness* (classical polytheism may even be said to be rooted in participial usages), while biblical Hebrew tended always toward a prolongation of *unified divine aliveness*.

As a result, in the very first line of Psalm 118, the LXX poet accomplished a tiny miracle of reconfiguration by using a plural Greek participle to translate a plural Hebrew indicative verb: μακά-ριοι . . . οἱ πορευόμενοι (*makarioi hoi poreuomenoi*, blessed . . . the "walking-ones"). What is new to Hebrew usage is that the LXX participle here enacts a Hebrew indicative—a usage whose primary effect is to incarnate *living divine unity* in (and as) *living earthly diversity*. No classical Greek poet would have employed the Greek participle in this fashion; and in so doing, the LXX psalmic poet or poets changed both Greek and Hebrew and thereby created what, in its totality, may be rightly seen as the theological grammar of the Incarnation.[3]

The Unity of Personhood Is Established

The incarnative movement in the LXX, signaled by small verbal events within Psalms, is most strongly felt in Psalm 118. By line 5 of stanza 1 of Psalm 118 (*Aleph*),[4] the hypostatic unity of the human person is established by a single stroke in the LXX Greek suffix and the MT Hebrew—strokes verbally tiny but hypostatically decisive in both languages. And this establishing of the human person in line 5 follows—as a direct result—upon the establishing of the divine "thou" in line 4; for in lines 1–3, God is (relatively speaking) remote as third-person singular—just as the human person is remote as first-person plural (*-oi* endings of first 3 words—and then words 6 and 7 of Psalm 118's first line).

Here are the opening lines of the Great Psalm in my translation:

1   Blessed are the blameless in the way,
    Who walk in the law of the Lord.
2   Blessed be those searching his testimonies,
    Who seek him with the whole heart.
3   For the workers of iniquity
    Have never walked in his ways.
4   Thou hast charged that thy commandments
    Be kept most diligently.
5   Oh that my ways be all directed
    To the keeping of thy statutes.

Note, too: In Greek, the *nomos* (νόμος, law) of line 1 is reflected in the *anomia* (ἀνομία, iniquity, sin, or lawlessness) of line 3: that is, all our iniquity arises from our uprooting God's *nomos* from our deep heart.

These sequences are crucial, therefore: plural humanity ("those") changes in the movement of this stanza to become the single unity of personhood ("my") in prayer; blessedness comes by way of blameless walking in the law, searching God's testimonies in fullness of heart; the divine "him" and "his" become "thou" and "thy"; and the two join—the human "I" (in "my ways" in l. 5) now able, in fervent prayer, to be directed to the "keeping of thy statutes."[5]

The Door Is Opened to *Theosis*

There are ten Hebrew words for *law*, God's holy Word, in Psalm 118: *law, way, statute, commandment, judgment, testimony, precept, righteousness, word,* and *saying.* These ten Hebrew words are, in the Septuagint, translated by nine (not ten) Greek words.[6] The two, and most often repeated, Hebrew words that become one Greek word are *statute* (Heb. חֻקִּים, *huqqim*) and *precept* (Heb. פִּקּוּדִים, *piqqudim*), translated by the single Greek word δικαιώματα (*dikaiōmata*). (NB: all three words, the two Hebrew and the one Greek, are plurals.)

- *Statutes* are the divinely created patterns within which all creation takes life and moves. They are, to us, incomprehensible and mysterious, for their roots are not in this world but in His infinite wisdom.
- *Precepts*, by contrast, are easily comprehended and readily appreciated, for they are the orders that God gives concerning things He has given into our care (e.g., our family).

In using one Greek word for the two Hebrew terms, the LXX translators create an astonishing revelation: that the practical care we give our families is *one with* the divine patterns of the created universe. In this single act, these wise men paved the way for family life to be understood as an *ascetic* practice. They saw that the daily and unceasing cycle of sacrifice in family can only be endured as and in the desert of deliberate surrender to God—a desert known fully by the Holy Orthodox Fathers who, several centuries later, described, precisely, how to live there and what to do; and who continue to be now for us our masters and guides in the deserts of our homes. For there in these deserts flow the rivers of pure and glorifying consciousness in God.

The student of the LXX Psalter may therefore conclude that the tiny icons of our ascetical lives are—*in practice*—not to be distinguished from their divine prototypes. And in this sense the LXX text of Psalm 118 is far more open as well to what Orthodox Christians understand as *deification* or *theosis*: as the direct communion, without intermediate steps, that we can achieve with the divine Creator through the long disciplines of Orthodox ascesis. For, as Hebrew *piqqudim* (precepts) vanishes, we can see that the Greek ἐντολαί (*entolai*, commandments) are the historically actualized and human patterns of the divinely shaped statutes.[7] And thus we can say this: that *once the statutes are actualized, the Messiah has arrived on earth.*

The Earth and the Earthly Day *Endure*

I make note of another example of this crucial difference of perception between the Hebrew and the LXX in discussing the *Lamed*-stanza of Psalm 118 in chapter 11. Here the LXX translators make no verbal distinction (as the Hebrew does) between the *enduring* of a day, of the earth, and of heaven itself, using the Greek verb διαμένει (*diamenei*) for all three. Each endures in the same way the Holy Mother's life endures: through the action of translation—translation to life. As I ask in the later chapter: how can any earthly day be said to endure in the very way that God's word endures in heaven? It can only be to emphasize that logically impossible fact that Psalm 118 is everywhere asserting: the earthly incarnation of the divine is raising all earthly things up, *and into direct participation in* God through His immeasurable love for us. And this can only be so *when the Messiah is actually arriving on earth.* Such knowledge is embedded in the Septuagint Greek.

The Compactness of the Hebrew Psalm

When faced with (say) five Hebrew words in Psalms, the first contemporary instinct of translation is to create comparable compactness. But contemporary English compactness most often is staccato and reductive; it loses, therefore, the essential quality of Hebrew sacred poetry: divinity amidst lightness. The density of sound and semantic energy serves entirely a sacred purpose: to hold God in speech. That is, only in this charged compactness can the terrifying *dimensionality* of God be held; only so can the dark rage and bright ecstasy find ground and take root in us. For all things on all heavens and all earths grow from Him—and die out in Him. And only in the charged thickness of the semantic/sonic energy that is sacred Hebrew can this ceaseless growing and dying be registered—once and for all—fully and exactly.

Thus the trim *compactness* of the Hebrew psalm is, apparently, untranslatable; the Hebrew prefix/suffix pattern has no reflex in English; hence, our translations get heavy—must so get—where Hebrew stays nimbly light. Not being able to translate the compactness means that the concentration of formal energy is dispersed. This is disastrous in all the psalms; it is intensely damaging in the alphabetic psalms; and it is a crisis of terminal proportions in Psalm 118. A glance at the Hebrew text of 118, even knowing nothing of the language, can reveal something of the problem.

> 'ashre themime-darekh
> > haholekhim bethorath yehwah
> 'ashre notsere 'edothayw
> > bekhol-lev yidreshuhu

'af lo-fa'alu 'awlah
  bidrakhayw halakhu
'attah tsiwwithah fiqqudeykha
  lishmor me'od
'ahalay yikkonu derakhay
  lishmor huqqeykha
'az lo-'evosh
  behabbiti 'el-kol-mitswotheykha
'odekha beyosher levav
  belomdi mishpete tsidqekha
'eth-huqqeykha 'eshmor
  'al-ta'azveni 'ad-me'od (Ps. 118[119]:1–8)[8]

These trim and shapely half-lines, with their two or three words in each (counting bound words as one), sprawl very badly in English; and their every concentration of formal energy is scattered in translation beyond any recognition. The King James AV is not a bad translation; in fact, it is abundantly beautiful. But its coherence of pattern has almost nothing to do with original Hebrew coherence—nor can it. The loss is so profound and total that we can only pretend not to notice:

1   Blessed are the undefiled in the way, who walk in the law of the Lord.

2   Blessed are they that keep his testimonies, and that seek him with the whole heart.

3   They also do no iniquity: they walk in his ways.

4   Thou hast commanded us to keep thy precepts diligently.

5   O that my ways were directed to keep thy statutes!

6   Then shall I not be ashamed, when I have respect unto all thy commandments.

7   I will praise thee with uprightness of heart, when I
     shall have learned thy righteous judgments.

8   I will keep thy statutes: O forsake me not utterly.
     (Ps. 119:1–8 AV)

Here is an example from the final (terrifying) line of Psalm
87[88]:

Lover and friend hast thou put far from me, and mine
acquaintance into darkness. (Ps. 88:18 AV)

In the Hebrew this is:

הִרְחַקְתָּ מִמֶּנִּי אֹהֵב וָרֵעַ
מְיֻדָּעַי מַחְשָׁךְ:

That is, four words in the first line, two in the second—six as against
fourteen in English. Latin (in the translation from the Hebrew)
does better—nine words:

Elongàsti a me amantem et socium; noti mei tenebrae.[9]

And the Hebrew sounds are far more compact and dense than the
English:

hirhaqta mimmenni 'ohev warea'
meyudda'ay mahshakh

Here the weave of *h* and *m* sounds is untranslated (and possibly
untranslatable) by either English or Latin.

The Letters of Torah Are the Shape of God

From Hartman's *Midrash and Literature*, we learn this: "All the letters of the Torah, by their shapes, combined and separated, swad-
dled letters, curved ones and crooked ones, superfluous ones and

elliptic ones, minute and large ones, and inverted, the calligraphy of the letters, the open and closed pericopes and the ordered ones, all of them are the shape of God. Blessed be He."[10] That is to say, the calligraphic activity of written Torah *is* the very activity of God Himself in the ceaseless operations of the living universe. The former is not a "mimicry" of the latter but is the very thing itself.

Hence, the vastly powerful (yet infinitely delicate) sounds and rhythms and semantic registerings that constitute the Hebrew of Psalm 87[88]'s final line: these sounds and rhythms and registerings are woven into the shapes of the letters, which are the shapes of the sound of psalmic consciousness.

And the overwhelming agony of this last line of Psalm 87[88] is a straight shock from Heaven's depths and heights: the desolated agony of pure abandonment. That is, the so-called subtleties of Kabbalistic perception are, in Psalms, always joined to the terror and urgency and joy and dread of God's actual living presence. This indissoluble joining of delicate linguistic sensitivity and profound spiritual power is unique to psalmic Hebrew: which is to say, to Torah—untranslatably unique.

Translating the Hebrew Sonic Figure

Consider Psalm 97[98], "Sing psalms to the Lord on a lyre, on a lyre and in psalmic voice" (in my translation).

In Hebrew the sonic figure is dense and tightly inwoven. The rhymes of the first and final sounds (forms of the same word) bind the line, while the second and penultimate words are conceptual rhyme (i.e., God and the psalm's voice); and the middle pair are the exact same preposition and word phrase:

הָרְמַז לוֹקוּ רוֹנכְּב רוֹנכְּב הָוהיַל וּרמְּזַ:

zammeru layhwah bekhinnor bekhinnor weqol zimrah

Typo: זַמְּרוּ לַיהֹוָה בְּכִנּוֹר בְּכִנּוֹר וְקוֹל זִמְרָה

The Greek catches some of this:

ψάλατε τῷ Κυρίῳ ἐν κιθάρᾳ, ἐν κιθάρᾳ καὶ φωνῇ ψαλμοῦ
psalate tō Kyriō en kithara, en kithara kai phōnē psalmou

The abstract pattern of sonic-semantic rhyming is held. But it is abstract in the sense that the Greek *freezes* the Hebrew's movements inside the pattern, makes the flow of Hebrew sounds and syllables light and quick and dance-like where the Hebrew motion is, in fact, slow and dense and inexorable.

The Greek is very beautiful in its performance, very pure and attentive to Hebrew patterning. That it *must* move as it must (i.e., balletically) does not diminish its profound mindfulness. When, though, we move to (say) the Latin, the loss grows:

Psallite Jehovae in cithara, in cithara et voce cantus.

The pattern is simply lost; only the mid-line expression of it remains. The AV follows the Latin loss:

Sing unto the Lord with the harp; with the harp, and the
voice of a psalm.

The Orthodox variant:

Chant ye unto the Lord with a harp, with the harp and
with the voice of a psalm.[11]

A sad business, seen aright. The Greek losses are enough: the reality of God-on-earth that the motion and weight of the Hebrew carry so massively—this reality the Greek abandons, *as it must*. But when we see and hear the Latin loss of primary Hebrew pattern, it is heartbreaking. Adding these to the further English losses of rhythm and semantic-sonic compactness, a compactness kept by Latin and Greek, the losses are truly devastating. But each loss *must* happen; that is, Greek must be as it is and nothing else; so, too, Latin and English. Yet the *inevitability* only increases the sadness.

The Actual God and the Mystery of the Biblical Future Tense

This tiny sentence ends line 48 in Psalm 118: וְאָשִׂיחָה בְחֻקֶּיךָ: (*we'asihah vehuqqeykha*). It also ends the *Waw* section of this alphabetic text. "And I will meditate in thy statutes" is how the AV rightly reads it. But the mystery of the biblical future tense: who can read it now wholly? *What is the relation of the historic time in the biblical texts to the historic time we now occupy?*

The verb holds the answer perhaps: שׂיח (*siah*).[12] Strange conjunction of meanings: "to muse," "to complain." The citations in BDB point to Psalm 77 (AV), where we see this: "I remembered God and was troubled: / I complained, and my spirit was overwhelmed" (77:3 AV). "I call to remembrance my song in the night: / I commune with mine own heart: / And my spirit made diligent search" (77:6 AV).

The verbs "complain" and "commune" are the same verb in Hebrew: *siah*. But where the AV has the past tenses both times, the Hebrew imperfect is best read as future in both. The overall AV sense of things is construably right, but it blurs the essential point that the verb is future: I *will* complain, I *will* commune.

Essential how? Essential, in that futurity here links the *remembered* holy past with the *envisioned* holy future through the inward process of (1) complaining-musing and (2) spiritual searching. Complaining-musing is biblical meditation. That is, rather than serving to bring the practitioner *out of* the dark swirl of history, biblical meditation plunges him or her directly *into* that fearful churning so as to reveal God as *the Presence-in-the-darkness* ("though I walk

through the valley of the shadow of death"; 23:4 AV). Biblical meditation doesn't smooth out the anxieties; it deepens them into God.
The first is fantasy, dangerous to the extent that such smoothings out
become a psychic craving—for then it is the basis of addictive religion. The second is real, for it compels you to stay *in* the historically
present and real until the truly Real, or the entirely and ceaselessly
Present One, is met finally and fully: that is, Christ Jesus our Lord.
This is a distinct and exact practice. How does it work, then?

To understand this, we must engage the second part of the
inward process: searching. In memory, the song is recalled: נְגִינָה
(*neginah*; BDB 618b)—and the word is several times used in the
title of individual psalms. That is, the psalmic narrator is self-
reflexively remembering the psalm itself; and this act of psalmodic
remembering initiates the search. Then comes the meditation—and
where is it held? It is held "in the night," בַלַּיְלָה (*vallaylah*), that is, in
the swirl of darkness of actuality within. And the meditation is
done "with my heart," עִם לְבָבִי ('*im-levavi*). The heart descends into
the darkness in the heart—but *only* in the active memory of psalmic
song: the heart goes into itself. And the heart does so *not because a
fantasized peace is there but because the actual God is there.*

And there, in that darkness, what does one find? One finds
the conditions for spiritual search. And the psychic content of
this search is psalmic words. As you plunge into the fearful swirl
of the inward darknesses, you can begin to follow the contours of
biblical—especially psalmic—words: how they are alive in a vibrancy
of connectiveness beyond imagining—and how this intense life is
lived along the lines of relations of sounds and meanings in Holy
Scripture.

In the valley of death's shadow within, we search the holy
words of Psalms: and their life bursts upon us, flooding us with
depth of connection, with intensities of meanings. Meditation is the

process of this search within complaint-song, a search at once suffused with the stillness of sacred study and churning with the heart's darknesses—and the stillness and the churning are one complex event within us.

Thus, each line is *deuterosemic*.[13] "Thou holdest mine eyes' waking" (Ps. 77:4 AV) means both (1) our anxieties have shattered our sleep, and (2) a contemplative attentiveness has now been fully awakened in us: both terrifying agony and genuine mindfulness. (The crucifixion would complete all deuterosemic circumstances—hence, we meditate *in* it.) The mindfulness of agony and the agony of mindfulness are inescapably one in biblical meditation. Thus, to "meditate in thy statutes" is the call to all inwardness in God and His holy Word.

What Is a Translator to Do?

The key to the Psalms is the presence of David. He is king, he is father, he is shepherd and son, adulterer and grieving father: heavy with crime, purest poet of God. To raise the issue of David's presence is also to ask the foundational question of all Hebrew sacred poetry: how is it composed? That is, how is it conceivable that a poet in one century can write a poem under the name of a poet from an earlier century? This is, for us, either insane egotism or dangerous naiveté: such a person is either a robot or a madman. Psalmic tradition affirms ten authors of Psalms. All are David. The logic of this is *prophecy*: David is prophetically the author of all the psalms. We do not have the category of prophecy.

That's the first problem. The second one is that the techniques of Hebrew poetry translate approximately, not precisely. Thus, we see the mid-ranges of Hebraic technique moderately well; but we cannot see the far horizons of it nor the details of its intricate surfaces.

To see the requisite distances we must see the whole of Hebrew verbal culture; to see the intricate surfaces we must stand open and alert before the actual Hebrew lines and rhythms. Only then can we begin to see finally what those long-perceived mid-ranges—that is, the parallelisms and repetitions—are actually about.

A third problem is the relation between the first two: Why is Hebraic technique the appropriate mode for Hebraic prophecy? In answering this, we come back to the question of David's presence: as David takes shape—literary shape—*by means of* the Psalms, that is, as he comes before our eyes in and through the sacred poems, *how is he composed?* For, regardless of whether the actual composer of any given psalm could have been the historical David, all the psalms—individually and all together—are compositions of David; that is, *they compose the presence we know as David.*

Thus, when we see prophecy and technique as the composing of David's presence, we will see why these poems were so essential in forming the sacred consciousness of our Lord: why, that is, He is the Son of David. Saint Paul writes "we have the mind of Christ" (ἡμεῖς δὲ νοῦν Χριστοῦ ἔχομεν, *hēmeis de noun Christou echomen*) (1 Cor 2:16): that is, we have—at least we *can* have—the Psalms. *Reading the Psalms is the composing of ourselves in Christ.*[14]

One answer to our dilemma, of course, is to learn Hebrew— or at least enough to enter the outer courtyard, as it were, of the holy temple of the Word. For once there, we may begin to approach the high place: with poverty, with (that is) the poor shreds of our miserable grasp of the sacred words: that is, with prayer. We must pray ourselves into Hebrew; our very study must be prayer—what could be righter?—if we are to enter the penumbra, the vivid brightness, of sacred words. For living in that brightness is an unceasing *connectiveness,* a praying without ceasing wherein each sound and syllabic shape connects once, twice, or more to surrounding sounds and shapes. This connectiveness is, first of all, a local "breathing," a kind of capillary or synaptic flow or humming, that awakens us wholly; and the further we probe this connectiveness the wider— and deeper—run the patterns of it. These patterns are plainest in the Hebrew but they are held almost entirely in LXX Greek—and (here is the essential point) they are *translatable* into any other language on earth. In other words, the psalmic student working solely, say, with English or German or French or Aleut has open before him the fullness of steady psalmic breathing.

That is, just as the lion softly and steadily growls as it consumes the prey it has brought down, so, too, psalmic meditation follows a softly "growling" rhythm that nourishes the one who prays the psalms. For this psalmic music is both the engine and the fuel of psalmic meditation. Much has been written on Hebrew poetics— much of it possessing great accuracy and deep insight. But what moves every Hebrew line of psalmic poetry is best comprehended as this "growl" of unceasing nourishment: a rhythmic growl that is softly audible and deeply pleasurable. And what is true of the Hebrew is perfectly re-created in the movement and sound of LXX psalmic Greek: a re-creation always deferential to Hebrew and yet completely nourishing all who attend to LXX psalmic music.

Just as there is no moment in the Gospels after which Jesus of Nazareth ceases being a Jew—for Jesus is steadily and wholly engaged in a process wherein Messianic Judaism is becoming *fully translated* into His Person—just so: there is nothing of psalmic music that cannot be made to breathe fully and beautifully in any other language—provided, of course, that the translator has searched deeply, noetically, in the darkness in the heart, in the active memory of psalmic song, both the Hebrew and the Greek patterns in form-ing his or her Aleut or French or English patterns: for "every breath praise[s] the Lord."

4

The Angels Sing

Reflections on a Rule of Prayer

These reflections are an assemblage of journal entries reflecting the author's experience of psalmic prayer: the place of personal prayer in the Orthodox Church as a taking home of the mystical union with God offered in each Liturgy; its routinizing of this in a regulated life (by following a Rule); its participation in and reflection of the ordered hierarchical drama that mirrors the creation itself; and its ascetic renunciation of the swarm of our emotional demands. How is this done, and why? Why do we chant? Psalms are the prayerbook of the Church, a participation in the Mind of Christ. Sobriety is a spiritual practice, a choosing of discipline and freedom over ecstasy and enslavement. And Psalms give us our personhood and joy. They lead us to the desert; their joy is in the rhythm and in sustaining the rule. The angels sing, each time, when one fulfills the Rule. —*Ed.*

How good to give praise to the Lord, to sing psalms to
thy name, O Most High,

To proclaim every morning thy mercy and thy truth
every night . . . (Psalm 91:1–2)

"Daily we rise with the Psalms, and imperceptibly,
inside the call of Christ, they lead us to look at ourselves, and into the way of repentance." (Mother Maria[1])

"For this reason, every devout man will pray to thee at
set times and seasons: when the floods of great waters
come they will not reach him." (Psalm 31:6)

1

The Holy Orthodox Church has two essential characteristics: it is a *mystical* and a *monastic* Church. By mystical I mean that the essence of its practice is to bring the participant into the direct experience of God. The Divine Liturgy is this practice; and in being this, the Liturgy accomplishes its end at once perfectly and approximately. That is, every celebration of the Liturgy brings about the mystical union with God at the very moment it can only point toward such a union as something that will occur beyond this time and place.

The Orthodox Church is *monastic* in that everything she says and does is doubly influenced by monastic life: the rules of fasting and prayer; the frequency, sequence, and length of services; the rituals and texts of devotion and praise. Where monasticism is unknown in Protestantism and remote in Roman Catholicism, it is visible, essential, and determinative in Orthodoxy. The aim of Orthodox monastery life may be described as the routinizing of the mystical; that is, it seeks to make union with God the form and content of every moment in the monk's life. This routinizing of the mystical is what the practice of "ceaseless prayer" seeks to effect. If the mystical describes the end of Orthodox practice, monastic describes the means to this end.

These two essential characteristics of the Orthodox Church give rise, in turn, to two more. The mystical in Orthodoxy creates the *hierarchical* as its truest outward expression. The double nature of the Liturgy—that is, its perfection and its approximation—means that every liturgical gesture and word by every liturgical participant is simultaneously in God and on earth. Thus, each gesture and each word is part of an ordered drama in which certain elements of voice and movement are valued far more than others, and it is therefore a hierarchical drama. This drama of Liturgy is hierarchical, of course, because in Orthodoxy the creation itself is understood to be such, with levels of sacred existence ranging far below and far above the human. This hierarchical nature of the creation is also reproduced within each element of it, so that every blade of grass as well as every human being and every angel is also hierarchical in nature. Yet, at the same moment that each element is hierarchically related to every other element, each is also simultaneously in God, perfectly and mystically co-inhered therein with every other created element, being, and angel. Hierarchy is Mystery.

Finally, in the Orthodox Church the monastic dimension gives rise to her *ascetic* character. If hierarchy is the outward form of the mystical, then asceticism is the outward form of the monastic. What is asceticism? Properly understood and practiced, it is a clarification of life. In following the Orthodox faith, for example, one finds that where previously the desire for food was followed by the consumption of it, now a new situation obtains. Now, between the desire and the satisfaction, a space is opened: the space of fasting. Into this space rush a swarm of emotional demands, alternately clamoring and whining and self-pitying, and bullying—and sometimes all at once. Simply wait, letting this swarm die of its own hysteria, and then will begin to open the possibility of *God-with-us*, of *theosis*.[2]

2

The Psalms as prayer, in their entirety *and only so*, give us our personhood. They are in this our private liturgy, enacted every morning and every evening of every day. Note well: the public liturgy is woven and woven with the Psalms, while the holy songs are shot through with psalmic light. What binds the private and public liturgies, then, is precisely what coheres each—and is what also cohered our Lord's life: the Psalms. The rule of prayer is activated and sustained by both our direct and full participation in the liturgical and sacramental life of the Orthodox Church, and the praying of the Psalter daily. The Psalms are essential; the life of the liturgy is essential. In many ways they are close to being one thing. Abba Philemon said that the Psalms "embrace everything in all the Divine Scriptures."[3]

3

The Psalms are the oldest and possibly the truest prayerbook in the Holy Orthodox tradition. They are the prayers that our Lord Himself prayed, they were on His lips again and again in His ministry, and they were among the final words He spoke as He died on the cross. Praying them, then, is perhaps the profoundest way to enter into His own life of prayer and *into our own personhood*. For as Psalms formed in Him the consciousness always latent in them, so He infused His presence into them. And just so our own personhood—*not* who we individually and accidentally are and experience, but that personhood which is who we are *in God*. He, in our encounter with Him in Psalms, brings that forth in us. One's personhood may feel a tiny bit impersonal at first; but the fire of prayer quickly burns away those attachments to our individualisms which are making it seem thin. And then we *are* in Christ; we are

Where we have always been but did not recognize and affirm as so.

As we pray the Psalms we participate in some way in this psalmic consciousness of our Lord. We enter the penumbra of psalmic light that He revealed and by it we see ourselves, nakedly, fully, lovingly.

4

In making His own life whole in and through the Psalms, our Lord made comparably whole the entire course of Israelite history, the history of God-loss and God-gain over and over.

5

Abba Philemon was asked by a brother: "Why, father, do you find more joy in the psalms than in any other part of divine Scripture? And why, when quietly chanting them, do you say the words as though you were speaking with someone?" And Abba Philemon replied: "My son, God has impressed the power of the psalms on my poor soul as He did on the soul of the prophet David. I cannot be separated from the sweetness of the visions about which they speak."[4]

This is an essential text, for it speaks directly of three matters of essence: the Psalms have the power to take hold of the whole soul and life; the Psalms are—in the sense of embracing (as lover embracing beloved)—all divine Scripture; and when "chanted quietly" the Psalms produce in us joy: that is, the wholeness of our inward life.

These three matters of essence Abba Philemon manifested in his rule of psalmic prayer: that is, the psalms are the whole of our soul; the whole of Scripture; and the whole of our inwardness. In doing so, dear Abba Philemon (how much I love him! across time and space to Egypt of the early seventh century: the eve before Islam)—dear Abba shows us the Way of Holy Wisdom.

6

The whole art of praying the Psalms lies entirely in the regular and sequential practice of doing so. That is, one simply begins at Psalm 1 and continues, each morning and evening, to pray them through to their conclusion in Psalm 150. Whether this takes a week or a month, or longer, is not at all the point. The point is the daily coming into the illumined psalmic consciousness that lives and breathes in these 150 poems.

This entry into the Psalms is, in Orthodox practice, beautifully established by the practice of chanting. Even the word "to chant" is properly ψάλλειν [*psallein*]—"to sing a psalm"—and the word for "chanter" is ψάλτης [*psaltēs*], a psalmist.[5] The simple plainchant of the Orthodox temple has several beneficial effects in private psalmic prayer. For one thing, the chant softens the harsher words of the Psalms while it strengthens the milder ones. The result is a great evenness of light in which, on the one hand, the poems' anger, dread, and defeat are more drastic and terrible and, on the other hand, their praise, joy, and holy presence become more breathtaking and alive. The chant establishes this great light.

For another thing, the chanting also connects one's private prayer with the public prayer of the Orthodox Liturgy. The Divine Liturgy is so deeply psalmic, with hundreds of phrases, scores of lines, and several long passages taken directly from the Psalms, that the private discipline of psalmic prayer converges with the public Liturgy. St. Isaac even refers to one's prayer as "the liturgy of your vigil"—as, for example, "while you observe your liturgy. . . ."[6] If

Divine Liturgy is the heart of the Orthodox faith, and if one's prayer is also (rightly) a liturgy, then the way of a life in Psalms is the way wherein the Psalter comes into one's heart and takes up abode there. From Saturday evening of Psalm 1 to Saturday morning of Psalm 118 is the way of the Resurrection of one's heart in Christ.

And one result of such convergence of private and public Liturgy is that the public Liturgy becomes a deeply inward experience while private prayer becomes an encounter with the community. For the Psalms are the substance that both worlds share.

The practice of psalmic prayer is so simple, then, and the consequences so profound, that it is clear why the Orthodox tradition has given such prominence to it. This very night each of us may enter into this wondrous way of encountering Christ. As a wise Orthodox monk once said, "Simply begin."

7

I began praying psalms sometime in May or June of 1983, on my way to becoming Orthodox. When I was chrismated Orthodox on September 8, 1984, I had been praying the Psalms every morning and evening for some sixteen months. At that point, I began the practice of softly *chanting* the psalms aloud, so as to bring my little experience into the far more immense experience of Orthodox liturgical life; and very soon I found that I could easily take on more and more psalms each morning and night. And so, by the spring of 1986, I was following the rule of prayer I have followed these twelve years: to pray through the whole of the Psalter each week. The pattern I follow is one long established in the Orthodox Church, one that begins the Psalter on Saturday evening and ends the following Saturday morning.[7]

8

My experience in praying the Psalms has given me a tiny, fleeting glimpse of a vast and very great subject. I can put the subject this way: the Psalms disclose the mind of David in the process of becoming the mind of Christ.[8] The phrase "the mind of Christ" is of course Saint Paul's, when, in First Corinthians, he writes this astonishing sentence: "We have the mind of Christ" (1 Cor. 2:16). Saint Paul's point in this chapter of the epistle is that we possess in ourselves the mind of Christ solely because God has given us this mind in order that we may know—in Saint Paul's own words—"the things freely given us by God" (1 Cor. 2:12). Itself a gift, the mind of Christ in us is thus the mode wherein we know God's gifts. For Saint Paul, then, the essence of our mental life can best be expressed as human gratitude for divine self-giving.

9

Prayer, regular prayer, is direct and urgent daily, even hourly, business: more, it is moment-by-moment urgency. We must *listen*—so as to hope; we must lift up our soul—so as to know where to go: these are (as everywhere in Psalms) explicit instructions. I hope—now, *because* I hope, let me hear thy morning mercy; I lift up my soul—now, *because* I am doing this, let me know the way I should go. The hoping and elevating are our work; His is the mercy and knowledge we do this in.

10

A rule of prayer is perhaps the simplest of all spiritual mechanisms on earth. One simply begins and then keeps on going: as if plunging into a river of pure pleasure and then swimming on the dominant current because that's how one moves in rivers. The mind—or that part of the mind that likes to chatter on and on and never think—will find a thousand million other things better (that is, more exciting) to do than this swimming the dominant current of prayer's great river. But, really the current's better. After a bit, life on the banks loses something of its obsessive appeal: and you learn then how really to see—and to love, and to let go of your hunger to arrange (to dominate)—it. For bank-life isn't carrying you; it never did; this warm, strong river is; and it always has.

Thus, "he shall be like a tree planted by the rivers of water" (1. 3, AV; "onrushing waters" in my own version[9]). For in prayer we are not, of course, simply rootlessly drifting. We are, in actuality, rooted. Our roots run to the nearby water. We are a tree.

11

Orthodox prayer in Psalms is like the ox in the field—slow, patient, undramatic work—and the field bears fruit. Psalm prayer is the ox-work; the field that flourishes is our life.

12

Because Psalms participate actively, moment by moment, in the ongoingness of Christ's divinely "en-statuted" mind—His mind formed fully in, and of, the holy statutes of the Father—this psalmic participation means that the one praying the Psalms is directly entering into the Mind of Christ in its ongoingness—its eternally dynamic movement in, below, above human time and action.

And praising the Father through the Psalms is voluntarily (always defying the demonic suggestion to do something else *now*) becoming "dynamized" by Christ's Mind—better: His *nous*.[10] The Psalms are therefore *always alive*—that is, they participate in the eternal aliveness of Christ's Mind.

Thus, in the Kingdom of Heaven, the Psalms continue to be prayed: and in that heavenly rule of psalmic prayer we will see everything in the Psalms fully and beautifully—in ways we can, here and now on earth, but faintly glimpse: glimpses nonetheless fully accurate and regnant with the glory of the King.

13

A life of Orthodox prayer is a life—I am convinced—devoted to exact spiritual realities. The *Philokalia*[11]—behind each phrase, each sentence (probably each syllable) lies an exact spiritual situation, either desired, condemned, or present. This exactness is the result of the Orthodox attitude of *sobriety*: an attitude that is a condition of consciousness deliberately created by an act of personal will and sustained by an act of deliberate surrender of the will to God: an attitude caught perfectly in Psalm 130: "My heart, O Lord, has not been exalted, I have not raised up my eyes, nor have I wandered about in things too great or too marvelous for me."

Sobriety as a spiritual practice becomes, when sustained over centuries, the ground for exactness in language. As when you live in the desert for a very long time you will come to find where *precisely* the sources of water lie: not approximately but *precisely and exactly* where they are—anything less is dangerous. "All my springs are in Thee."

14

Many misconceive religious life in the same way they misunderstand married life: They expect spontaneous ecstasy where there is really the practice of discipline, and they see bondage where there is perfect freedom. Ecstasy and bondage can most assuredly arise in a marriage or in a vocation. But far more likely one will experience instead discipline and freedom. Why are so few of us taught to desire discipline and freedom; why do we hunger so for ecstasy and enslavement?

One answer, of course, is that as creatures caught in the cycles of elation and bondage we are perfect *consumers*: that is, creatures who will pay *anything* to be constantly elated. But we can be made so because our predisposition is so: that is, we live in the consequences of universal "faulting," that great slippage into misaligned will that we know as *sin*. And thus we only very painstakingly and very slowly and very deliberately begin to see how discipline and freedom are—in a marriage, in a religious vocation—at once the conditions for and the consequences of love: and how correspondingly ecstasy and bondage stem from hate (of self or other) and despair.

15

A rule of prayer is characterized above all by *rhythm*, and the experience of a rule is that of submitting to the rhythm of it. You pray at certain times and in certain words; and these times and words begin fairly soon to give a definite pattern to one's days. When a rule of prayer is first begun, there is usually an ecstatic period in which the prayers are resonant, profound, and extremely moving. It is exactly like falling in love: an extraordinary sweetness gives one's days vividness, depth, and perfection. You wake up into joy—not merely into happiness but into genuine joy, into something richer, sharper, and more actual than any happiness ever can be. Happiness is feeling, but joy is something greater in the same order of magnitude that a child's happiness at play is something far greater than the stuffed teddy-bear he plays with. And just as the child's happiness at play may be expressed by only the tiniest outward signs, so a person experiencing the first joy of prayer may in fact be quite subdued. For the first work of spiritual joy is often very largely inward. So it was for me.

But as our loving cannot remain ecstatic, nor our children play happily forever, so a rule of prayer soon moves us beyond this first joy. For the experience of prayer that follows the first joy is the experience of failure, an experience in which one's own prayer is a very poor thing, with nothing to recommend it. Prayer becomes a place of struggle, not triumph, a place where you just barely keep your head above water. And most of the time you sink and are engulfed again and again by the world you have so badly made and keep on making: your world of work and family and friends and enemies. This disastrous failure also is entirely undramatic and thoroughly unspectacular. Where it once was vast, gathered, and profound, prayer now becomes mean, scattered, and flat.

There is no way out of this. It is what the early Orthodox Fathers called *the desert*. You cannot survive in this merciless place unless you submit to the conditions of it: that is, unless you meet its implacable demand for an ever deeper spiritual poverty. For what the rule is drawing you toward is what Mother Maria calls the End-Point, that point wherein—as at your bath—you are stripped of absolutely all you possess—"except your sins, and the cry for mercy."[12] With a slowly growing awareness—or else with a sudden shock of insight— you see that this desert is, in fact, the place where you live now— and will live for the rest of your life. Where is joy? *In* the rhythm.

Into this desert come the voices of the great Orthodox masters of prayer, the saints, fathers, monks, and nuns of the holy tradition. Saint Innocent of Alaska says in *The Art of Prayer*: "The Holy Spirit teaches true prayer. . . . A man with the Holy Spirit dwelling in him knows God and sees that He is his Father. He knows how to approach Him, how to ask and what to ask for. His thoughts in prayer are orderly, pure, and directed to the one object alone—God; and by his prayer he is truly able to do everything."[13]

If we feel something like despair in hearing such a voice (for our thoughts in prayer are anything but "orderly, pure, and directed"), we are also instructed. I haven't the slightest idea what sustains one in a rule of prayer. Certainly, it isn't pleasure of any easily recognizable variety, for desert life is scarcely anyone's formula for personal happiness. Yet what Saint Innocent here says—"by prayer he is truly able to do everything"—is illumined by a joy so profound, strong, and vivid that all our notions of pleasure simply vanish in the way flickers of candlelight vanish in the glaring immensity of the desert sun. You die into the joy.

All the time the *rhythm* of the rule keeps on working.

16

To be broken, and in poverty, is to be at the starting point of dwelling in the house of psalmic prayer: broken by depression, to be poor in spirit, low in mind, heart, and soul. Here is the way of "making straight" one's way.

17

I see: this feeling of no-feeling is a sign of God's mercy and will. The sign comes right when the absent "feelings" are in fact anxiety, fear, anger, etc. For example, in silent prayer, there are often times when, in the midst of the longish list of petitions for others that I pray each morning and night, I lose my place: that is, other thoughts quite irrelevant to the names and petitions claim my attention—and

I follow these interruptive thoughts to the point where I suddenly am aware that I've *lost my place*: I don't know the person's name for whom I am at this moment praying and I don't know the name of the new person. What I do is this: I give up the interruptive thought and ask for help—especially the Holy Mother's help. Always, *unfailingly*, she restores me to my right place in prayer, the right next name.

Now (and here's the point) the *feeling* that accompanies this restoration is a feeling of emotional diminution, of the shrinking of feeling to the point of nonexistence. The feelings simply go away— that is, all the stirrings that accompanied the charged interruptive thoughts. What is left is the emotional neutrality, of—in effect—no-feeling. I believe entirely, without reservation, that this no-feeling is God's merciful will for me in this moment of prayer.

The moment of restoration: this is crucial. The restoration never occurs if I attempt willfully to remember the list. I must try to do this—but only (I think) as a signal of assent, a signal to God that I wish to continue in rightful prayer now and to give up my swirl of obsessions. This signal *does not cause* the restoration to occur; it merely signals that I desire it to happen. God, in the Holy Mother, makes it happen.

18

Do not change—do not surrender—the rule of prayer. Persist— even the dryness is of great moment.

19

How *easy* it is to fall! to give up, to let go one's rule of prayer: and how idiotic, how self-absorbed! Yet the Psalms are stronger by far than all this; they ride beautifully above and beneath the currents of distraction. How did these poems come to *be*?

20

To ponder God's commandments is fully to achieve a sharp deepening of the capacity to pray while simultaneously avoiding the mental chatter. Every rule of psalmic prayer knows this action; and most of us experience psalmic prayer as long stretches of nearly empty chatter illumined by sharp and sudden depths. These moments of depth are moments of comprehension: the sudden descent into the *nous*, the heart's depths, where David's song becomes our own.

21

That one's Rule is one's true teacher in Christ is, surely, the difficult ecstasy of Orthodox practice. My Rule: a joy, a burden—a lightness of heart, a heaviness of time. Actually to *choose* to go to prayer is to assume a burden unknown to any whole life that is without Rule: a burden compounded of severity, joy, tedium, restlessness, failure, love, exhaustion, melody. The Psalms know, from within, the *fullest* reality of each element in this astonishing compound—and *why* the burden exists, and *who* is carrying it.

22

A life in Psalms means a life given entirely *into* the text of the Psalms: into the very words and shapes and events and voices of these loveliest of poems.

The key experience is shape. The shape of each psalm is uniquely and permanently beautiful: apt, joyous, magnificent in shape. And this psalmic shape enters the life of the one praying—each morning and evening—the Psalms: the only way so to enter and *be entered*.

23

This: that merely *completing* a Rule is itself of some spiritual victory, for so many are the steady distractions and exhaustions that would have you stop. The angels sing, each time, when one fulfills the Rule. And if one does so with true presence before God, then the triumphal song is resounding. Nevertheless, if one only just gets through to the end, enduring all the devilish callings into silence and cessation of praising God, one still hears the angelic singing, if only as a faint echo of the past and future singing in the heart.

Psalms know all this.

24

Who is God save our Lord? Who is a rock save our God? Dumb-steadiness just keeping on going one foot in front of the other not *thinking*: this is part of prayer life's power in the Psalms.

The Psalms' steadiness is deepest fact—steadiness that holds their catastrophes and their exultations (the nightmare of actual historic disaster and the undying vision of Lord God's redemptive love) in perfect composure. I keep praying them and they me.

5

Chiastic and Temporal
Movement in Psalms

Psalms 1, 136, and 50

Every psalm, and the Psalter itself, moves forward temporally in response to "the upward call of God in Christ Jesus" (Phil. 3:14). As the Psalter progresses, as at the hands of a sculptor, our stony excess is gradually trimmed off so that Christ, in accordance with whose image we existed in the beginning, may be formed anew in us. Thus, in the final psalms, the angels rejoice in songs of praise and clashing cymbals as our nature joins with theirs. Psalms' second and primary movement, however, is spatial rather than temporal. Each psalm has a chiastic shape, with a center from which and toward which its movement tends and its body grows, and by which it is able to hold and govern severe oppositions—antinomies of evil and good, despair and resurrection. In this chapter, readers will learn to read chiastically, following the author through Psalm 136. Then, through Psalm 50, we will learn to discern the interactions of the chiastic and temporal movements in what the author calls a "psalmic helix." He compares this method of reading with Ezekiel's prophecy of bringing the dry bones to life at Holy Saturday Matins and with St. Isaac's third mode of knowledge: "noetic resurrection as a true witness of the universal renewal of all things." He concludes: "To discern and then enter the chiastic heart of any psalm is to walk away—in full repentance—from ungodliness, sinfulness, and scornful contempt." "The eschatological 'authentic personhood' the psalmist attains in the penitential process thus unites the human and the angelic natures." —*Ed.*

S aint Gregory of Nyssa (*c.* 335–95) was much, though by no means exclusively, concerned with the forward, temporal, or ascending movement of the psalmic narrative. He inherited the tradition of dividing the Psalter into five books, paralleling the five books of Torah:

I.   Psalms 1–40: Separation from what is evil; Christ emerges

II.   Psalms 41–71: Thirst for participation in God by the one who has devoured his passions

III. Psalms 72–88: Begin to see things the way God sees them: *synapheia* (conjunction)

IV.   Psalms 89–105: Attained *synapheia*; Prayer of Moses (89), reaching to sublime heights; become generative of goodness in others (*Shuvah*, Return)

V.   Psalms 106–150: Proclaiming the complete return of humanity to the good: "redeemed from the enemy's hands"[1] (i.e., from death itself)

What *moves* the whole sequence of Psalms 1–150 is *epectasis*: the continual straining forward to direct participation in the Divine nature. In *De vita Moysis*, Gregory of Nyssa will quote Philippians 3:13–14: "Brethren, I count not myself to have apprehended: but this one thing I do, forgetting those things which are behind, and reaching forth unto those things which are before, I press toward the mark for the prize of the upward call of God in Christ Jesus."

Saint Gregory uses the metaphor of the sculptor shaping stone to become a statue:

> [S]ince our nature has become stone, as it were, through our propensity to what is material, the Word which is hewing us in relation to the divine likeness proceeds methodically and orderly to the end of the aim. First it separates us, as it were, from the attached rock (I mean evil, of course) to which we have been attached by participation. Then it trims off the excesses of the material. After this it begins to form that which lies within in relation to the likeness of the aim, by stripping off those things which hinder the representation. And thus it scrapes and polishes our understanding by means of more delicate teachings of ideas. Then, by means of the forms of virtue, it forms Christ in us, in accordance with whose image we existed in the beginning, and in accordance with which we again come to exist.[2]

The conclusion of the Psalms, in Psalm 150, is accompanied by resounding cymbals as the angelic and human natures join in a single song, showing that:

> Whenever the whole creation, consisting of all things superior and all things inferior, has been united in one choir, both the spiritual creation and that which has been separated and has been at a distance on account of sin will produce the good sound, like a *cymbal* (150:5), from our concord. Whenever our humanity unites with the angels, and the divine company has taken itself up from the confusion at the slaughter of the enemies and loudly shouts the song of victory to the one who holds the trophies, then the *praise of every breathing creature* (150:6) occurs, which continues the

gratitude for ever, and causes the *blessedness* (1:1) to abound, through increase, in perpetuity, I mean of course, the true *blessedness.*[3]

A *spatial* art primarily, psalmic music is not governed only by the forward, temporal movement but also by the psalm's *chiastic center.* Each psalm sounds a *single complex sound* that possesses a "shape," in which the aesthetic pattern and the theological significance converge in *one shape.*

Think of Psalm 50, so omnipresent in Slavic-based Orthodox liturgical life, in which joy and repentance *as antinomies* form one "shape" of experience.[4] That shape is one that, over and over, brings the one who walks in the way of the Lord, through great wickedness, into intimate communion with the God of heaven and earth; it raises up the poor and humble, casts down the proud, and turns the pit of despair into a place of resurrection. It is a shape that can hold all of this. Hence, cadential shape is what makes of each psalm a spiritual instrument that God is using upon both the Davidic psalmist and the psalmic hearer.

The Chiastic Method

Let me now sketch this chiastic method of reading, in three closely related—in fact, continuous—stages. The first stage is finding and entering into the chiastic heart of the psalm. This heart is found very near, and often exactly at, the psalm's midpoint, as a single line or small group of lines. Hence, this finding and entering may best be described as *discernment*, a spiritual gift that permits us to discriminate the center from the psalm's other lines and to assess them with what I wish to call a *swiftly accurate lightness of touch.*

If at all labored—if the touch of comprehension grows too heavy or moves too slowly—this discernment of the psalm's chiastic heart will begin to thicken into a widening and deepening inaccuracy. Now, this swiftness I am trying to describe is not at all what we normally call having a "quick mind." For by "quick mind," we are almost always signifying the triumph of one's autonomous will. By discernment, on the other hand, we are signifying the exact opposite: that is, we mean the self-emptying and penitential submission of one's own will to the living reality of the psalm's chiastic heart. And the first stage becomes complete when we enter into this psalmic heart in—and as—an act of self-giving and penitential love.

The second stage of psalmic reading then immediately begins: letting the psalm's "body"—that is, all the other lines of the psalm— arise from the psalm's heart. This second stage finds its most fitting and most beautiful analogy at the Matins of Holy Saturday, in the reading from the Prophet Ezekiel (37:1–14). This reading begins with Ezekiel being set by God's Holy Spirit in the "midst of the plain" (ἐν μέσῳ τοῦ πεδίου, *en mesō tou pediou*) as if at the very heart of it; and the plain all around is filled with human bones, exceedingly dry and dead. Then God says to Ezekiel: "Shall these bones live?" And He commands him: "Prophesy to these bones; say to them: 'I will bring upon you the breath of life [πνεῦμα ζωῆς, *pneuma zōēs*], I will lay sinews upon you, and will raise up flesh upon you, and will spread skin upon you, and will put my Spirit into you, and you shall live; and you shall know that I am [ἐγώ εἰμι, *ego eimi*] the Lord'" (Ezek. 37:1–6). The bones then begin to move, each one drawing near its . . .

Its what? The usual English translation of this phrase in Ezekiel is: "each bone drew near its joint." Yet the Greek word that the LXX translators used was *harmonia*: "each bone drew near its harmony." And when one considers the Hebrew word that was being translated by the Greek one finds it to be עֶצֶם (*etsem*; BDB 782b), signifying "bone, limbs, substances, and (in the plural) the entire person," then one arrives at an astonishing place, for we can now easily construe the phrase as saying that each bone was drawing near its *harmonic and substantial aliveness.*

And here is the point of my analogy. As we begin to let all the lines of the psalm live and move in their substantial and harmonic relation to the psalm's heart, the dry bones can begin to arise into a new and vivid life. The Lord continues to Ezekiel: "I will open your tombs, I will put my Spirit within you, and you shall live" (Ezek. 37:12–13). Here, then, is the significance of the second stage in reading Psalms: as the "body" of the psalm arises from the chiastic heart, the psalm is resurrected into vivid meaningfulness in which the tombs of our incomprehension are opened in such a way that we experience (with Ezekiel) being placed by God upon our own true land (cf. Ezek. 37:14). Thus, the reading of Ezekiel focuses not only the Matins of Holy Saturday but also what I am calling the second stage of psalmic comprehension: a focus that arises in us by our neither extracting nor imposing meaning but, rather, by our giving ourselves wholly to the resurrectional meaning that is moving to embrace us.

The third, and final, stage of psalmic understanding can be perhaps best approached through Saint Isaac the Syrian's description of the third mode of knowledge, which he calls the mode of perfection:

> When knowledge is raised above earthly things and the cares of earthly activities, and its thoughts begin to gain experience in inward matters which are hidden from the eyes; and when in part it scorns [the recollections of] things (whence the perverseness of passions arises), and when it stretches itself upward and follows faith in its solicitude for the future age, in its desire for what has been promised us, and in searching deeply into hidden mysteries: then faith

itself swallows up knowledge, converts it, and begets it anew, so that it becomes wholly and completely spirit.

Then it can soar on wings in the realms of the bodiless and touch the depths of the unfathomable sea, musing upon the wondrous and divine workings of God's governance of noetic and corporeal creatures. It searches out spiritual mysteries that are perceived by the simple and subtle intellect. Then the inner senses awaken for spiritual doing, according to the order that will be in the immortal and incorruptible life. For even from now it has received, as it were in a mystery, the noetic resurrection as a true witness of the universal renewal of all things.[5]

Such a state of knowledge is therefore very close to what Saint Gregory of Nyssa describes as "the union [συνάφεια, *synapheia*] of our nature with the angels," referring to the "resounding cymbals" at the end of Psalm 150 as "the sweet sound of thanksgiving through [the human and angelic] meeting with one another"[6]—an image also chiastic in meaning, as the cymbals represent the two halves of the psalm and their moment of sounding is the chiastic heart. But in Saint Isaac's description, the human mind (or *nous*) is resurrected "as a true witness of the universal renewal of all things"—a noetic resurrection certainly implied by Gregory but only asserted by Isaac.

And in the light of Saint Isaac, we may say that the third and highest mode of psalmic comprehension begins when we have garnered experience in "inward matters which are hidden from the eyes";[7] that is, when we have first clearly discerned the psalm's chiastic heart and then directly entered into the psalm's resurrected body. Once we have so discerned and so entered, then we begin to move (says Isaac) in two opposed directions at once: we soar to the highest realms of heaven, and we plunge into the unfathomable depths of the sea. This opposition between heaven and ocean suggests, of course, the opposition between the psalm's spatial (or chiastic) movement and its temporal (or forward) movement. And just as the discernment of the psalm's chiastic heart required a *swiftly accurate lightness of touch*, so, too, the purposive fulfillment of that discernment now calls forth in us the capacity for deep *stillness*. Isaac puts it this way: "the third [stage] is rest from labour, which is the type of the age to come, for the soul [now] takes delight solely in the mind's meditation upon the mysteries of the good things to come."[8]

In this way, then, the third stage of psalmic comprehension brings together the psalm's body, heart, and spirit. As we begin to discern the chiastic heart of the psalm, and then enter into and experience the resurrected body of the psalm, we then begin to probe (says Isaac) "the depths of all the mysteries of the Spirit": and we are then, Isaac continues, "caught away to a state higher than nature in the divine vision [or θεωρία, *theōria*[9]] of God."[10]

Thus, in this movement through the three stages of psalmic comprehension—from entering and knowing the psalmic heart; to seeing and loving (with Ezekiel) the psalm's resurrectional aliveness of meaning; to experiencing (with Isaac) "the wondrous and divine workings of God's governance of noetic and corporeal creatures"— in this movement, wherein we come to comprehend the psalm, we are experiencing fully the movement of the first three lines of Psalm 1. Line 1 is: "Blessed is the man who walks not in the counsel of the ungodly, nor takes the way of the sinful, nor sits in the seat of the scornful."[11]

To discern and then enter the chiastic heart of any psalm is to walk away—in full repentance—from ungodliness, sinfulness, and scornful contempt. For walking in "the counsel of the ungodly" is precisely to pour toxic scorn on the heart of the psalm—better: such toxic scorn is the violent eating away of that heart. For the etymology of the Greek word for "blessed" (μακάριος, *makarios*) is, as Fr. Pavel Florensky reminds us, "do not devour the heart."[12]

The second stage of psalmic comprehension thus parallels the second line of Psalm 1: "But his will is in the law of the Lord and in his law he will meditate day and night." As the dry bones begin to stir into life, our autonomous will is given over into the law, or Word, of God. Again, a detail in Ezekiel's experience in chapter 37 is crucial to our understanding. As the hand of the Lord sets Ezekiel in the chiastic "midst of the plain" where the dry bones are (37:1), the Lord "led me," says Ezekiel, "round about them every way" (37:2). The Greek phrasing here is extraordinary: περιήγαγέν με ἐπ' αὐτὰ κυκλόθεν κύκλῳ (*periēgagen me ep' auta kuklothen kuklō*)—literally, "he led me around them circularly in a circle." Being set in the center, Ezekiel is then guided in a circle of what I shall call chiastic comprehension. This is a circle defined by the question God asks Ezekiel—"shall these bones live?"—a question then answered by God in words to the bones themselves, resurrectional words (*note well*:) that God gives Ezekiel to say. And the bones become substantial life. Ezekiel's circularity of movement around the bones beautifully parallels our chiastic circularity around the psalm. And in the second line of Psalm 1—"in His law he will meditate day and night"—we see a fine illustration of psalmic meditation: the lion growling over its prey is practicing the resurrection of flesh into nourishment.[13]

In the first stage, we have left behind the toxicities of scorn; in the second, we achieve sustenance. Then line 3 of Psalm 1 illustrates the third stage of psalmic comprehension: "And he shall be like a tree [planted by the onrushing waters,] whose fruit comes forth in its season and whose leaf shall not wither, and whatever he does shall flourish."

By the time I'd completed translating the Psalter in May of 2002, I'd become persuaded—and still remain convinced—that the entire Psalter possesses a living cadential shape: that is, that the Psalter possesses an artistic shape in the same way (and for precisely the same reason) that the Divine Liturgy may be said to possess a shape: it begins and progresses and concludes for our salvation in Christ.[14]

Let us look now at the shape of a psalm that is central in the life of the Orthodox Church.

A Chiastic Reading of Psalm 136

A psalm of David, concerning Jeremiah in the captivity.

1 By the rivers of Babylon, there we sat down and wept when we remembered Zion.

2 Upon the willows in her midst, we hung up our harps.

3 There, our captors asked us for some words from our songs, our plunderers demanded and said: Sing us a psalm of Zion.

4 How shall we sing the Lord's song in a strange and alien land?

5 If I forget thee, O Jerusalem, let my right hand wither,

6 Let my tongue cleave to my mouth if I do not remember thee, if I do not keep Jerusalem as the fountainhead of my joy.

7 Remember, O Lord, Edom's sons on that day in Jerusalem, saying: Destroy it, destroy it, down to the very foundations.

8 O wretched daughter of Babylon, blessed the one who shall deal to thee what thou hast dealt to us,

9 Blessed the one who shall seize thine infants and smash them against the rock.

A chiastic reading of Psalm 136 can most usefully begin with considering line 5, the poem's center: "If I forget thee, O Jerusalem,

let my right hand wither." Living in exile as a slave to those who
have wrecked his home, the psalmist touches the heart of the psalm:
memory of Hebraic holiness is *alone* salvific. For such memory holds
the key not simply to physical health and prowess ("let my right
hand wither") but, more deeply, to the very act of articulation itself:
"Let my tongue cleave to my mouth if I do not remember thee, if I
do not keep Jerusalem as the fountainhead of my joy" (l. 6). Jerusalem is the fountainhead of joy even amidst the savagery of enslavement; and the articulation of that remembered joy is the only way to
withstand such violence. But this now "alien land" of our sin (l. 4)
is precisely the place where salvific joy can no longer be sung. Here
is the context to comprehend the Orthodox understanding of this
psalm as the gateway to Great Lent: the memory of joy is a way
through the violent enslavement of our sinfulness.

Then, moving outward from this center, we encounter the chiastic pair of lines 3 and 7. First the captors demand "a psalm of
Zion"—a demand that would, if acquiesced in, give into the hands
of the violators the sole (and complete) source of Hebraic salvation:
the action of psalmic memory. Then, in chiastic pairing, line 7 calls
the psalmist into the ontological accuracy of all redemptive psalmic
memory: into, that is, the knowledge that your killers genuinely
hate you, that they seek to unmake your life "down to the very foundations." In Orthodox penitential terms, the psalm urges us *never* to
be deceived as to our demonic enemies' unshakeable intentions: that
is, *never* to see our sins as attractive friends.

Then the next chiastic pair out from the center—lines 2 and 8—
deepen the experience. To hang up our harp (l. 2) means that we
will no longer give over to violence our power of psalmic joy. Instead
we will remember the immense, saving psalmic word: "Blessed"
(Heb. אַשְׁרֵי,*ashre*; Gk. μακάριος, *makarios*). This word initiates the
entire Psalter: "Blessed is the man ..." (Ps. 1:1), and the vast

radiance of its meaning illumines all of Orthodox penitential and artistic ethos. Blessedness begins in remembering the demonic violence of our enemies to the very extent we remember—in tears—the joy of Zion, on the very banks of the waters of our own evil enslavement.

Then we at last come to the astonishing *edges* of this key Orthodox psalm: lines 1 and 9. Line 1 focuses on what Saint John Climacus calls, in *The Ladder of Divine Ascent*, "tears of all-holy love."[15] Tears are the beginning, and much of the way into repentance. For only in such weeping can we even begin to engage the memory of the violence our sinfulness has wrought in our lives: it has murdered even the most defenseless among us, our helpless, vulnerable infants (the murder of babies is confirmed by all modern biblical scholarship on the Babylonian destruction of Jerusalem; and is of course visibly rampant in modern life and warfare). The psalm conceives the act of remembering the violence as blessed because such memory restores to us the reality of actual events: our violent sinfulness actively slaughters even the tiny babies in our lives. So understood, this final line of Psalm 136 is not at all a cry for vengeance but is, rather, the restoration of the only reality that can yield repentance: the reality of our full complicity in what most genuinely destroys us. And—as all of Orthodox Lent exists to demonstrate—such reality can be endured *only* in the saving action of genuine memory.

The Psalmic Helix: Temporal and Chiastic Movements in Psalm 50

Chiastic movement runs along with, interacts with, deepens, and fulfills the forward temporal movement Saint Gregory describes, as perhaps most beautifully revealed in Psalm 50. Here is the psalm, in my translation:

Psalm 50

A psalm of David, when Nathan the prophet came to him, after
he had gone in to Bathsheba, the wife of Uriah.

1 Have mercy on me, O God, according to thy great mercy; according to the abundance of thy compassion blot out my transgression.

2 Wash me thoroughly from my iniquity and cleanse me from my sin.

3 For I know my iniquity and my sin is always before me:

4. Against thee, thee alone, have I sinned; I have done evil before thee: that thou mayest be justified in thy words and victorious when thou art judged.

5 Behold, I was conceived in iniquities, in sins did my mother bear me.

6 Behold, thou hast loved the truth, thou hast made manifest to me wisdom's hidden and secret things.

7 Thou shalt sprinkle me with hyssop and I will be made clean, thou shalt wash me and I will be made whiter than snow.

8 Thou shalt make me hear joy and gladness, my humbled bones shall rejoice.

9 Turn thy face from my sins and blot out all my iniquities.

10 Create in me a pure heart, O God, and renew a right Spirit within me.

11 Do not cast me away from thy presence, do not take thy Holy Spirit from me.

12 Restore to me the joy of thy salvation and uphold me by thy guiding Spirit.

13 I will teach transgressors thy ways and the godless shall turn back to thee.

14 Deliver me from bloodguiltiness, O God, the God of my salvation, and my tongue shall rejoice in thy righteousness.

15 O Lord, thou shalt open my lips and my mouth shall declare thy praise.

16 For if thou hadst desired a sacrifice I would have given it; thou wilt not be pleased even with whole burnt sacrifices.

17 A sacrifice to God is a broken spirit, a broken and humbled heart God will not count as nothing.

18 Do good in thy good pleasure to Zion, and may Jerusalem's walls be built up.

19 Then thou shalt be pleased with a sacrifice of righteousness, with offering and whole burnt sacrifices; then shall they offer young bulls on thine altar.

The Temporal Movement of Psalm 50

The forward or temporal movement of Psalm 50 (as opposed to the chiastic movement) is the movement of repentance, beginning with the psalmist beseeching God's mercy in the first line, moving through his growing awareness of his deeply sinful nature (ll. 2–5), to his seeing that God, in His infinite love, desires to reveal all truth and wisdom (l. 6), and then to the central prayers of repentance and the direct encounter with the God who forgives and heals (ll. 7–12). Then, in the final movement of the Psalm (ll. 13–19), the psalmist achieves full comprehension of the joy-giving sadness of repentance, a comprehension that begins with his first becoming teacher and guide for others (l. 13) and then enacting true sacrificial repentance (ll. 14–19).

In this way, then, Psalm 50 enacts what Fr. Sophrony, in his book *Saint Silouan the Athonite*, terms pure prayer: "In the ascetic experience of pure prayer the mind, divested of all images and concepts, is vouchsafed, after deep repentance and much weeping, authentic vision of God."[16]

In the scriptural narrative of the David and Bathsheba episode, two crucial moments in David's repentance are described. The first occurs just after the prophet Nathan has declared that the sinful man in the parable he has just told David is, in fact, David himself; and David says—and this is the crucial moment—"I have offended against the Lord."[17] In LXX Greek, the verb is in the present perfect: a tense best understood as signaling the entire state of completion of (as opposed to a mere moment in) an action. That is, David's action of sinning against God began at a definite point in the past, then it continued on until—now, at the present moment—the action has become so full that it constitutes not merely a discrete act (or even an extended series of acts) but a *complete state of existence*: and this completeness is the meaning of the tense's "perfection." David's repentance begins in this awareness of his ontological state—of his "perfectly" sinful state.

The second crucial moment in his repentance occurs when the male child born of his and Bathsheba's adultery dies—as prophesied by Nathan—despite David's having fasted, wept, and prayed that the child live. The instant he is told the news, David gets up, bathes, changes his clothes, and eats a meal. The servants are shocked, saying: "What is this thing that you have done? For the sake of the living child you fasted and wept, and when the child was dead, you arose and ate food?" David answers them by saying that he wept and fasted while the child lived, but such things now are of no avail—and then arrives the crucial moment in repentance: "Can I bring him back again? I am going to him and he will not come back to me."[18]

Robert Alter beautifully says of these words of David's:

> If the episode of Bathsheba and Uriah is the great turn-
> ing point of the David story, these haunting words are the
> pivotal moment in the turning point. . . . David speaks for
> the first time not out of political need but in his existential
> nakedness. The words he utters have a stark simplicity . . .
> and his recognition of the irreversibility of his son's death
> also makes him think of his own mortality.[19]

That David has now completely accepted God's will is, in fact, signaled precisely by doing what shocks—even stuns—his servants:
he masters his own emotional passions and entirely surrenders
self-will. This self-mastery is what Psalm 50 calls "broken spirit"
(πνεῦμα συντετριμμένον, *pneuma syntetrimmenon*), a heart that has
achieved humility (καρδία τεταπεινωμένη, *kardia tetapeinōmenē*).
The spiritual brokenness wherein the heart is humbled is the "deep
repentance" Fr. Sophrony sees as the prelude to pure prayer. And
in Psalm 50, after David's weeping comes to an end, he is "vouchsafed," in Fr. Sophrony's magnificent sentence, an "authentic vision
of God": a vision in which God Himself now opens David's lips and
causes his tongue and mouth to sing perfect praise (l. 15). Thus the
deep corruption of Psalm 11:4—"Our lips are our own, who is Lord
over us?"—is set right in this act of deepest repentance: the giving
over of one's lips to God. Jerusalem is then made perfectly whole
(l. 18) and divine wisdom is made perfectly manifest (l. 6). In seeing
clearly his own mortality through the death of his infant son, David
thus beholds the immortality of God.

The Chiastic Movement of Psalm 50

Taken together, then, these two narrative moments in David's
repentance directly inform the forward—or temporal—movement
of Psalm 50. Equally clearly, the chiastic (or spatial) movement of

Psalm 50 interlocks with this temporal movement to create a spiral or helical effect. That is, as the psalm chiastically moves into the poem's center in line 10—"Create in me a pure heart, O God, and renew a right spirit within me"—the spatial pattern becomes fully clarified at the very moment the temporal forward movement of repentance is still being unfolded. What clarifies, in line 10, the spatial pattern of the psalm are the aorist imperative verbs: that is, the intense *specificity* of the two aorists brings about the direct vision of God. And simultaneously, this spatial center is what is moving the whole penitential process forward. As God creates a purified heart in David, and as He renews the Holy Spirit within him, He is directly revealing to David His very face and whole presence. In line 9, David beseeches God to turn His face (πρόσωπον, *prosōpon*) from David's sins, thereby entirely cleansing him of the leprosy of iniquity; in line 11, David begs God not to cast him away from "thy presence"—and the Greek is again *prosōpon*, thereby deepening the significance of beholding God's face by making it be the experience of entering God's entire *presence*. In this way, then, lines 11 and 9 set forth a strong chiastic interaction, one wherein the eleventh line simultaneously reverses and fulfills the ninth line: for such is the power of line 10, the chiastic pivot of the psalm.

As a result, the psalm's forward movement now becomes explicitly chiastic as the meaning of repentance now emerges. For the joy and gladness of line 8 connect with, and are fulfilled by, the salvific joy of line 12. Similarly, we see now that the cleansing of line 7 is chiastically preparing for the psalmist to become the spiritual teacher in line 13. The point, I think, is very plain. Once the psalmist enters the chiastic center in line 10, his forward movement into complete repentance becomes simultaneously a chiastic spiralling. And in this way, the deeply *antinomical* experience of genuine repentance—that is, the spiritual experience of joyous sadness and agonized gladness—thus finds its perfect poetic form in (and indeed *through* and *by*) this fiftieth psalm.

And so perfect is this poetic form that we can say, with Gregory of Nyssa, that this perfect form is also a *perfective* form: that is, the form is capable of producing penitential perfection in others. It is this *perfectiveness* of Psalm 50 that brings the poem to the very heart of the Slavic Liturgy, at the consecration of the holy gifts. For as the celebrant prepares for the calling of the Holy Spirit "upon us and upon these gifts" he enters into the deep repentance of Psalm 50, praying, with David, "Do not cast me away from thy presence" (l. 11), now that thou hast purified my heart and renewed the Holy Spirit within me (l. 10). In this way, then, the liturgical context of Psalm 50 gives the poem a profound *eucharistic* significance. That is, just as David directly encounters God's presence in the psalm, so we, too, directly enter into Christ's body and blood in the Liturgy: and the psalm's perfective form helps to shape for us the Liturgy's perfectiveness. We are thus called into perfection by the Liturgy—just as, says Gregory, we are called by the Psalter into sharing in the perfective life of the angels.[20]

An astonishing line in Psalm 59 helps clarify the penitential experience described in Psalm 50: "Thou hast shown thy people harsh things, thou hast made us drink down the wine of deep repentance" (59:3). The word translated "deep repentance" here is, in Greek, κατάνυξις (*katanyxis*), often translated "compunction." The glossary to the *Philokalia* beautifully defines compunction this way: "The state of one who is 'pricked to the heart,' becoming conscious both of his own sinfulness and of the forgiveness extended to him by God; a mingled feeling of sorrow, tenderness and joy, springing from sincere repentance."[21]

Saint Gregory Palamas explicitly connects the wine of deep repentance in Psalm 59 to the wine that gladdens man's heart in

Psalm 103:15, saying that the wine of compunction "crushes the passions . . . and fills [the soul] with blessed joy."[22] In this way, even the "harsh things"—in Greek, σκληρά (*sklēra*), meaning "hard, unyielding, cruel, unbending, dried up"—are understood as being the direct gifts of God, and they are therefore experienced as *harsh yet joy-bearing blessings*, ones wherein we become conscious (as the *Philokalia*'s glossary says) of both the depth of our leprous iniquity and the infinitely greater depth of God's loving forgiveness. Thus, in drinking down the wine of deep repentance, we enter into the eucharistic joy of Christ's Body and Blood: and Psalm 50 enters into the Liturgy.

One final point concerning repentance in Psalm 50. In his beautiful chapter titled "Personhood and Being," J. D. Zizioulas discusses what he terms "the encounter between the ecclesial and the biological hypostases," an encounter wherein, writes Bishop John, one experiences "authentic personhood" as paradox—or, as we might now put it, as *chiasm*. For, Bishop John says, "Man [in this encounter] appears to exist . . . not [merely] as that which he is but as that which he *will be*; the ecclesial identity is linked to eschatology, that is, with the final outcome of his existence."[23]

This ontological encounter is precisely the penitential experience the psalmist undergoes in Psalm 50. As a result, the eschatological power of line 15 is manifestly clear: "O Lord, thou shalt open my lips and my mouth shall declare thy praise." This condition of ceaseless praise enacts the complete cleansing of the psalmist's mouth, a cleansing that fully heals the psalmist even of *inherited* iniquity (see the line's chiastic "match" in line 5: "Behold, I was conceived in iniquities, in sins did my mother bear me"). And in becoming so cleansed in mouth, the psalmist in Psalm 50 attains to the unending song of the angels, a song that ceaselessly deepens and broadens the angelic experience of blessedness. Saint Gregory of Nyssa says this: "Whenever our humanity unites with the angels . . . then 'every breath [will] praise the Lord' [my translation], which continues the gratitude forever, and causes the blessedness to abound, through increase, to perpetuity."[24]

The eschatological "authentic personhood" the psalmist attains in the penitential process thus unites the human and the angelic natures. And in this way the paradox of the hypostatic encounter is given perfect—and perfective—form in Psalm 50's twin chiastic and temporal movements. As these two psalmic movements—the chiastic (or spatial) movement and the forward (or temporal) movement—interlock at the center of Psalm 50, then each becomes fully open to the other: and what David *is* becomes imbued with what he *will be*. As Dostoevsky writes at an essential moment in *The Brothers Karamazov*, "The silence of the earth seemed to merge with the silence of the stars; the mystery of the earth touched the mystery of the stars."[25] Such is the abounding of penitential blessedness in Psalm 50.

6

Psalmic Enemies: Absalom

Psalms 3 and 142

The psalmic enemy seeks not only to destroy the divine inwardness of the human person but to violate the whole of creation and the Creator Himself. The author here sees Psalms 3 and 142 (based on the Davidic narrative in LXX 2 Kings /AV 2 Samuel) as a frame for all the psalms. Amnon has raped his sister Tamar after receiving a gift of bread from her, and then immediately turns to hating her; two years later their brother Absalom kills Amnon. After a period of desperate confusion and contention between Absalom and their father, David, Absalom himself is killed, against David's orders, in a brutal piercing of his heart as he hangs in the heart of an ancient oak. The author sees this intense tangle of love and hate within the family and the kingdom, and even within and against the tree, as mirroring the spiritual warfare that underlies all political struggles: that is, earthly warfare is rooted in the heavenly as branches are rooted in a tree. Psalm 3, analyzed chiastically, shows the psalmist sustaining his divinely given personhood, his communion with God (in accepting God's gift of courage and crying out to Him) in the face of escalating affliction, and against the contemptuous scoffers who say there is no salvation for him in his God.

In Psalm 142, David, fleeing his son's violence, falls into deep depression, known in Psalms as the Pit. The arrival of grief begins for him a path through his darkness that will lead him to remember the land where God's creation is deeply seen and held, and he prays for mercy, as dry land cries for water. Returning to his right relation with God, he knows he will be quickened to life and his enemies completely unmade. The psalmic enemy is thus at once both highly dangerous and wholly ineffectual. The danger lies in the enemy's capacity to inflict depression upon the psalmist; his ineffectuality arises from the fact that the swift flight of psalmic prayer can part the very veil of the high holy place to call down God's mercy. —*Ed.*

To many casual or first-time readers of Psalms, what most strikes the eye is the widespread focus on enemies. Indeed, the LXX Greek word ἐχθρός (*echthros;* Heb. אֹיֵב, *'oyev*), meaning "enemy," occurs in 57 of the 150 psalms; and close synonyms for these words occur in dozens more. For the casual reader, the alienation is almost instantaneous: what does all this dark, violent talk have to do with the blessed Kingdom of God? And the Psalter is slammed shut, with a quick gasp of relief.

The question, therefore, must be put to every serious or would-be student of the Psalms: Why are the enemies so focused upon? And probably much more to the point: How is this psalmic focus achieved and sustained? Can we speak, in other words, of a psalmic *esthetics* of evil?

The answer to *Why this focus?* is—or can be—fairly straightforward. We really do have enemies who really do seek to destroy us: both literally and psychically to destroy us. That is, because enemies really exist in the world, they must be in the Psalms, for the Psalter is the divine poem of the real world. Yet this response largely begs the question, for the great and weighty matter of theology is therefore raised: Why is there evil in the world if God is good and creates the world in His goodness? Easy answers miss everything.

I want to approach the question of psalmic enemies through consideration of two psalms: 3 and 142. The LXX title of Psalm 3 is: "A Psalm of David, when he fled in the desert from his son Absalom," while the title of Psalm 142 reads: "A Psalm of David, when his son Absalom pursued him." A striking fact emerges: the Psalter, as a whole, seems to be using this event from the Davidic narratives as a kind of frame for all the psalms.

The narrative of Absalom's murder of his brother Amnon for the rape of their sister Tamar; his flight from his father's wrath; his exile and eventual return to his father's palace; his being superficially forgiven by his father but remaining actually unforgiven: all this is powerfully told in the Septuagint in 2 Kings (in the Hebrew, 2 Samuel) and provides the background for the narrative of Absalom's rebellion.

I want to focus on two moments in this powerful narrative. The first moment is from the account of Amnon's rape of Tamar. The account begins when Amnon feigns sickness so as to ask his sister Tamar to bring some food to him while he lies in bed. When she brings two small cakes to her brother, Amnon seizes her hand as she holds out the bread to him, forcing her into his bed. "No, no, my brother, do not force me," she cries (13:13). "But he would not listen, and being stronger than she, he forced her, and lay with her" (13:14). The next verse reads: "Then Amnon hated her with a very great hatred; so that the hatred with which he hated her was greater than the love with which he loved her" (13:15)—and the LXX adds: "for the last [ἐσχάτη, *eschatē*] wickedness was worse than the first [πρώτη, *prōtē*]."[1]

The Destruction of Inwardness

Here is our moment. Amnon's instantaneous hatred of Tamar after raping her is not merely a psychological maneuver whereby he can dissociate himself from the victim of his assault—and from his crime—by blaming it on her. More deeply, this hatred destroys in Tamar her very *inwardness*, wrecking her capacity to experience God as truly alive *within* her. In Psalm 3, the second line reads: "Many are they who say to my soul: there is no salvation for him in his God." The key phrase here is "in his God"; there is no God-Who-Is-In-Me, no inwardness that is God; there is only this violence wherein I am being psychically wrecked. Here, then, is the inner reality of what it means to have an enemy: there exists a person who seeks to wreck your soul in such a way that you will lose all inward capacity to know God directly, to be in direct communion with Him. This wreckage of communion is signaled by the narrator having Tamar offer bread to her brother: here is the dark "anti-communion" of violent hatred, a communion that destroys the very heart of any genuine relationship.

One further detail here is striking. The LXX Greek verb used in line 14, "he forced her" (meaning: he raped her), is *tapeinoō* (ταπείνοω), meaning he humiliated her, he afflicted her. Yet the same verb is widely used in patristic and ascetical writings to mean "to become humble," "to find genuine humility." As Saint John Climacus says, using the noun: "Humility [ταπεινοφροσύνη, *tapeinophrosynē*] is a tower of strength against the face of the enemy" (*Ladder* 25:26). As either noun or verb, the word is spiritually charged with the power either to debase or to illumine the person undergoing the experience—or (perhaps better) to illumine *because* it debases. Tamar is, then, in her wreckage, also a figure of illumination.[2]

We may thus say that this Davidic moment reveals the crucial action performed by one's real enemy: the action whereby physical violence escalates into a psychic violence that seeks to destroy in you your living communion with God. In this way, then, the rape of Tamar sheds immense light on what the psalmic enemy is actually—and very terribly—doing.

The Murder of Absalom

The second moment from the Davidic narrative occurs at the murder of Absalom. The narrative events connecting the rape of Tamar and the murder of Absalom are beautifully given. For two years after the rape of his sister by his brother, Absalom bides his time, finally striking Amnon down at a sheep-shearing festival; and then he flees, staying in a neighboring land for three years (2 Kings 13:39). Initially seeking to punish Absalom for Amnon's murder, David in time gives up his desire for vengeance. Joab, David's shrewd military advisor (and a highly experienced killer), then persuades David to allow Absalom to return, no doubt at least as much for reasons of preventing Absalom from stirring up rebellion against David as for any desire to reconcile father and son. Absalom returns—but David refuses to allow his son into the palace, never even permitting Absalom to see his face. As a result, Absalom resentfully begins to collect a band of secret malcontents, and does this so successfully that he leads a rebellion that causes his father to flee (hence, Psalms 3 and 142).

Once in the wilderness, David recovers his love for his son as he reassembles his scattered palace guards into a potent military force against the (temporarily) successful rebels, who briefly occupy the palace and declare Absalom to be the new king. Yet the rebellion very quickly disintegrates, and Absalom shortly becomes a man running for his life as David retakes the kingdom. David himself then leads his newly triumphant army in pursuit of the now-solitary Absalom, saying to his commanders, "Deal gently for me with the lad Absalom" (2 Kings 18:5). The pursuit intensifies.

Now the moment we are awaiting draws near. Absalom's long

hair becomes tangled in the branches of a great oak tree as the mule he is riding passes on, leaving Absalom dangling "between heaven and earth" (2 Kings 18:9). Joab and his men come upon this bizarre scene, and Joab orders them to kill Absalom. They refuse, shocked, saying they could not disobey their king who had said, "Watch for me over the lad Absalom" (18:13). Joab seizes three blunt sticks, saying, "Then I'll begin this; I'll not wait for you." The moment arrives: "he took three sticks in his hand and he thrust them into Absalom's heart, still alive in the heart of the oak tree" (18:14).

The Two Hearts

Robert Alter astutely says of this moment: "The two hearts, one a vulnerable human organ, the other the dense center of the tangle of branches, produce an unsettling effect."[3] The two hearts. What is indeed unsettling about Joab's act of murder is its width and its depth. Joab's hand, in piercing simultaneously the heart of the old oak and the heart of the young man, becomes a hand seeking to destroy a highly specific victim at the same instant it becomes a hand enacting violence against *the heart of all creation*—an escalation in violence signaled by the very next verse: "And the ten lads, Joab's armor bearers, surrounded Absalom and together finished him off."[4] Taken with the moment when Tamar is raped, this moment reveals the width and depth of the enemy's violence. For, in Psalms, the enemy is seeking to destroy the divine inwardness of the human person at the same instant it escalates into violating the whole of creation—and thereby to escalate further into assaulting the Creator Himself. To defend against such assault therefore becomes, at depth, a defense of both the creation and the Creator: nothing less.

For this reason, then, Psalms 3 and 142 rightly see the spiritual warfare that underlies all the political struggles. Or, to say it another way, we see how the earthly warfare is rooted in a heavenly warfare the way—in the psalmic metaphor—branches are rooted in a tree. In other words, good and evil truly exist; and the Psalms are, at every moment, manifesting their existence as acts of warfare.

Remembering the Statutes

We are now in a position to understand the psalmic heart of the great Psalm 118, a single line occurring not at the arithmetically exact midpoint of the poem but some four lines later:

> I shall never forget thy statutes,
> In them thou hast quickened me to life. (118:93)

In rabbinic commentary, as we saw in chapter 3, statutes are the foundational patterns of the created world, the patterns with which God first created and still sustains the entire creation.[5] Therefore, the statutes are the patterns that we cannot fully comprehend with our minds, for their actions and operations reach far beyond—wider, higher, and deeper than merely human thoughts can even conceivably begin to reach. Yet these statutes constitute the very inwardness we possess and, in doing so, they provide the ways whereby we actually live, they are the divine patterns of our earthly souls, the way we remember God and, hence, remember who we are in Him. And at the same time, the statutes are the divine patterns of aliveness within all created things, within each tiny blade of grass or the heart of every tree. To remember the statutes is therefore to know—deeply and widely—who you truly are and also who all created beings truly are: and therefore to have divinely given aliveness within you. To forget the statutes is to die to both the creation and the Creator.

Now, the Hebrew text of Psalm 118, as we saw in chapter 3,

distinguishes the statutes from the precepts (פִּקּוּדִים, *piqqudim*), the Rabbis seeing the latter term as indicating specific acts taken by us that sustain our communion in the statutes: for example, fasting and prayer. In this sense, then, the Hebrew precepts can be seen as tiny icons we make of the divinely shaped statutes: they are the *ways* we thus make our personal lives harmonize with the divine aliveness.

But the LXX translators make no distinction in their Greek between statutes and precepts, using the same word (*dikaiōmata*) for both. The student of the LXX Psalter may therefore conclude that the tiny icons of our ascetical lives are—*in practice*—not to be distinguished from their divine prototypes. And in this sense, as we saw in chapter 3, the LXX text of Psalm 118 is far more open to what we as Orthodox Christians understand as *deification* or *theosis*: as the *direct communion* we can achieve with the divine Creator through the long disciplines of Orthodox ascesis.

And from this perspective we may usefully approach Psalm 3.

Psalm 3

*A psalm of David, when he fled in the desert
from his son Absalom.*

1 Lord, why do they that afflict me keep multiplying? Many are they that rise up against me.

2 Many are they who say to my soul: There is no salvation for him in his God.

3 But thou, O Lord, art my protector, my glory and the one who lifts up my head.

4 I cried to the Lord with my voice and he heard me from his holy hill.

5 I lay down and slept; I awoke, for the Lord will protect me.

6 I will not be afraid of ten thousands of people who set
themselves against me all around.

7 Arise, O Lord, save me, O my God, for thou hast struck all
those who are my enemies without cause, thou hast broken the
teeth of the sinners.

8 Salvation is from the Lord and thy blessing is upon thy people.

The chiastic heart of the poem is lines 4 and 5.[6] To cry out with
your voice is to pray aloud to God; and therefore it is to sustain communion with God as divinely given inwardness. Note the verb tense
in the second half of line 4: the LXX Greek and the MT Hebrew
concur in using the past tense, thereby establishing firmly the vivid
actuality of the divine response to David's prayer. Rashi believes
that, in his first night fleeing his son, David approaches psalmic terror in this line, while RaDak disagrees with Rashi, holding that
the next line—"I lay down and slept"—indicates David's complete
assurance in God's bounty even during this night of terror.[7] Either
way, the significance is clear: at the psalm's chiastic heart, David
sustains his divinely given communion with God; he sustains the
inward aliveness his enemy is seeking to destroy.

Hence, in lines 3 and 6, we see the immediate consequences of
sustaining this inward communion:

3   But thou, O Lord, art my protector, my glory and the
      one who lifts up my head.

6   I will not be afraid of ten thousands of people who set
      themselves against me all around.

In line 6 we see the escalation in violent attacks ("ten thousands
of people" against the single "I") at the same moment we see the
inward stillness of ascetic courage in the face of vast hordes of the
enemy. This courage is not at all an attribute of David's personality.
Rather, the courage is a gift directly given by God to David: the gift

of personhood. Hence, the glory (δόξα, *doxa*) is at once uniquely David's and entirely God's bounty: it is *who* David is in direct communion with God. And this personhood is what the psalmic enemy actively seeks to unmake.

The next pair out from the psalmic center thus provides a direct contrast, the first line indicating the enemy's action, the second declaring God's power against this action.

2   Many are they who say to my soul: There is no
     salvation for him in his God.

7   Arise, O Lord, save me, O my God, for thou hast
     struck all those who are my enemies without cause,
     thou hast broken the teeth of the sinners.

As we have now come to understand, line 2 reveals in vivid clarity the psalmic enemy's constant target: the very soul, or inward aliveness, of the psalmic speaker. Note, too, the *way* wherein the psalmic enemy seeks victory: by using words of contempt and scorn. The LXX Greek word for contempt (ὄνειδος, *oneidos*; and ὀνειδισμός, *oneidismos* as a close synonym) occurs over twenty times in the Psalter, most significantly at the conclusion of Psalm 88:

50   Remember the contempt, O Lord, I suffered in my
     heart, contempt all thy servants suffer from all the
     nations,

51   Contempt, O Lord, thine enemies have used to darken
     that reconciling exchange given by thy Christ.

Contempt is the fuel that drives the engines of all psalmic violence; and in calling God to remember this contempt, the psalmic speaker is seeking to drain the fuel from all engines of violence. Note, too, that contempt "darkens that reconciling exchange [ἀντάλλαγμα, *antallagma*[8]] given by thy Christ." That is, contempt destroys the divine communion given to us for our participation in God, and in so doing, contempt unmakes all the creation. The seventh line of Psalm 3—"thou hast struck all those who are my enemies without cause, thou hast broken the teeth of the sinners"—therefore strikes at the very instrument of this terrible psychic darkening: at the mouth of the enemy.

Psalm 3's first and final lines perfectly—and contrastively—frame the whole psalm:

1 Lord, why do they that afflict me keep multiplying?
   Many are they that rise up against me . . .
8 Salvation is from the Lord and thy blessing is upon thy people.

The poem begins with stating the escalating nature of all psalmic violence, the way wherein an exponential multiplying of terror characterizes the enemy's action—an escalation in which one son, Absalom, becomes almost instantly ten thousands of people surrounding the solitary "me." This solitary psalmic "I" nevertheless sustains divinely given personhood, and in so doing, the speaker comes, in the final line, to experience the salvation (σωτηρία, *sōtēria*) and blessing (εὐλογία, *eulogia*). This salvation therefore directly responds to line 2's attempt to destroy it, while the blessing is exactly the "well-speaking" (*eu-logia*) that unmakes the enemy's contempt.

It is worth noting, too, that the verb form of this noun *eulogia* is used on the Holy Mountain as both a welcoming greeting and a kind of farewell: *eulogite*. For such usage of one's own tongue—one's instrument of deeply comprehended noetic understanding—beautifully unmakes in us every impulse to speak those words of contempt that would assault the personhood of another—and, through that assault, to attack the very heart of the creation itself: both hearts at once.

In Homily 4, Saint Isaac the Syrian has this passage:

> Consider yourself a stranger all the days of your life, wher-
> ever you may be, so that you may find deliverance from the
> injury which is born of familiarity. In every matter consider
> yourself to be totally ignorant so as to escape the reproach
> which follows the suspicion that you wish to set aright other
> men's opinions. Let your lips always utter blessings, and you
> will never be reviled; for revilement begets revilement, and
> blessing begets blessing.[9]

1 Cor 2.— (handwritten margin note)

This sheds considerable light, I think, on Psalm 3's depiction of the
enemy. The fuel of contempt that drives all psalmic violence is first
drilled for in our desire "to set aright other men's opinions"; while
lips that "always utter blessings" (*eulogite*) give rise to more blessings.
In this way, then, Abba Isaac here posits a divinely positive escalation, one that—in direct contrast with the dreadful multiplication
of contempt—proceeds in the way God's creation proceeds: the way
of incarnation. That is, the multiplying of blessings has the result,
says Saint Isaac, of becoming *an entire way of actually living in God*:
a life, that is, in direct participation in Him. Here indeed is what
Psalm 3 calls salvation and blessing.

Psalm 142 again engages the issue of David's fleeing his violent
son, Absalom.

Psalm 142

A psalm of David, when his son Absalom pursued him.

1　O Lord, hear my prayer; in thy truthfulness heed my
　　plea, answer me in thy righteousness.
2　Do not judge against thy servant, for no man living
　　shall be found to be righteous in thy sight.

3 For the enemy has tormented my soul, he has laid low my life to the earth, making me dwell in dark places like one who has been long dead,

4 And my spirit has fallen into depression, my heart deeply troubled within me.

5 I remembered the days of old, I meditated on all thy works, and deeply on the creations of thy hands.

6 I spread out my hands to thee, my soul thirsts like dry land for thee.

7 Hear me speedily, O Lord, my spirit has forsaken me; turn not thy face from me or I shall become like one who goes down into the pit.

8 Grant that I may hear every morning thy mercy, for in thee I have hoped; and grant me, O Lord, to know the way wherein I should walk, for I have lifted my soul up to thee.

9 Deliver me, O Lord, from my enemies, for to thee I have fled.

10 Teach me to do thy will, for thou art my God, thy good Spirit shall guide me into the land of uprightness.

11 For thy name's sake, O Lord, thou shalt quicken me to life, in thy righteousness thou shalt bring my soul out from these afflictions.

12 In thy mercy thou shalt destroy my enemies, thou shalt completely unmake all those tormenting my soul, for I am thy servant.

But the effects of the terror have now become more drastic for David. Here is the chiastic heart of Psalm 142:

6 I spread out my hands to thee, my soul thirsts like dry land for thee.

7   Hear me speedily, O Lord, my spirit has forsaken me;
     turn not thy face from me or I shall become like one
     who goes down into the pit.

The "pit" (Greek λάκκος, *lakkos*; Hebrew בּוֹר, *bor*[10]) is widely used in Psalms—indeed, throughout Scripture—to indicate the place of isolated emptiness: darkness, depression, inward wreckage and outward bondage: in brief, the pit is the place of living death.

LXX Psalm 87 is the most devastating exploration of the pit in all the Psalter, vividly matching even the pit into which Joseph is cast in Genesis 37. There are two details in Psalm 87's depiction of the pit that can help our understanding of it in Psalm 142. The first detail occurs in line 7b: "shall anyone give an account of . . . thy truthfulness in a wrecked place?" Now, the LXX Greek for *wrecked place* is ἀπώλεια (*apōleia*);[11] while the Hebrew is אֲבַדּוֹן (*avaddon*[12]), a place situated in deepest Hell, the place vividly described by Job as the place that stands naked to God's chastising eye, the place of total wreckage that is completely uncovered (Job 26:6). Saint John Chrysostom, in fact, says that the cause of *apōleia* is the desertion (ἀπωταξία, *apōtaxia*) of God.[13]

The second detail from Psalm 87 concerns line 13: "O Lord I cried out to thee." The *Zohar* differentiates between a cry (שׁוֹעַ, *shoa'*) and a scream (צְעָקָה, *tse'aqah*), saying the cry is a form of prayer that articulates salvation (יְשׁוּעָה, *yeshu'ah*); while the scream is merely an inarticulate wailing.[14] Note carefully this Hebrew wordplay: *shoa'* is read as cognate with *yeshu'ah*, which is precisely the wordplay used in Matthew 1:21: "you shall call His name *Iēsus* because He will save [*sosei*] His people from their sins."[15] In Psalm 87:13, then, the speaker finds his capacity for salvific prayer still exists even at the very bottom of the pit. Taken together, these two details register a crucial fact about the psalmic pit: although it is the place of total inward devastation, this very totality can cause the pit to become

*1.6. God no longer covers, looks away from the sin and offenses, while still being present.

the way to psychic resurrection: for every power is taken away so completely from the person in the pit that God can thus directly work His redemptive will for him.

With these details in mind, let us return to the center of Psalm 142. Line 7 ends in LXX Greek this way: εἰς λάκκον (*eis lakkon*)— a phrase that uses the slightly but distinctly emphatic form of the preposition plus the accusative to show *direct motion all the way into* the pit (an emphasis the Hebrew also shows). That is, the accusative case stresses the action of *going into* a place, as opposed to the dative case's emphasis upon *resting in* that place. This grammatical detail of emphasis is then given greater urgency by the phrase being placed in the sentence's highly emphatic final position (again, the Hebrew achieves the same emphasis in a similar way). The point is clear. The grammars of both the Hebrew and the Greek act to sharpen a crucial fact about Psalm 142: the poem is conceiving David's action as *in-flight movement*, a conception that emerges only in the final two lines of Psalm 3. We may therefore put the point this way: In Psalm 3, as David *begins* his flight from his son Absalom, he is increasing the speed with which he is moving through the land as the poem moves toward the velocity of lines 7 and 8. In Psalm 142, the velocities of movement start from the level reached at the end of Psalm 3 and steadily increase throughout the poem's movement.

We may thus put two key questions. First, how precisely is Psalm 142 increasing the velocity of Psalm 3's movement? Second, what do these increases in movement signify in Psalm 142 about both the psalmic enemy and God's response?

At the heart of Psalm 142 we see this: "I spread out my hands to thee," where the LXX Greek verb is διεπέτασα (*diepetasa*), a word formed from the preposition *dia*, meaning "all the way through," and the noun πέτασμα (*petasma*), meaning both the *veil* of the Temple and the *flight* of a bird. The LXX verb thus creates a vivid etymological image of movement: the hands of David, like birds in flight, are parting the very veil of the Holy Temple. The critical point is surprisingly made: psalmic prayer actively opens a way in and through the enemy so that he may be successfully fled from: indeed, prayer *is* this swift flight. Line 7's first word then powerfully emphasizes this action: ταχύ (*tachu*), the adverb "speedily," made doubly emphatic by being placed in the initial position.

Yet, these velocities of redemptive movement through prayer are matched in the psalm by the counter-velocities of demonic movement into the pit: "thy spirit has forsaken me." Spirit (πνεῦμα, *pneuma*) is to be distinguished from soul (ψύχη, *psychē*) in the same sense we distinguish spiritual power from emotional power: the loss of the first power is far more drastic than is the loss of the second. This more drastic loss is radically signaled in line 4: "my spirit has fallen into depression" (ἀκηδιάω, *akēdiaō* [verb]). Depression in the

Psalms (ἀκηδία, *akēdia* [noun]) is directly connected to the work of the enemies; and perhaps the most important explication of it is Saint John Climacus' in *The Ladder of Divine Ascent* 13:2: "Despondency [depression] is a paralysis of soul, an enervation of the mind, neglect of asceticism, hatred of the vow made. . . . It accuses God of being merciless and without love for men."

Saint John connects this definition to "the midday demon of catastrophe" in Psalm 90 (l. 6). Etymologically, the Greek word *akēdia* is formed by prefixing the alpha-privative to the word for heart (κῆρ, *kēr*);[16] hence, depression means to move one's heart into a state of complete absent-heartedness, to become a-hearted—a condition that line 4 then emphatically underlines: "My heart is deeply troubled within me." Thus, the redemptive movement of Psalm 142 collides with this movement into psalmic depression.

The pit locates, in the Psalms, the *place* of depression: the place where a-heartedness has become a-ontological: that is, the place

Hebrew: עטף : faint, hide away, withdraw

Latin: fatless

where all being has been consumed by the psalmic enemy. Psalm 87 employs a unique and startling image of this depression: the speaker has become "like mangled men lying in graves" (87:4)—a unique mass murder so complete that God Himself is seen as the perpetrator: "Thy wrath leaned heavy on me, thy waves all crashed down on me" (87:7). And as in Psalm 142, Psalm 87 is filled with high-velocity movements: *cry out; come before; draw close; snatched from; crashed down; took away; stretch out; draw very near; cast away; brought down; swept through; swirling; took . . . far*—nearly every verb in Psalm 87 conveys the catastrophic movement of swift disintegration: the movement, that is, of psalmic depression.

Yet the whipsaw progression of these two movements in Psalm 142—a whipsawing perfectly held and sharply developed by the chiastic pattern—finds its resolution in redemptive movement. This resolution is illustrated in the psalm's penultimate line: "For thy name's sake, O Lord, thou shalt quicken me to life, in thy righteousness shalt bring my soul out from these afflictions" (142:11). The key verbal movement is "thou shalt quicken me," the same verb that occurs at the chiastic center of the great resurrectional Psalm 118: "I shall never forget thy statutes, / In them thou hast quickened me to life." Just as the psalmic enemy seeks to compel the psalmist's soul to enter all the way into what Psalm 87 calls "oblivion's land," so, too, redemption occurs for the psalmist as an act of spiritual remembering of the divine statutes: of, that is, the foundational and generative patterns of the created world. Here, in Psalm 142, the statutes are beautifully described in line 5: "I remembered the days of old, I meditated on all thy works, and deeply on the creations of thy hands." The "days of old" are indeed "the creations of [God's] hands," and these divine foundational creations are indeed His statutes. To remember the statutes is therefore to reintegrate the creation so broken by the enemy that the psalmist's "spirit ha[d] fallen into depression" (l. 4)

*EJ... ME /תְּחַיֵּנִי — "enlivened"

but has now fully comprehended "the way wherein I should walk" (l. 8). If psalmic depression is a downward falling into the pit of the heart's oblivion, then psalmic redemption is being guided into a rising up into "the land of uprightness"—the place, that is, where the demonic depression is lifted up into salvific joy.

In Homily 42, Saint Isaac writes this extraordinary passage:

> The trials that are inflicted by the paternal rod for the soul's progress and growth, and wherein she may be trained, are the following: sloth, oppressiveness of the body; enfeeblement of the limbs; despondency [or depression]; bodily pains—or suspicion of bodily illness; temporary loss of hope; darkening of thoughts; absence of help from men; scarcity of bodily necessities; and the like. By these temptations a man's soul feels herself lonely and defenceless, his heart is deadened and filled with humility, and he is trained thereby to come to yearn for his Creator. Yet divine providence proportions these trials to the strength and needs of those who suffer them. In them are mingled both consolation and griefs, light and darkness, wars and aid. In short, they straiten and enlarge. This is the sign of the increase of God's help. (42:209–10)

This remarkable passage perfectly expresses the whipsaw double movement of Psalm 142. The nine trials listed by Saint Isaac can all be subsumed into what we might term *clinical depression*: and the range of these symptoms is fully matched by the depth of comprehensive understanding. The "enfeeblement of the limbs" and the "suspicion of bodily illness" are indeed classic symptoms experienced by almost any seriously depressed person. Similarly, what Psalm 142 describes as an "a-hearted-ness" of spirit is fully seen by Abba Isaac as "loss of hope" and "darkening of thoughts." Also, the *relational*

[handwritten margin note: Read Isaiah 53:10? Hebrews (chastening) etc. In this light]

effects of depression are described by Saint Isaac as "absence of help from men," a description fully concurring with the powerful line from Psalm 141, a psalm entitled "Instruction by David, when he was in the cave, praying": "I looked on my right and I saw that no one had recognized me, that all flight had failed me, that no one saw deeply my soul" (141:4). Here, again, is the total triumph of the psalmic enemy: he has led the psalmist into a depression so severe that all relational reality has been unmade in him, *no one* sees deeply his soul, *all flight* has failed him. Hence, the cave where David is praying in Psalm 141 is fully congruent with the pit in Psalm 142: it is the psalmic place of deepest depression.

And yet, says Saint Isaac, this deadening of the heart is simultaneously—and above all else a filling with—humility, for it is, first of all, a training, he says, in coming "to yearn for the Creator." In this sense, then, depression in the Psalms is *fundamentally* a reconfiguring of desire; it is, if you will, an emotional rewiring wherein both the ways and the goals of all our desires are entirely redirected. To use Saint Isaac's important insight, depression is a straitening and an enlarging of the soul: an entering-into a tightly constructed place that is simultaneously an entering-into a place that enlarges.

The fourth (*Daleth*) stanza of Psalm 118 beautifully illustrates this insight of Saint Isaac's—and thereby sheds considerable light on Psalms 3 and 142:

Daleth

25 My soul lies prostrate on the earth,
   Quicken me according to thy word.
26 I declared my ways, and thou didst hear me,
   Teach me thy statutes.

27 Make me comprehend the way of thy statutes,
    I shall ponder thy wondrous works.

28 My soul has fainted from depression,
    Strengthen me with thy words.

29 Put the unjust way far from me,
    With thy law have mercy on me.

30 I have chosen the way of truth,
    I have never forgotten thy judgments.

31 I have clung to thy testimonies,
    O Lord, put me not to shame.

32 I have run the way of thy commandments
    When thou didst enlarge my heart.

Here, indeed, is expressed the double movement in Psalm 142, as the psalmist's soul, beginning in prostration (an image of total wreckage and deepest humility), moves to being quickened into life by the way of God's statutes: from depression to the heart's enlargement by means of pondering God's "wondrous works" (θαυμάσιοι, *thaumasioi*) of creation, which is "the way of truth," of *a-lethia*, of *a-forgetfulness*. Note, too, that the speaker of this stanza *clings* (a vivid verb in both Greek and Hebrew) to God's *testimonies* (Gk. *martyria*; Heb. עֵדָה, *'eduth*), one of the ten Hebrew words used to incarnate God's holy word. The *'eduth* (BDB 730a), say the Rabbis, are the historically revealed and culturally retained forms of God's holy word; as such, the *'eduth* incarnate the statutes as historical realities that can be—indeed, *must* be—held in and as the action of the spiritual ceremony; for in such tenacious acts of memory lies the defeat of the psalmic enemy.

The final line of Psalm 142 enacts this complete victory over the enemy: "In thy mercy thou shalt destroy my enemies, thou shalt completely unmake all those tormenting my soul, for I am thy servant" (142:12). The psychic torments inflicted by depression are now "completely unmade" in and by the action of God's mercy, an action that completes all the high-velocity movements in the psalm: and God's truthfulness in line 1 (Gk. ἀλήθεια, *alētheia*) becomes incarnate in line 12 as God's mercy. And in this psalmic incarnation the unmaking of the enemy occurs in *and as* the psalmist's spiritual resurrection into *servanthood*. The Hebrew word עֶבֶד (*'eved*) and the Greek word δοῦλος (*doulos*) are crucial, placed in their respective poems; and the Greek exhibits an especially striking syntax: δοῦλος σού εἰμι ἐγώ (*doulos sou ego eimi ego*, servant-thine-I-am), with the highly charged ἐγώ εἰμι (*egō eimi*) recalling the divine Name revealed to Moses and here, in Psalm 142, placed in emphatic final position. This syntax thus serves to heighten the religious significance of servanthood; for the psalmist here quite literally takes on the holy Name of God at the very moment he achieves the humility of servanthood.

The psalmic enemy, then, is at once highly dangerous and wholly ineffectual. The danger lies in the enemy's capacity to inflict depression upon the psalmist; his ineffectuality arises from the fact that psalmic prayer can part the very veil of the high holy place to call down God's mercy. In Psalms 3 and 142, David flees the violence of his son Absalom: and in so doing, he learns to pray past even the brutal murder of his pursuing son. After Joab thrusts the blunt sticks into Absalom's heart and then has his men join him in finishing off Absalom, he orders his men to fling the corpse into the woods and heap over it a big pile of stones (see 2 Kings 18:19; paraphrase by Alter). When David hears the news, he cries out:

> My son, Absalom!
> My son, my son, Absalom!
> Would that I had died
> In your stead!
> Absalom, my son, my son! (2 Kings 19:1)

(ἀντι σου : תחתי)

There are probably no more heartbreaking words in all Scripture, heartbreaking in their simplicity and their depth of grieving: heart-breaking in their psalmic intensity. The enemy is deeply injured, and the arrival of great grief begins for David a path through the darkness of great depression that will lead to the land of uprightness: the land where the creations of God's hands are deeply seen and held.

7

The Sword of Depression and the Shield of Psalmic Prayer

Psalm 101

The sword of depression is the despondency that cuts off prayer, which in turn cuts off our living connection with the Creator. To combat it we must engage in spiritual (not psychological) warfare, meeting the sword of depression with the shield of psalmic prayer with such strength and personal presence that the enemy's sword breaks against our shield. As penitents, we live on earth as guerilla fighters in enemy territory. The fighter's starting point in repentance is the knowledge that his own strength is weak; only God's strength is truly good and right. Thus his chief weapon is supplication, spoken outcry to God. The author looks first at Psalm 136 and then at Psalms 1 and 101, citing Psalm 1 as indicating the way into the endpoint of blessedness: first, separating from evil; second, bringing our will into the law of God; and third, achieving the perfected life in union with God. He says depression, vividly described in Psalm 101, triumphs when we lose this way and thereby lose *who* we are by identifying ourselves with *how* we are. "In the day I am afflicted, . . . I call out to thee," the psalmist cries, and by so doing sharpens the distinction between his (temporary) spiritual condition of affliction and his personhood. That is, in seizing hold of the unceasing aliveness of God, the psalmist pushes back against the overwhelming condition (the how he is) and calls forth the deeper reality of who he is in relation to who God is. —*Ed.*

A s we have seen so far in our reflections upon the actions of the psalmic enemy, the single most devastating weapon the enemy possesses is the sword of depression: the despondency that cuts off prayer—and this cuts off our living connection to the Creator. That we must engage in spiritual (and *not* psychological) warfare means that we must meet the sword of depression with the shield of psalmic prayer: and must do so with such strength that the enemy's sword breaks against our shield.

This is the approach I shall employ as we begin to reflect upon LXX Psalm 101. But—before we turn to Psalm 101, let us first consider this:

1. The single most vivid date in Hebrew history is August 586 BC—the destruction of Jerusalem by the Babylonian imperial army, with the slaughter of thousands of men, women, and children and the mass deportation of the survivors some eight hundred miles on foot to the Babylonian empire. For the next seventy years the Israelites are an enslaved people. Especially important to this experience is Psalm 136 (discussed in chapter 5). Also significant is the title to LXX Psalm 64: "A Psalmic Ode of David when Jeremiah, Ezekiel and the captive people were about to depart."

2. David, king some five hundred years before, succeeding Saul (the first king). The key experience of all 150 psalms is David's ten years as a guerilla leader in enemy territory, hunted, hated, and hungry. See 1 and 2 Samuel (LXX

1 and 2 Kings) and Chronicles for the account of David's life and work.

3. Approaching Orthodox Great Lent, we sing Psalm 136, and also these lines (17 and 18) from Psalm 68: "Turn not thy face from thy child, for I am afflicted, hear me speedily. / Draw near to my soul and redeem it, deliver me because of my enemies." The Orthodox Church thus raises the psalm to a new level (yet one that was always there): as penitents, we live on earth like guerilla fighters in enemy territory. The guerilla fighter must survive in the bleakest lands—like David during his ten years in the wilderness—yet fully trusting God: *because*, here's the point, David knew in his deepest heart, in every least fiber of his being, that all was happening in God's way, all was in His hands; that no strength was his own but every strength was God's strength. The guerilla fighter's starting point in repentance is that his own strength is weak in every serious encounter with the enemy; that *only* God's strength is truly good and right.

4. Hence: Psalms show *the way into blessedness*. Saint Gregory of Nyssa believes that the entire Psalter discloses such a way to us and shows us that way in the first three lines:[1]

Psalm 1:1: Blessed is the man who separates himself from evil. Here, says Gregory, begins that blessedness that is likeness to God: *that is the definition of psalmic blessedness*. Note well: There are three elements to be *separated from*: (1) "the counsel of the ungodly"—that is, the whole realm of violent discourses we know as the media and indeed our whole cultural discourse: discourse given entirely to ways of darkness; (2) "the way of the sinful"—the key word is "way" (ὁδος, *hodos*)—that is, actually proceeding in the practice of violence to self and/or to others; and (3) "the seat of the

[margin note: shared ("reality")]

scornful": here is the culmination of the separation: actually to renounce all our scorn (which is the verbal/psychic precondition of all habitual violence and sin).

Psalm 1:2: Then, in line 2 of Psalm 1, Gregory of Nyssa says we begin to participate in divine blessedness by bringing our will (τὸ θέλημα, *to thelēma*) actually into the λόγος (*logos*, law) of God: and this, says Gregory, "produces [in us] the capacity for what is better."[2] Here "meditation day and night" is what we know as *prayer without ceasing* (cf. Ps. 71:15, which uses this phrase: "They shall pray to him [Solomon] without ceasing, all the day long shall they bless him"). As an aside, we can see that the source for Saint Paul's famous phrase in 1 Thess. 5 is probably psalmic.

Psalm 1:3: And once we do this, then line 3 opens for us: we become "like a tree" whose "leaf shall not wither": that is, says Gregory, we achieve the life that has been perfected, we achieve *theosis*.

Psalm 101

*A prayer of a poor man, when he is depressed and
pours out his supplication before the Lord.*

1 Hear my prayer, O Lord, and let my cry come to thee.
2 Do not turn thy countenance from me; in the day I am afflicted, incline thine ear to me; in the day I call out to thee, hear me speedily.
3 For my days have vanished like smoke, my bones consumed like wood in a fire.
4 I have been cut down like the grass, and my heart has become so withered I have forgotten to eat my bread.
5 Because of the sound of my groaning, my bones have

clung to my flesh.

6   I have become like a desert pelican; like an owl perched in the ruins,

7   I kept watch and have now become like a sparrow alone on a housetop.

8   My enemies reproached me all day long; even those who once praised me kept swearing falsely against me.

9   For I kept eating ashes like bread, kept mingling my drink with weeping,

10 Because of thy countenance's furious wrath, for thou didst lift me up, then throw me down.

11 My days are a lengthening shadow, I have withered away like the grass.

12 But thou, O Lord, shalt forever endure; thy memory is from generation to generation.

13 Arising, thou shalt have compassion on Zion, for the time of mercy for her has come, the right moment has come.

14 For thy servants took pleasure in her stones, they shall have compassion even for her dust.

15 So the nations shall fear thy name, O Lord, all the kings of the earth thy glory.

16 For the Lord shall build up Zion, he shall appear in his glory.

17 He has regarded well all humble prayer, he has not despised their pleas.

18 Let this prayer in psalm be written down for the generation to come, that the people yet to be created may give praise to the Lord.

19 For he looked down from his high holy place, the Lord looked from heaven to earth

20 To attend to the prisoners' groaning, to set free the
    sons of the slain,

21 To declare the Lord's name in Zion, and his praise in
    Jerusalem,

22 When the peoples are gathered together, and the
    kingdoms, to serve the Lord.

23 From his strength's path, he said to him: Tell me the
    fewness of my days,

24 Take me not away, O my God, in the midst of my days;
    thy years are throughout all generations.

25 In the beginning, O Lord, thou didst found the earth;
    the heavens are the works of thy hands.

26 They will perish but thou shalt endure; all things will
    wear out like a garment, and like a cloak thou shalt
    change them, and they shall be changed.

27 But thou art the same, and thy years shall never fail.

28 Thy servants' sons forever shall dwell, their seed guided
    rightly forever.

To begin: the title of Psalm 101 carries three important insights
for us. The title's "poor man" is (say the Fathers) the one named most
blessed by Christ in the Beatitudes (Matt. 5:3).[3] For such complete poverty of spirit signifies the complete absence of any arrogance before God the Father. In other words, the poor man of the
psalm—like the guerilla warrior in the Davidic narratives—knows
his own weakness apart from God.

The second insight of the title is the verb "depressed" (ἀκηδία,
akēdia): in construe, "a-hearted-ness."[4] This condition is called in
Psalm 90:6 "the midday demon of catastrophe" and is seen, says
Saint John Climacus, to afflict especially those who pray the psalms:
"When there is no psalmody, then despondency [*akēdia*] does not
make its appearance,"[5] adding: "despondency visits ascetics about

noonday"[6]—direct references to Psalm 90:6. For the guerilla fighter to be weakened at midday is to lose all possibility of engaging in any spiritual warfare.

The title's third insight is the noun "supplication." This noun is best glossed by Saint Paul in his first letter to Timothy, where he says (in 2:1) that "supplication, prayers, intercessions, and giving of thanks be made for all men . . . that we may [all] lead a calm and peaceful life in all godliness and sanctity"—and uses the same noun, δέησις (*deēsis*), that is used in the title of Psalm 101. The guerilla fighter's weapon against the demon of depression is, then, *supplication*: spoken outcry to God. For (as we see in Psalm 101) supplication is the basis of all psalmic poetics.

Most of the opening third of Psalm 101 (from lines 3 to 11) is given to describing the terrible effects of depression: the complete vanishing of time as a dimension of struggle (1. 3); greatly decreased appetite (1. 4) and weight loss (1. 5); a sense of desolated isolation (11. 6 and 7); total self-hatred (1. 8); the wreckage of all sensory enjoyment (1. 9); weeping (1. 9); the devastating sense that God hates you (1. 10); and the overwhelming sense that total darkness is now descending inescapably upon you (1. 11).

In this bleak, terrible light, rabbinic tradition sees special significance in line 14: "For thy servants took pleasure in her stones, they shall have compassion even for her dust." This line (the Rabbis hold) refers directly to the destruction of Jerusalem in August 586 BC; and in this line, they say, King David is prophesying—some five hundred years before the event—the εὐδοκία (*eudokia*, pleasure) and οἰκτηρμός (*oiktērmos*, compassion) even for the stones and dust of the wrecked city—pleasure and compassion that will rebuild the city from wreckage.

The first two lines of Psalm 101 describe the psalmist's shield against the sword of depression:

1   Hear my prayer, O Lord, and let my cry come to thee.
2   Do not turn thy countenance from me; in the day I am
    afflicted, incline thine ear to me; in the day I call out to
    thee, hear me speedily.

The primary characteristics of this shield can be described as: spoken prayer charged with personal presence. That is, the psalmist *articulates* his great need, pouring into that articulation the full reality of who—and *how*—he is. The *who* he is can then be said to be this man praying at this moment; and the *how* he is can therefore be said to be a man who is now, at this moment, depressed. The LXX verb for "depressed" in the title is, interestingly, in the aorist subjunctive—aorist, to indicate definite actuality of the moment; subjunctive, to signal the temporally conditional nature of his attack—that is, "depressed" describes not *who* he is but only *how*, at this moment, he is. This tension between ontologically permanent personhood and temporal condition shapes the entire psalm.

The second line heightens this tension by twice using the phrase "in the day": "in the day I am afflicted"; "in the day I call out to thee" (Ps. 101:2). The effect of this repetition is to sharpen the distinction between the psalmist's personhood and his (temporary) spiritual condition; between, that is, the *who* and the *how*. And the sharpness of the distinction inclines, in line 2, toward the psalmist's seeing who he is as defined by how he is. Here, then, is the leading edge of depression's sword: *depression triumphs when it causes you to see—and to experience—your condition as your personhood.*

As the next nine lines show (ll. 3–11), the psalmist has succumbed to the enemy's sword, describing in vivid detail the effects of depression. Especially to be noted are lines 6 and 7:

6   I have become like a desert pelican; like an owl perched
    in the ruins.

7   I kept watch and have now become like a sparrow
    alone on a housetop.

The rabbinic tradition describes the "desert pelican" (πελεκὰν ἐρη-μικός, *pelekan herēmikos*) as an "undomesticated bird who lives in the wilderness and . . . issues a sighing sound," adding: "The cries of Israel in exile resemble this mournful sighing"[7]—again emphasizing the wreckage of Jerusalem. The Rabbis further say—in reference to the "sparrow alone on a housetop" (Ps. 101:7)—that "when this bird alights upon the roof of a comfortable home, it yearns to enter the home but does not lest it be captured and killed."[8] The depressive feels, above all, homeless and isolated: here is the triumph of *how* over *who*; of condition over personhood.

Fr. Pavel Florensky, in his magnificent book *The Pillar and Ground of the Truth*, describes to his spiritual father a nightmare he once had:

Once in a dream I experienced the second death in all its concreteness. I did not see any images. The experience was a purely interior one. Utter darkness, almost materially dense, surrounded me. Powers of some kind dragged me to the edge and I felt this to be the edge of God's being, that beyond it is absolute Nothing. I wanted to scream but could not. I knew that in one more moment I would be expelled into the outer darkness. The darkness began to flow into my whole being. Half my consciousness of self was lost, and I knew that this was absolute, metaphysical annihilation. In ultimate despair I cried with a voice that was not my own: "From out of the depths, O Lord, I have cried out to thee, / O Lord, hear my voice . . ." (Ps. 129:1–2). My whole soul was in those words. Someone's hands gripped me, a drowning man, powerfully and threw me somewhere, far from the abyss. The jolt was sudden and powerful. Suddenly I found myself in my usual surroundings, my room. From mystical non-being I was thrown back into ordinary, everyday life. Here at once I felt myself in the presence of God and then I awoke, drenched in a cold sweat.[9]

Fr. Pavel's nightmare perfectly describes the first third of Psalm 101, where depression has turned the psalmist's sunlight into deepening darkness: "My days are a lengthening shadow" (Ps. 101:11), a shadow in which God Himself is seen as the One inflicting the darkness: "For thou didst lift me up, then threw me down" (Ps. 101:10).

But, with lines 12 and 13, the darkness lifts suddenly; and like Fr. Pavel in his dream, the psalmist is powerfully gripped and thrown "somewhere, far from the abyss":

12   But thou, O Lord, shalt forever endure; thy memory is from generation to generation.

13   Arising, thou shalt have compassion on Zion, for the time of mercy for her has come, the right moment has come.

What powerfully grips the psalmist is prayer—in particular, the supplicatory prayer for mercy. As the lights flicker and threaten to go out completely, the psalmist suddenly seizes hold of (or, better, is *seized by*) the unceasing aliveness of God, an aliveness that brings with it the divine compassion that is the antidote to the poison of depression. And in so seizing hold, the psalmist instantly pushes back against the overwhelming condition (the *how* he is) and calls forth the deeper reality of *who* he is in relation to *who* God is.

Line 27 says: "But thou art the same, and thy years shall never fail." By beholding God's *permanence*, the psalmist sees also his own way past depression's toxic assertion of total darkness. And, in

*This is one way to read the name Hezikiah חזקיה (Isaiah 38:10-20 "makes strong" d" + "Jah" and he had a similar experience 2 kings 20:1-11 = "grabs on firm"

a reversal of the moment in Fr. Pavel's nightmare when "darkness began to *flow into* my whole being," Psalm 101 begins and ends in a *pouring-out* (ἐκχέω, *ekcheo*)[10] of supplication before God. And the darkness recedes; the toxicity vanishes; and the psalmist sees, in the final line, the reality of *who*, exactly and deeply, he is in relation to who, mercifully, God is: "Thy servants' sons forever shall dwell, their seed guided rightly forever." In this line, the emphatic "forever" reflects the LXX Greek of εἰς τὸν αἰῶνα (*eis ton aiōna*), literally, "all the way into the age."

In conclusion, let me refer once again to line 14: "thy servants took pleasure in her stones" (Ps. 101:14a), which the rabbinic tradition sees as representing the Israelites taking with them into their captivity the stones of the wrecked Temple—stones, the Rabbis say, carried back to Jerusalem some seventy years later when the Temple was rebuilt.

On Wednesday, January 7, 2004, my son Rowan [Benedict], our Orthodox seminarian friend Mark Montague [from Vermont], and I were in Paramythia, Greece, in the northern mountains up near the Albanian border. We were on pilgrimage to visit the home of my name saint, Donatos (fourth-century Bishop in Epiros). We had spent the morning visiting Geromeriou Monastery some 40 kilometers away; by the afternoon I was tired and needed to rest. The afternoon sun was descending as we drove back to Paramythia. When we reached the hotel, Mark said to me: "Would you mind if Rowan and I try to find the saint's holy places while you rest?" Very tired yet very happy, I said it would give me great joy for them to do that.

Some three hours later they returned, faces flushed with excitement. They had indeed found the site that tradition identifies as the spot where Saint Donatos had slain a water-poisoning dragon by making the sign of the cross in the air; and they had also found the ruins that the historical record describes as those of the saint's original church. Rowan held out his hand to me; in his palm was a small stone. "This," he said, "is from the central column of Saint Donatos's own church." His eyes were filled with love. "You should have it." Since that day in Greece, I have had this stone at my prayer-corner. Each morning and evening I lightly touch it, always with deepest spiritual pleasure.

8

The Sons of Korah and the Way of Psalmic Poetics

Psalm 44

This chapter begins with the repentant sons of Korah, placed by God on a precarious ledge high above His fiery destruction of the rebels who had participated in their father's rebellion against Moses and Aaron. There, as with one mind, these sons of the rebel leader begin to compose psalms, and the author asks how this series of psalms and their backstory can serve as a model for us of the way of psalmic poetics. Following a path of meticulous linguistic, scriptural, and midrashic analysis of Psalm 44, he concludes that psalm composition begins in a stirring of the heart to repentance that transforms the heart's trangressive desires into an overflowing love for the Word's goodness and the beauty of the divine King. Through intermediate stages of fervent penitential remembrance of God, the psalmist ends in praise that never ceases, through which the praisegiver becomes one with the divine Person being praised. Thus is consummated the marriage union of divine and human, figured here by the Christlike King (or Christ Himself) and the earthly Queen (traditionally understood as the Church); and even the beholder of Psalms becomes himself psalmic. This, the author says, is the way of psalmic poetics. —*Ed.*

"Notwithstanding, the sons of Korah did not die."
(Num. 26:11)

B eginning with Psalm 41, there is a series of eight psalms with the inscription "for the sons of Korah" (Psalms 41–48). Identifying Psalm 44 as the center, Gregory of Nyssa sees the series as proclaiming the everlasting throne of Christ; the "appearance of the Lord in the flesh"; the descent and ascent of Christ; the day of resurrection; and the wind of the Holy Spirit coming upon the Apostles. It concludes in Psalm 48:1–2, where "all human beings become one hearing and one heart when the Word resounds in them all."[1]

Four later psalms bear the same inscription, "for the Sons of Korah" (83, 84, 86, and 87). Exodus (6:24) names the three sons—Assir, Elkanah, and Abiasaph—whom rabbinic tradition identifies as among the ten poets who, besides David, composed the Psalms: Adam, Melchizidek, Abraham, Moses, Heiman, Jedusun, Asaph, and the three sons of Korah. Hence, we may consider taking the inscription "to the sons of Korah" as an attribution of authorship.

In Numbers 16, we are given the narrative of Korah's rebellion against the authority of Moses. Korah, the son of Levi, persuades Dathan and Abiram—along with two hundred fifty other highly respected leaders of the Israelites—to join with him in challenging Moses and Aaron. Moses responds to them: "Why do you exalt yourselves above the assembly of the Lord?" (Num. 16:3) and calls upon God to reveal His truth and gracious will to all of them.

The argument continues with considerable heat, with Dathan and Abiram saying to Moses: "Why did you bring us out into the wilderness and make yourself prince over us?" Moses responds, not to them but to God Himself: "I have not harmed one of them," saying to Korah: "Tomorrow, you and all your company assemble at the entrance to the holy tabernacle—and bring with you, every one of you, your censer with incense in it." They all meet in the morning.[2]

Then the Lord commands Moses and Aaron to separate themselves from the assembly so that, He says, "I may consume them in a moment." Moses pleads with God: "Shall one man sin, and wilt thou be angry with all the congregation?" (Num. 16:21–22). God responds, commanding Moses to tell everyone to flee from the dwellings of Korah, Dathan, and Abiram. Moses does so, saying further: "if the ground opens its mouth, and swallows them up, with all that belongs to them, and they go down alive into Sheol, then you shall know that these men have despised the Lord" (Num. 16:30).

Then: "As he finished speaking all these words, the ground under them split asunder; and the earth opened its mouth and swallowed them up, with their households and all the men that belonged to Korah and all their goods" (Num. 16:31). In chapter 26 of Numbers, however, we have this important verse: "Notwithstanding, the sons of Korah did not die" (26:11). Rashi explains it by saying that, while the three sons at first supported the rebellion, they repented. A modern Jewish scholar of Psalms sums up Rashi's astonishing and crucial point:

> In the midst of the rebellion, however, they [the three sons] realized their folly and repented. When the earth opened its mouth to swallow the entire assembly of Korah, and to transport them to Gehenna, God miraculously provided a place of refuge for Korah's three sons. They landed on an elevated niche within the earth high above the flames [of Gehenna]. It was on their precarious ledge that they composed these psalms.[3]

The descendants of Korah's sons thus fully sustain (in the rabbinic view) this divinely given gift of psalmic inspiration and composition. And what begins as an attack upon God becomes, in His hands, the way of psalmic poetics.

The Way of Psalmic Poetics

Here, then, is our key to Psalm 44: it is the way of psalmic poetics. Now, the usual definition of the term "poetics" is that it is a culturally held set of assumptions about what constitutes a poem. This definition has clear and obvious value, for surely poetics in this sense *guides* any poet in composing any poem: guides but does not determine: that is, the poet—not the culture—composes the poem. This, however, cannot account adequately for two key factors in Psalm 44: *where* in the poet are the assumptions held? and *how* does what we call "inspiration" actually operate in psalmic composition? To respond to these questions is to begin to sketch what I am calling the way of psalmic poetics. Here is the psalm:

Psalm 44

For the end of the struggle, in alternating verses, concerning instruction for the sons of Korah, an ode about the Beloved.

1   My heart has overflowed with a good word, I myself say my works to the king, my tongue is the pen of a swift-writing scribe.

2   Thou art fairer than the sons of men, grace has been poured on thy lips, therefore God has blessed thee forever.

3   Gird thy sword upon thy thigh, O mighty one, in thy splendor and thy beauty.

4 And string thy bow, prosper and reign because of truth, gentleness and righteousness, and wondrously shall thy right hand guide thee.

5 Thine arrows are sharp, O mighty one, in the heart of the king's enemies; the peoples shall fall under thee.

6 Thy throne, O God, is for ever and ever, thy royal scepter is a scepter of uprightness.

7 Thou hast loved righteousness and hated iniquity; therefore God, thy God, has anointed thee with the oil of gladness more than thy companions.

8 Myrrh and aloes and cassia exhale from thy garments, and from the ivory palaces they have gladdened thee,

9 These daughters of kings in thine honor. At thy right hand stood the queen dressed in gold-woven raiment richly embroidered.

10 Listen, O daughter, behold and incline thine ear: forget thine own people and thy father's house.

11 For the king shall greatly desire thy beauty, for he is himself thy Lord.

12 And the daughters of Tyre shall worship him with gifts, the rich among the people shall entreat thy countenance.

13 The king's daughter is all glorious within, her clothing is woven with gold.

14 The virgins who follow after her shall be brought to the king, those near her shall be brought to thee.

15 They shall be brought with gladness and rejoicing, they shall enter into the king's palace.

16 In place of thy fathers are sons born to thee, whom thou shalt make princes over all the earth.

17 I will make thy name to be remembered from

generation to generation; all peoples shall give praise to thee unto ages of ages, forever.

Transformation of the Heart's Transgressive Desires into the Word's Goodness

The first and final lines of Psalm 44 are the only two lines in the LXX Greek text that use the first-person singular verb; every other line in the poem has persons other than "I."[4] These two lines provide the outer chiastic framework for the psalm:

1   My heart has overflowed with a good word, I myself
     say my works to the king, my tongue is the pen of a
     swift-writing scribe. . . .

17 I will make thy name to be remembered from
     generation to generation; all peoples shall give praise to
     thee unto ages of ages, forever.

Now, the LXX Greek word for "heart" in line 1 is glossed in the *Philokalia* this way: "not simply the physical organ, but the spiritual center of man's being, man as made in the image of God, his deepest and truest self, or the inner shrine, to be entered only through sacrifice and death, in which the mystery of the union between the divine and the human is consummated."[5]

Fabre d'Olivet—in his curious and seminal 1815 work entitled *The Hebraic Tongue Restored* (a book that, in the hands of Benjamin Whorf, helped form the foundations of modern linguistics)—says that the Hebrew word לֵב (*lev*) "constitutes a root whence emanate all ideas of vitality, passion, vigour, courage, audacity: literally, it is *the heart*, and figuratively, all things which pertain to that centre of life; every quality, every faculty resulting from the unfolding of the vital principle."[6]

The seat of "the power"
« δυναμιοτηριον »

Both the Hebrew and the Greek concur: the heart is not merely the physical organ or the psychological dimension but is, most importantly, the *spiritual* center of the human person. As such, the heart is (again, d'Olivet) the "image of every interior activity, every appetent, desirous, generative force" in the person.[7] The *Philokalia* glossary also quotes Saint John Climacus, who refers to Psalm 118:145: "I have cried with my whole heart" (ὅλη καρδίᾳ μου, *olē kardia mou*)—adding, "that is, with my body, soul and spirit."[8] In sum, then, the heart constitutes the very essence of the human person. And this essence is where—again, the *Philokalia*—"the mystery of the union between the divine and the human is consummated."[9]

The psalmist then says, "My heart *has overflowed* with a good word" (l.1). My translation—"*over*flowed"—reflects the Greek verb ἐξηρεύξατο (*exēreuxato*) with its strong prepositional prefix. The LXX translator is, in turn, looking at the Hebrew verb רָחַשׁ (*rahash*), which literally means "is stirred, moved."[10] Jewish scholars note that here, in Psalm 44, is—and I quote—"the only place in Scriptures where *rahash* is employed as a verb rather than as a noun meaning a creeping reptile."[11] A crucial midrash observes "that when the sons of Korah were swallowed in the earth, they were [struck] dumb"— but "their hearts were stirred to repentance and God . . . saved them."[12] The same scholars also note that the Hebrew uses the singular form of "my heart" "to emphasize that the three sons were simultaneously around and developed identical thoughts at the same time and their hearts were as one."[13]

The Hebrew further contains an implicit transgressive jolt: to have one's heart stirred into overflowing is to risk touching the slithering insects and snakes strictly and explicitly forbidden by Torah.[14] Yet this transgressive jolt becomes, in the first line of Psalm 44, transformed into "a good word"—λόγος ἀγαθός (*logos agathos*) in

Three persons with one essence...
how strange! ... for this to be in Jewish commentary.

Greek, דָּבָר טוֹב (*davar tov*) in Hebrew. *This transformation of the heart's transgressive desires into the word's goodness thus constitutes the first step in the way of psalmic poetics*: a way signaled by the repentance of Korah's sons. As they see their father and his whole violent company of rebels plunging into the flames, these three sons, literally on the edge of disaster, find their hearts are all at once overflowing with the word of deepest repentance. The awestruck nature of this moment cannot be overstated: they watch their father being consumed in the fires they themselves feel keenly—and they choose the penitential way of psalmic poetics.

The King to whom the psalmist speaks in line 1 is (says Saint Gregory of Nyssa) Christ Himself. Rashi identifies this King as a Torah scholar, while RaDak sees him as the Messiah.[15] In line 2 of the psalm, the primary quality the King possesses is *beauty*.[16] "Thou art fairer than the sons of men": hence, the King is the whole focus of the poetics of Psalm 44. By saying his works to the King, the speaker thus affirms the penitential nature of psalmic poetics: that is, in turning away from the flames of transgressive desire, the sons of Korah are turning toward the beauty of the divine King.

Thus, the first step in the way of psalmic poetics is a stirring of the heart to repentance, transforming the heart's transgressive desires into an overflowing love for the word's goodness and the beauty of the divine King.

The Tongue

"My tongue," the first line concludes, "is the pen of a swift-writing scribe" (1.1). Now, in Psalms, *tongue* signifies deeply felt noetic comprehension; as such, the psalmic tongue is the king of personhood. A midrash illuminates the importance of the psalmic tongue by quoting a parable of the Persian king:

Thoughts:
לָשׁוֹן sounds similar to לִשׁוֹן
(tongue) (first)

《 לְשׁוֹן לְמִרְמָה 》 of Psalm 120 is therefore the king, chief, first liar. It is the fallen nature of the self

I said: I will take heed to my ways, that I sin not with my tongue (Ps. 39:2). It happened once that a king of Persia was about to die. As he grew exceeding weak, his physicians said: "There can be no remedy for thee until they bring thee the milk of a lioness, which thou must drink until thou art healed." So the king sent his servants, who took much money with them, to Solomon, son of David. Thereupon Solomon sent and summoned Benaiah, the son of Jehoiada, whom he asked: "How can we get the milk of a lioness?" Benaiah replied: "Give me ten she-goats." Then Benaiah and the king's servants went to a lions' den, in which a lioness was giving suck to her whelps. The first day he stood afar, and threw one goat to her, which she devoured. The second day Benaiah drew a little nearer and threw another goat. And thus he continued day by day. At the end of ten days he was close to the lioness, so that as he played with her, he touched her dugs and took some of *... new word ..* her milk and went on his way. Then the king's servants went back to Solomon; he dismissed them in peace and they went on their way.

While they were midway in their journey, the physician [who was with the king's servants], had a dream in which he saw the parts of his body arguing with one another.

The feet were saying: "Among all the parts, there are none like us. Had we not walked, he would not have been able to fetch any of the milk."

The hands replied, saying: "There are none like us. Had we not touched the lioness, he would not now be carrying any of the milk."

The eyes said: "We are of greater worth than any of you. Had we not shown him the way, nothing at all would have been accomplished."

The heart spoke, saying: "I am of greater worth than any of you. Had I not given counsel, you would not have succeeded at all in the errand."

But the tongue spoke up and said: "I am better than you. Had it not been for speech, what would you have done?"

Then all the parts replied, saying to the tongue: "Art thou not afraid to compare thyself to us, thou that art lodged in a place of obscurity and darkness—thou indeed in whom there is not a single bone such as there is in all the other parts?"

But the tongue declared: "This very day, you are going to acknowledge that I rule you."

As the physician woke up from his sleep, he kept the dream in his heart, and went on his way. He came to the king and said: "Here is the milk of a bitch which we went to get for thee. Drink it."

Immediately the king became angry with the physician and ordered that he be hanged. As he went out to be hanged, all the parts began to tremble. The tongue said to them: "Did I not tell you this day, that there is nothing to you? If I save you, will you admit that there is nothing to you?"

They said: "Yes."

Then the tongue said to those who were about to hang the physician: "Bring me back to the king." They brought the physician back to the king, and he asked the king: "Why didst thou order to have me hanged?"

The king replied: "Because thou broughtest the milk of a bitch to me."

He asked the king: "What does that matter to thee? It

will cure thee. Besides, a lioness can be called a bitch."

The king then took some of the milk, and drank, and was healed. And so, since it was proved that the milk was the milk of a lioness, the physician was dismissed in peace.

Thereupon all the parts said to the tongue: "Now do we confess to thee that thou rulest all the parts." Of this it is written *Death and life are in the power of the tongue* (Prov. 18:21). And so David declared: *I said: "I will take heed to my ways, that I sin not with my tongue."*[17]

The Hebrew rhyme in this parable—לְבִיָּא (*leviyya*, lioness) and כְּלַבְיָּא (*kilbiyya*, female dog)—playfully makes the important point: *if the heart is the very center of personhood, then the tongue is the articulation of that center.* The tongue is thus the noetic center of the center, dwelling, says Saint Diadochos, as "the grace of God . . . dwells in the very depths of the soul"[18]—provided, of course, that the tongue is seeking only the beauty of the King.

The Penitential Action of Memory

Saint Diadochos continues: "For it is written: 'The King's daughter is all glorious within,' and [this glory] is not perceptible to the demons. Thus, when we fervently remember God, we feel within us from the depths of our heart."[19]

In this way, Saint Diadochos focuses on the meditative, or contemplative, aspect of the way of psalmic poetics. And the key to this meditation is *memory of God*. Inwardness in psalms is thus the action of memory wherein God incarnates in the human mind as the human mind becomes deified: an action that has both esthetic and penitential meanings at the same moment. The action is esthetic in the sense that grace (Gk. χάρις, *charis*; Heb. חֵן, *ḥen*) becomes instantly seen as having been poured out upon the very lips of the

King of beauty. It is a penitential action of memory in the sense that the King's beauty is chosen over the father's destructive transgression. And the primary result of such action is disclosed in the final line: "all peoples shall give praise to thee unto ages of ages, forever" (Ps. 44:17). And the end of psalmic poetics is praise that never ceases but always—for all the ages and for the time beyond—remains alive and perfective, praise wherein the praisegiver becomes one with the divine Person being praised. *The way of psalmic poetics is the way wherein the union of divine and human is consummated.*

The Palaces of Eden

The chiastic heart of Psalm 44 is line 9 (taken along with the final half of line 8):

8   . . . and from the ivory palaces they have gladdened thee,

9   These daughters of kings in thine honor. At thy right hand stood the queen dressed in gold-woven raiment richly embroidered.

The ivory palaces are read in rabbinic commentary as the very palaces of Eden: hence, even the Queen's garments gladden the King. The LXX Greek verb has a lovely etymological aroma in itself: it is formed of the prefix εὐ- (*eu-*, meaning "well") and the noun φρήν (*phrēn*, meaning "mind"); hence, to gladden means to make the mind completely—indeed, paradisiacally—well. The daughters of earthly kings provide the divine King with His bride, the Queen, who is then dressed in "gold-woven raiment richly embroidered" (44:9)—a fact echoed in line 13: "Her clothing is woven with gold."

These garments of the Queen signify that beauty the Queen achieves in the light of the King's overwhelming love for her; and thus the Queen becomes the icon of the Orthodox Church, the entire *ecclesia*, as the Bride of Christ. And the beauty bestowed by the King upon His Bride therefore becomes the beauty He most greatly desires: "The King shall greatly desire thy beauty, for he is himself thy Lord" (44:11). That is, as the King makes beautiful His Bride by His great love for her, His love for her is increased by her beauty. Here is the union between the bestower and the bestowed through the gift that is given.

In line 10, the psalmist directly addresses the Queen: "Listen, O daughter, behold and incline thine ear: forget thine own people and thy father's house." The three imperative verbs in this line of the LXX Greek define a crucial sequence: *hearing* (ἄκουσον, *akouson*) the "good word" becomes a vivid *seeing* (ἰδέ, *ide*) of it, which in turn, becomes the *inclining* (κλῖνον, *klinon*) of the whole person toward the word, a *leaning-into* Christ. This sequence thus perfectly embodies every esthetic experience: for it expresses the way wherein the beholder of Psalms becomes himself psalmic: first by simply hearing, next by visualizing, and finally by leaning all the way into the Psalms. εδω: perspective hold internally, in

And what the Queen is told fulfills the experience of Korah's sons: she is to forget her own people and her father's whole house. In this way, the psalm recalls the moment in Deuteronomy when the pious Levites refused to join the rest of all Israel in idolizing the golden calf. The Deuteronomic text reads: "Who said of his father and his mother: 'I have never seen them,' neither did he acknowledge his brothers nor know his own children" (33:9). At the root of Korah's rebellion is idolatry, and *the root of all idolatry is precisely the substituting of human relationships for the relation to God.* If the psalm's salvific conclusion resides in remembering God's holy name, then the way to that salvation lies in forgetting all relational idolatry.

The chiastic match to line 10—"Listen, O daughter, behold and

incline thine ear: forget thine own people and thy father's house"—
is the first half of line 8: "Myrrh and aloes and cassia exhale from
thy garments" (44:8). These three herbs are identified, in rabbinic
commentary, as native to the unfallen paradisiacal garden, and they
all possess intensely fragrant odors that entirely fill any space. The
Talmud significantly associates *myrrh* with the words spoken by
God, for God's words "spiritually purify and refresh the soul, just as
fragrant spices revive the body."[20] The Hebrew word for "aloe" (*aha-
los*) comes into Hebrew by way of the word אֹהָלִים(*'ohalim*), meaning
"tents," because, say the rabbis, "it spreads in the tent" when used as
incense in the Holy Service;[21] and, again, we clearly hear an echo to
the censers carried by Korah's priestly rebels. Besides being an
exceptionally aromatic herb, *cassia* is also the name of one of Job's
three daughters, who are, along with their seven brothers, part of
Job's resurrectional life on earth.[22] In giving off these three pun-
gently beautiful odors, the King's garments possess the beauty of
the unfallen Edenic garden, a beauty lost to Job and then restored
fully to him.

Tsedeq: The Sword of Ascetic Clarification and Scepter of Uprightness

Line 11 then chiastically matches line 7:

7   Thou hast loved righteousness and hated iniquity;
     therefore God, thy God, has anointed thee with the oil
     of gladness more than thy companions.

11   For the king shall greatly desire thy beauty, for he is
     himself thy Lord.

In line 7 we encounter the great psalmic word "righteousness"—in
LXX Greek, δικαιοσύνη (*dikaiosynē*); in Hebrew, צֶדֶק (*tsedeq*). The

[handwritten marginal note: "Myrrh" resembles "to say" (Hebrew) and "Word" (Aramaic), hence the association]

Hebrew word combines three crucial consonants. According to d'Olivet, the first letter, צ (*tsade*), means "scission," "solution," "goad"; and when used initially, *tsade* signifies movement toward the word's concluding consonant. The middle consonant, ד (*daleth*), indicates abundance that occurs in and through division, while the final one, ק (*qof*), indicates astringency and sharpness. Taken together, the three consonants of צֶדֶק (*tsedeq*) can be said to be: the urgent movement wherein earthly actuality becomes sharply divided, the swift movement of the sword of ascetic clarification: this is psalmic—indeed, Scriptural—righteousness. The Greek word *dikaiosynē* also sustains the notion of straightness of going; but the Hebrew is by far the more vivid. Now, the primary effect achieved by the sword of ascetic clarification is *beauty*—specifically, "the oil of gladness" is poured upon the Son by the Father. This oil in Hebrew is שֶׁמֶן (*shemen*), a liquid that is clear, rich, thick, soft, highly aromatic, and holy.[23] In LXX Greek, the word chosen was ἔλαιον (*elaion*), a profound and far-reaching choice, for *elaion* not only carries in Greek the same rich associations as does the Hebrew word, but *elaion* closely rhymes in Greek with ἔλεον (*eleon*, mercy). Thus, the Greek "oil of gladness" in line 7 perfectly prepares for the pungent herbs of line 8, while the gladness prepares for line 8's ivory Edenic palaces.

The Union of Divine and Human

The eleventh line matches the seventh by declaring the King's desire for the Queen—that is, Christ's desire for the Church—to be an overflowing with a good word. That is, the LXX Greek verb used in the line, ἐπιθυμέω (*epithymeō*, to long for, desire), is one that, like the Hebrew verb it translates, can go in one of two sharply opposed directions: either toward carnal hungering or toward blessed desiring (Lampe divides the Patristic usages about equally). Just as the Hebrew verb in line 1—רָחַשׁ (*rahash*), "is stirred"—implicitly suggests a transgressive jolt but then veers sharply away from it, so, too, the Greek verb in line 11 raises but then turns away from a comparably transgressive meaning. The Hebrew verb here employed is אוה (*'awah*),[24] a verb, says d'Olivet, whose sense is appetite, passion, desire, and where the first two consonants (א, *'aleph*, and ו, *waw*) join pure potentiality to actualized being.[25] In this sense, the verb perfectly expresses the union of divine and human as fully consummated: for the King desires the *beauty* of the Queen, a beauty He Himself has bestowed upon her as her "gold-woven raiment richly embroidered" (l. 9): and the beauty is therefore wholly relational in its very nature, belonging at once to both the King and the Queen, a beauty simultaneously past, present, and future.

The way of psalmic poetics thus emerges further. Not only is this way penitential but it is also relational—better: the way is relational *because* it is penitential. That is, the way of psalmic beauty is the way of consummated union, the marriage of the heavenly King with the earthly Queen, Christ with the Church, a relationality that is therefore ontological in its nature: the very being of both Bridegroom and Bride is rooted in this union. The way of psalmic poetics lies in entering into this union.

The sixth and twelfth lines match chiastically:

6   Thy throne, O God, is for ever and ever, thy royal
    scepter is a scepter of uprightness . . .

12 And the daughters of Tyre shall worship him with
    gifts, the rich among the people shall entreat thy
    countenance.

The "scepter of uprightness" (Gk. εὐθύτης, *euthytēs*) in line 6 echoes the moment in 3 Kings 3:4 (1 Chronicles) when the Lord comes to Solomon in a dream, saying to him: "Ask me something for yourself," and Solomon beautifully responds:

> You have dealt very mercifully with Your servant my father David, for he walked with You in truth and in righteousness and in uprightness [*euthytēs*] of heart, and You have given him this great mercy, that he see his son upon his throne. And, O my God, I am a little child and I do not know when to go out or when to come in, but I am in the midst of this great people You have given me: give me now the heart to hear and to discern Your people justly, to understand good and evil: for who else is there to judge Your great people?[26]

Solomon's dream of his father David's *uprightness* of heart—along with David's righteousness (Heb. *tsedeq*) and truth (Gk. ἀλήθεια, *alētheia*)—perfectly shapes the meaning of line 6's "scepter of uprightness": it is the heart's capacity to discern truly the persons whom God has given you to love and to rule: and in this discernment lies the very beauty of psalmic truth and psalmic righteousness. Note, too, the genuinely *penitential* nature of Solomon's dream: "I am a little child"—a repentance that, once again, illumines the sons of Korah, as icons of penitential beauty. For in thus honoring his father, David, Solomon is honoring the uprightness of heart that underlies all psalmic beauty as the source for the λόγος ἀγαθός (*logos agathos*, good word) in line 1. The forgetting of the "father's house" in line 10 is wholly redeemed—indeed, is resurrected in and as this Solomonic remembering of the Davidic father: and the sons of Korah behold the restored and divine "scepter of uprightness" in the earthly King's hand.

The Noetic Ray Grows and Abides

We are now in a position to understand two brief but crucial texts from *The Ascetical Homilies* of Saint Isaac the Syrian. The first text is from Homily One: "Those who in their way of life are led by divine grace to be enlightened are always aware of something like a noetic ray running between the written lines [of Holy Scripture]."[27] Note well: this noetic ray runs not *in* but *between* the lines: it is pure background and genuine depth. We can "read" such rays *out*; we can banish depth; we can reduce the salvific potency to an empty zero. For example, we can attend Divine Liturgy or perform our private prayer—and simply not *be* there, absent-spirited, psychically flat, numb in mind and feeling—and scarcely even begin to notice our paralyzed state. Saint Isaac says that the start of such noetic darkening "(once a sign of it is visible in the soul) is to be seen, first of all, in slothfulness with regard to the [church] services and [[private]] prayer."[28] He continues, saying that if, on the other hand, we do remain awake in the church services and our rule of prayer, then we "cannot be led in the way of error."[29] For the noetic ray running between the lines of the church services and our psalmic prayer helps to realign our minds and psyches (better: our *nous*) to fit our entire inwardness *into* the words in their depth and power, for these words, says Isaac, give "the heart a most sweet taste through intuitions that awe the soul."[30]

In this way, then, the heart in line 1 of Psalm 44 overflows with a good word as *response* (in Saint Isaac's terms) to the noetic ray running within that good word: a response so profound that it causes that word to take up residence *within* the psalmist's own heart, to root itself there and to grow and abide in the heart, as the word being spoken by the psalmist. The relation between the good word and the psalmist thus beautifully parallels the union between the divine King and the earthly Queen, between Christ and the Church.

The second text from Abba Isaac is from the long and magnificent Homily 37: "[I]f a man passes his time in the study of divine Scriptures, seeking out their meanings, [then] the understanding of the divine Scriptures . . . grows and abides in him. . . . [And] being engrossed in these marvels and continually struck with wonder, [he] is always drunken and he lives as it were in the life after resurrection."[31] Then Abba Isaac adds: "Blessed is the man whose meditation this is both day and night! Blessed is the man who dwells upon these things and their like all the days of his life! . . . [For] there will be no place in his mind for a foreign memory that could remove him from his continuous memory of God."[32]

The study of Scripture thus exhibits three crucial properties. First, it "grows and abides," entering into the student's whole being and nourishing it literally as well as spiritually with life-giving sustenance that becomes the "continuous memory of God"—that is: he becomes what Psalm 1:3 calls the tree whose fruit never ceases. Second, the study of Scripture causes that unceasing inebriation—"[he] is always drunken"—wherein every sacred word—indeed, every syllable and each sacred letter—vividly gives life to every other word at the very moment it is receiving life from all other words. Noetic inebriation is thus the state of unending significance, that state in which meaning ecstatically never ceases its increasing. Third, the study of Scripture therefore yields an entire way of life, a way that we are now calling the way of psalmic poetics.

Noetic Swiftness

These two texts from Saint Isaac help shed considerable light on the adjective describing the scribe in line 1: "swift-writing" (ὀξυγράφος, *oxygraphos*). This adjective is unique in LXX Greek—indeed, in all Greek, ancient and modern—apparently here coined by the psalmist to express a unique psalmic idea: the idea of noetic *swift-ness* in psalmic poetics. The Hebrew word the Greek translates is מָהִיר (*mahir*), a word with only three other occurrences in Hebrew Scripture, all three usages expressing strong connection to the swiftness of *tsedeq*, "righteousness."[33] The notion common to all four usages is, says d'Olivet, "that which changes, varies, passes, flows off rapidly."[34] In other words, *mahir*—that is, noetic swiftness—overflows with a good word, one shaped by *tsedeq*, the sword of swiftly moving ascetic clarification.

The Action of Psalmic Meditation

The fifth and the thirteenth lines together deepen our understanding as we broaden the chiastic circle of comprehension:

5   Thine arrows are sharp, O mighty one, in the heart of
     the king's enemies; the peoples shall fall under thee.
13 The king's daughter is all glorious within, her clothing
     is woven with gold.

The sharp arrows from the bow of line 4 focus the meaning of ascetic clarification in line 5: the total defeat of those vast enemies of psalmic beauty who seek to unmake every clarifying action. And the primary meaning of that clarifying action is revealed by the Queen in line 13: the action of psalmic meditation. That is, as Gregory of Nyssa notes, the Queen's inward glory is like the lion growling over its prey, consuming "every creeping form of desire" and "with the teeth of self-control" devouring "the passions" and thereby achieving that "participation in God" wherein there is an unending fullness that (in Gregory's words) "transforms the one who has embraced it [in]to itself, and imparts to this person a portion of its own power."[35] The psalmic end of all ascetic clarification is precisely this victory of deification. Here is where the way of beauty in psalmic poetry always leads.

The fourth and the fourteenth lines then contribute substantially to our understanding:

> 4   And string thy bow, prosper and reign because of
>   truth, gentleness and righteousness, and wondrously
>   shall thy right hand guide thee. . . .
> 14 The virgins who follow after her shall be brought to the
>   king, those near her shall be brought to thee.

The Queen's inward clarification is joined to the King's ascetic arrows of "truth, gentleness and righteousness" (l. 4): three nouns that contribute greatly to our growing comprehension of psalmic beauty. The Hebrew for "truth" (אֱמֶת, *'emeth*) unites, says d'Olivet, potentiality to exterior activity, producing a sign whose root (*'em-*) signifies the formative faculty, maternity: "mother, origin, source . . . matrix" are some of its key meanings; while its final consonant (*-th*) conveys "the idea of perfection."[36] In Hebrew, then, *truth* signifies the mothering of every perfection. The LXX Greek word for Hebrew *'emeth*—*alētheia*—adds a powerful dimension to the Hebrew: *a-lethe*, "a-forgetting," that is, the reality of active remembering. Thus, combining Greek and Hebrew, psalmic truth can be said to signify the active memory of the perfect and perfective motherhood. And, when joined to "gentleness" (Gk. πραΰτης, *praütēs*, Heb. עֲנָוָה, *'anwah*;[37] meaning, in both languages, the voluntary affliction of true humility), as well as to "righteousness," truth—*alētheia* and *'emeth*—gains extraordinary significance: truth is, we may say, the clarifying and generative action of perfective ascetic remembering.

* often, 'meekness'

Leaning into Christ

In the fourteenth line, we see this definition of psalmic truth *enacted* as obedience. That is, the earthly virgins follow after the Queen in her "consummated union" with the King—into, that is, the Queen's *leaning-into* Christ. And in so obeying her, the virgins become themselves beautiful and are, as a result, brought to Christ Himself, blessed in and by the union of Christ and His Bride, the Church. And in the fifteenth line—"They shall be brought with gladness and rejoicing, they shall enter into the king's palace"—the virgins enter into the immense splendor of the King's heavenly palace on earth: in Greek, ναός (*naos*), meaning "temple, holy place (as distinct from the holy of holies)," and in Hebrew, הֵיכָל (*hekhal*), "palace of God."[38] The virgins' entry into the palace thus signifies their return to the Edenic palaces of the psalm's chiastic heart, the "ivory palaces" from which these daughters of kings first proceeded and into which their virginity—that is, their swords of ascetic clarification and divine memory—now carries them in the beauty of "gladness":—the beauty of εὐφροσύνη (*euphrosynē*), of "well-mindedness," a beauty (says Saint Dionysius the Areopagite) enjoyed by the very angels.[39] In fact, the luminous sentence in Saint Dionysius sheds wonderful light on this way of psalmic beauty: "They undergo a truly divine sense of well-being, the good and generous delight [*euphrosynē*] at the providence and salvation of those who are returned to God."[40]

The virgins' beauty is, in the Dionysian term, *good* in the unique sense of ἀγαθοειδής (*agathoeidēs*), a word used of the highest angelic choir, signifying "having the form of goodness"—the εἶδος (*eidos*, form or idea in Platonic philosophy) of the highest good.[41] *Agathoeidēs* is a term from Neo-Platonism that had become, in Saint Dionysius as interpreted by Saint Maximos, fully and beautifully Orthodox. The well-mindedness of the virgins thus becomes, in Psalm 44, joined to that essential goodness who is Christ Himself.

In this way, then, the *euphrosynē* of the virgins is joined to the *euthytēs* of the King's scepter; for just as their *euphrosynē* is one with their *sōphrosynē* (σωφροσύνη, i.e., their chastity), so the King's scepter—held by Solomon—is one with David's mercy and righteousness. The chiastic circling and recircling with which we enter into and read the psalm thus follows the festal joy of the virgins who enter into the King's palace.

A Most Sweet Taste

In line 16, the joy takes an extraordinary turn: "In place of thy fathers are sons born to thee, whom thou shalt make princes over all the earth." What is extraordinary is what cannot be translated but only paraphrased clumsily: "In place of thy [singular, the Queen herself] fathers [plural—thus gathering in all the fathers of all the virgins] sons are born to thee [again, singular; the Queen] whom thou [singular, the Queen] shalt make princes over all the earth." That is, the Queen who is the Church shall become the mother of princely sons who shall, in wisdom of heart, rule over the earth.

When, in his dream, Solomon asks God to give him "the heart to hear and discern . . . justly," God beautifully responds: "Because you have not asked anything for yourself—not wealth, not victory over your enemies—but only for the understanding to hear justly, behold, I have given you a comprehensive and wise heart—and there has not been, nor ever again will be, anyone like you."[42] Here is the sword of ascetic clarification perfectly manifest. "And," God continues to Solomon, "I have also given you what you have not asked for, wealth and glory, such that there has not ever been a man like you among all the kings" (3 Kings 3:12). In his voluntary self-abnegation—"I am a little child and I do not know when to go out or when to come in" (3 Kings 3:6)—Solomon achieves true ascetic kingship: the comprehensive heart of wisdom.

Here, then, is the extraordinary turn taken by line 44:16: the ascetic union between the many virgins and the one Queen who, in her beautiful uniqueness, fosters forth on earth the way of the heart's wisdom. The "splendor and beauty" of the King's sword in line 3—the clarifying sword of ascetic beauty and active memory—thus becomes for us what Saint Isaac calls "a noetic ray running between the lines" of Psalm 44, a ray (as Isaac says) that gives our heart "a most sweet taste" of the very air of the resurrection itself, the "continuous memory of God." We may say, then, that the sons of Korah—as they stand on the elevated niche and gaze down at their father plunging into the flames of Gehenna—these sons behold a noetic ray. The *Yalkut Shimoni* says: "At that moment, the spark of sincere repentance began to flicker in their hearts"[43]—and in that moment, they begin to fall deeply in love with *tsedeq*, with penitential righteousness.

"They Have Changed the King's Decree"

And, in this light, then, we may come to see something of the immense significance of the phrase in the title: "In alternating verses." In Hebrew, the word used for "alternating" is שָׁנָה (*shanah*), derived from the verb שָׁנָא (*shana*), meaning, "to change, to alter."[44] Now, the noun is variously defined in rabbinic commentary either (in the plural) as *roses*, signifying the scholars of Torah, or (in the singular) as an ancient musical instrument.[45] The Greek plural participle used by the LXX translators is ἀλλοιωθησομένων (*alloiōthēsomenōn*), from the verb ἀλλοιόω (*alloioō*), signifying "to change" in the redemptive and positive meaning of the word.[46] There is an important LXX usage of this verb in Psalm 72: "My

[handwritten margin note: ⌐ PS 72 (73):21]
[handwritten margin note: MT: אַשְׁתּוֹנָן]

mind had been ἠλλοιώθησαν [*ēlloiōthēsan*]," meaning "seared" in penitential flames, a psalmic usage echoed in Daniel when, after beholding God's miraculous deliverance of the three youths from the fiery furnace, King Nebuchadnezzar cries out: "they [the three youths] have changed [ἠλλοίωσαν, *ēlloiōsan*] the king's decree" (Dan. 3:28).[47] That is, the Babylonian king's violent words have penitentially become the "good word" of Psalm 44.

And the significance of the phrase in Psalm 44's title thus comes into sharp clarity. The instrument upon which Psalm 44 is being played is the mind's steadfast gaze down into all transgressive fires—and realizing, at that very moment, that (as Psalm 72, in line 22, continues) "I had become nothing and I did not understand": realizing, that is, that one's voluntary self-abnegation under the ascetic sword of clarification is the only way whereby one can achieve the glory of lines 23 and 24 of Psalm 72:

23 And I am continually with thee, thou hast held fast my
   right hand,
24 In thy counsel thou hast guided me, with glory thou
   hast received me.

The Way of Orthodox Ascetic Beauty

The way of psalmic poetics is entirely the way of Orthodox ascetic beauty. The first step is the transformation of the heart's trangressive desires into the word's goodness, signaled by the repentance of Korah's sons and their turning toward the beauty of the divine King. The second is the penitential action of memory wherein God incarnates in the human mind while the human mind becomes deified. And the end is praise that never ceases but always—for all the ages and for the time beyond—remains alive and perfective, praise wherein the praisegiver becomes one with the divine Person being praised. It is a way not only pentitential but relational—relational *because* it is penitential—wherein the union of divine and human is consummated. Thus even the beholder of Psalms becomes himself psalmic: first by simply hearing, next by visualizing, and finally by leaning all the way into the Psalms and entering into the union of the earthly Queen with the heavenly King.

In this way of psalmic poetics, you become (as l. 22 concludes in Ps. 72) "as a beast before thee," O God—and instantly "I am continually with thee," "the God of my heart" (Ps. 72:23, 26). And, in the glory of a beauty that is entirely bestowed upon you, you "shall enter into the King's palace" (44:15). Martin Buber perfectly says it: "as in the dark a father takes his little son by the hand, certainly in order to lead him, but primarily in order to make present to him, in the warm touch of coursing blood, the fact that he, the father, is continually with him."[48]

9

"In Their Very Midst He Judged among the Judges"

Psalm 81

What happens to us when we encounter a corrupt judiciary? And what happens to the judges when they encounter the judgment of God? Psalm 81 answers: when the judges are corrupt, "all earth's foundations will be shaken." Employing a chiastic analysis of this psalm, the author describes the antinomic condition of the corrupt judges as "sons of the Most High" who shall yet "die like any earthly prince" and fall like Lucifer and his angels when God comes to judge the earth. Were the judges to judge truly, as sons of God, they would comprehend the nature of their sonship, know who the true judge is, and use their (His) power to "rescue the poor and needy," as He does. Pointing to these adjectives as used at times in the Psalter to describe the Incarnate Christ Himself (following Gregory of Nyssa), the author shows the earthly courtrooms to be given us as arenas of our deification in which we must learn to advocate for God. He describes the particular attributes of true judicial *ischyros* (ἰσχυρός, strength), whose light must flood the darkness of our courtrooms and bathe all our earthly judgment. And he points to the two dimensions of earthly time revealed in Psalm 81: that which is seen from the divine perspective wherein every human action responds to every human need with God's mercy and truth; and that wherein such knowledge is entirely darkened and the earthly foundations disastrously shaken, creating a history that is no longer the arena of divine-human interaction. The choice between these, the psalmist shows, is entirely ours to make. —*Ed.*

C. S. Lewis once noted that the English-speaking have become so long accustomed to a judiciary that is fundamentally not something for sale—that is, we cannot buy the court judgments we most want—so long accustomed, he says, to a fundamental judicial fairness that we find it difficult, if not impossible, to enter into the circumstances of much of the Psalter. For in the Psalms we often find a deeply corrupt judiciary, one that treats its judgments as goods to be sold to the ruling powers in exchange for political and social prestige and power. What happens to us when we encounter such a judiciary? And what happens to it when it encounters the judgment of God? Psalm 81 explores these questions, and its responses are surprising and powerful.

Psalm 81

A psalm of Asaph.

1   God has stood in the mighty assembly, and in their very midst he judged among the judges.
2   How long will you judge unjustly and favor persons who are wicked?
3   Defend the poor and orphaned, be just to the oppressed and needy;

4   Rescue the poor and needy, deliver them from the
    sinner's hand.

5   Neither knowing nor comprehending, they have gone
    on in darkness; all earth's foundations will be shaken.

6   I said: You are gods, you are all sons of the Most High.

7   But you shall die as men die, you shall fall like any
    earthly prince.

8   Arise, O God, judge the earth, for thou shalt inherit
    all nations.

We can best begin to understand Psalm 81 by considering its first and final lines together. The tense of the first Greek verb in line 1—"has stood"—is the aorist of an immediate reality vividly achieved, while the tense of the second verb—"he judged"—is the Greek present, a tense used to signify that its action is fully present to the first verb's action. The result, in this opening line, is that God has already fully judged the corrupt earthly courtrooms. The eighth line, by contrast, calls upon God—with a present imperative verb—precisely to make this very judgment; and the line (and whole psalm) concludes with a future verb: "thou shalt inherit." A sharp contradiction (indeed an antinomy) plainly emerges: The divine judgment has already happened (l. 1); the divine judgment needs to happen (l. 8). How are we to understand this antinomy?

To answer this question, let us first look at the psalm's center in lines 4 and 5. Line 4—"Rescue the poor and needy, deliver them from the sinner's hand"—continues from the third line with a sharpened articulation of what the earthly judges *should*, in God, actually be doing. And what they most directly need to do is to intervene on the side of the one who is "poor and needy"—adjectives used in the Psalter to describe the Incarnate Christ Himself (cf. Heine 57). But—and now we encounter the psalm's central antinomy—the corrupt judges of earth do precisely the opposite: "Neither knowing nor comprehending, they have gone on in darkness; all earth's foundations will be shaken." Justice is, says rabbinic commentary, "one of the three pillars upon which the earth rests."[1] If justice is corrupted, the earth collapses—as Solomon says in Proverbs (4:29): "By justice a king gives stability to the land." Thus, lines 4 and 5 together form, not simply a contradiction (they should do X; they instead do Y) but, more deeply, again, an antinomy: a contradiction that must be resolved *without losing either pole*. That is, the judges of the earth must be biased in favor of God if they are to be truly impartial; yet their judgeship cannot merely be overthrown by God.

And this central contradiction of the psalm then immediately takes the form of yet another contradiction.

6   I said: You are gods, you are all sons of the Most High.
7   But you shall die as men die, you shall fall like any
     earthly prince.

To be like God, to be a son of the Most High, is to participate in immortality; to die "like any earthly prince" is to become (says Rashi) one of the celestial angels that fell from heaven (*Tehillim* 2:1039). The corrupt earthly judges thus re-enact the fall of angels into that demonic darkness wherein they see and comprehend nothing whatever, so dark is their delusional belief that they themselves possess the true power of judgment. And yet: all these corrupt judges are nevertheless "sons of the Most High" in that they, too, can indeed love and care for those whom God truly loves and attends to—"the poor and orphaned, the oppressed and needy"—for these are "sons of the Most High." And the sole means by which such instruction in redemptive mercy occurs is the full awareness of one's own certain death. Such awareness in us immediately and completely ends our delusion that we ourselves are in the driver's seat; and once that delusion ceases, we can begin to see *who* is truly in command. The shock of line 7 coming, in a chiastic reading, instantly after line 8 thus helps to focus the psalm's great meaning: to the extent we rescue the poor and needy we can fully know our sonship in God at the same moment we can truly comprehend that it is God—and not we ourselves—who is genuinely the judge. To know and comprehend this is to *choose* God.

And this decisive moment of awareness and choice—occurring, as it were, in the space between lines 6 and 7—prepares for the triumph of the psalm's final line: "Arise, O God, judge the earth, for thou shalt inherit all nations." The psalmist now, in the fullness of this moment, comprehends that God is Himself the Judge who is described in Psalm 7 as "just, gentle, and patient" (7:11). The middle ✝ adjective of these three is, in Greek, ἰσχυρός (*ischyros*), a word used to describe the divine attribute of *might* or *strength* in the sense of an *infinite* delicacy and an *unceasing* lightness of touch. For this quality of God's judicial *ischyros* reveals the very range and depth of the divine judgments themselves, a range and depth that can be said to possess five aspects—for, in their quality of *ischyros*, His judgments are:

1. *exact*: the precision of the divine judgments is most often indicated in Scripture by the metaphor of an extremely sharp knife, where the primary meaning that the metaphor conveys is razor-edge sharpness;

2. *powerful*: the power of God's judgments at once intensifies their sharpness and is intensified by it; that is, the sharpness grows continually sharper by means of God's vast power at the same moment the power is increased by the intensification of the sharpness;

3. *delicately beautiful*: the delicate beauty of God's judicial *ischyros* is often described in Scripture as the infinite magnificence of the creation itself; see, for example, the great Psalm 103, which opens with the phrase *emegalynthēs*

✝ MT has one word: צֶדֶק (שׁוֹפֵט) , comparble form to (סוֹדוֹ) עַרְתָּה in Psalm 44(45)

sphodra (ἐμεγαλύνθης σφόδρα): "How [*very exceedingly*] *magnificently* dost thou exist"—a magnificence of an endlessly patterned depth of aliveness;

4. *infinitely enduring*: the *ischyros* of God's judgments gives them their infinite capacity to endure throughout all the ages of both heavenly and earthly existence, a capacity that psalms everywhere praise as touching the very essence of God Himself; and

5. *unceasingly light-bearing*: that is, the *ischyros* of His judgments causes them to be forever light in themselves and the cause of light in the beholder, and in this sense, the "light-bearing-ness" is perfective: both perfection in itself and the cause of perfection in others.

These five aspects of God's judicial *ischyros*—that His judgments are *exact, powerful, delicately beautiful, infinitely enduring*, and *unceasingly light-bearing*—thus stand in direct contrast to the judgments of the corrupt earthly courtrooms, and they are thereby equally revelatory of those courts: clumsily *brutal*; yet inherently *weak*; deeply *ugly* to both the heart and the eye; very quickly *disintegrating*; and instantaneously *dark*.

In this sense, then, the trisagion prayer's initial triplet—Holy God, Holy Mighty, Holy Immortal—helps shed light on the final line of Psalm 81.[2] God's mightiness (His *ischyros*) participates in His divinity (θέος, *theos*) and His immortality (ἀθάνατος, *athanatos*) in the sense that all its five qualities—its exactness, its power, its beauty, its endurance, its "light-bearing-ness"—are manifest in *and as* His judgments of and upon all the earthly nations. Hence, God will inherit from us, His sons and daughters, the earthly courtrooms He has freely given us as the arenas of our deification: the places, that is, wherein we can become like Him by becoming the advocates for the poor and the needy: advocates, that is, for God Himself.

We may say, then, that the golden beauty of God's judgments is the primary quality we are called by Him to bathe all our earthly judgment in, allowing its magnificent light to flood into the darkness of our courtrooms. This is the golden beauty the psalmist chooses in Psalm 81.

Now we see the meaning of the psalm's central antinomy: God's divine judgment has already happened (1. 1); the divine judgment needs to happen (1. 5). In the course of the poem, the psalmist (and we with him) moves from the divine judgment having happened (1. 1) to the corrupt earthly judges persisting in their darkness, to (in 1. 3) the true earthly judge becoming advocate for God, to (in 11. 4 and 5) the full reality of the true earthly courtroom and the full reality of the corrupt one, to the shocking awareness of human deification (1. 6) and human death (1. 7), an awareness that triggers in the psalmist the power to *choose actively* to participate in the divine judgeship. In other words, the poem's whipsaw motion reveals the dynamic wherein the truest and deepest choice can occur: the choice to love the golden beauty of divine creation so fully that we, still in this life, give over our very nations—our entire actual lives—into this beauty. And God thereby *legally inherits* from us what He has already given us. The judgment has already occurred; we must, one by one, in the actuality of our courts, *choose* this judgment, rescuing the poor, the oppressed, the orphaned, and the needy: all of whom, says the psalmist, are God Himself.

In this sense, then, we can see that Psalm 81 expresses two dimensions of earthly time. The first is earthly time as seen from the divine perspective, time wherein every human action responds to every human need with God's mercy and truth: defending the poor, rescuing the needy and oppressed. In this dimension of time, the earthly courtroom becomes the place of illumined earthly deification: "You are gods" (1. 6). The second dimension is one wherein such knowledge is entirely darkened and the earthly foundations disastrously shaken, with the result that a poisonous delusion is thereby produced: the delusion of self-glorification. This delusion takes the form of hungering (in Martin Buber's important insight) "to conduct the history of the human race as a continuation of the history of nature."[3] That is, once we begin to glorify ourselves, and no longer glorify God, we enter into a history in which God no longer acts, and history therefore becomes merely an extension of empirical tangentialities and no longer the arena wherein the divine and the human fruitfully interact. These two dimensions of time thus together create the condition of actual human choice: in order to avoid becoming trapped in darkness, we must recognize—fully know and comprehend—that judgeship is either divinely grounded or it is entirely dark. And the choice, says the psalmist, is entirely ours to make.

Martin Buber paraphrases the closing lines of Psalm 81 in this way:

> In my vision . . . I have seen how Thou [O Lord] dost bring to destruction the rule over history of Thy rebellious governors [the corrupt judges]. So be it, Lord. Since those who were entrusted with the office of judge succumbed to injustice, do Thou abolish [their] intermediary rule, renounce the useless work of underlings and Thyself judge the world immediately in Thy justice. Thine are the nations, lead them as thine own! Close the history of man which is a prey to delusion and wickedness, open his true history![4]

Buber has it entirely aright. In all of the psalms, God is "working salvation in the midst of the earth" (Ps. 73:12)—not apart from our dark condition but in the very midst of it: exact, powerful, beautiful, enduring, and illumined salvation. If we choose it.

10

The Chiastic Heart
of the Psalter

Psalm 77

Psalm 77 is shown here to be the whole Psalter's center. The author points out that it contains nine eight-line "stanzas" and he arranges these into two interior "psalms," one composed of the first, fifth, and ninth stanzas, the other comprising the ones between them. The first depicts what the author calls "the deep structure of history as divine Presence"; the other reveals, without relief, the historic human twisting away from God that ends in total human destruction. In the full resurrective and Christic psalm, however, the fathers' twistedness is unmade (here as in the entire Psalter) in the free and joyful choosing of Davidic "integrity of heart" in the face of this twisting—choosing, that is, the heart of Christ Himself. The chapter and the Psalter begin with blessedness. This crucial word St. Gregory of Nyssa sees as "the aim of the entire Psalter," increasingly gathering depth and intensity through its sixty-two occurrences, as the antinomies grow sharper and the mind of David becomes increasingly illumined. The author shows Psalm 77 (and specifically its center in lines 34–38) to be the chiastic center of this entire psalmic journey. The first line of the psalm is "Give heed, O my people, to my law"; that is, to the words of creation, the words that establish in us, in and as our heart, "the wondrous works He has done," in order that we may remember His works in our hearts in the keeping of His commandments. The model given here: to listen to what God is saying is (1) to keep in one's heart the things hidden from the foundation of the world; (2) to "walk in his law" (i.e., one's whole way of going is always into God); (3) to remember and to speak to one's children. Hence, Psalm 77 is subtitled "An Instruction of Asaph." —*Ed*.

S aint Gregory of Nyssa sees the "aim of the entire Psalter in the first word of the Book of Psalms":[1] "*Blessed* is the man who walks not in the counsel of the ungodly." The Greek word used by the Septuagint to translate the Hebrew is *makarios* (μακάριος). As the Psalter proceeds, each of the successive sixty-two occurrences of blessedness gathers in all the prior experiences, deepening and intensifying the entire significance of blessedness. For the whole Psalter unfolds in the very same fashion every psalm does. And as it does, the antinomies grow always sharper and more dire as the mind of David continues to grow correspondingly more illumined in blessedness.[2]

This means, plainly, that the Psalter as a whole possesses a chiastic center: it is Psalm 77, lines 34–38, five lines, preceded by the crucial line 33, concluding the first half of the psalm: "And so all their days ended in emptiness, all their years in fear":

34 When he slew them they sought him and repented and rose up early in their prayers to God.

35 They remembered that God is their helper, the Most High God their redeemer.

36 So they loved him with their mouths but were lying to him with their tongues,

37 For their hearts were not straight with him, they were
   unfaithful to his covenant.

38 But he is compassionate and will be gracious to their
   sins and will not destroy them, again and again
   forgoing his wrath, never kindling all his anger.

Prayer of psalms—steady, unfailingly regular psalmic prayer
morning and night—is steadily and always attacked: the demons
seek above all to "thin" the words of psalms into passing and fleeting "meanings" as rote familiarities; and the attack always has this
result: depression as ἀκηδία (*akēdia*), "a-heartedness"; that is, as
fleeting semi-states of decaying "meanings." At the center of the
Psalter is this: "And so all their days ended in emptiness, all their
years in fear." Emptiness (ματαιότης, *mataiotēs*) and fear (σπουδη,
spoudē): here is the terrible core of depression that unmakes all
God's "wondrous works" (θαυμάσια, *thaumasia*; 77:32) on earth. For
mataiotēs is the experience wherein psalmic prayer becomes fleeting
words, rapidly meaningless words.

Thus fear breaks every connection to prayer in the psalmist—
and therefore breaks connection to every experience of being alive.
The attack is always ordinary; the warfare is always invisible; but the
defeats are always bitterly dramatic: the psalmic sweetness becomes
invisible and flat.

Here is the whole of the psalm:

Psalm 77

An instruction of Asaph.

1 Give heed, O my people, to my law, incline your ears
   to the words of my mouth.

2 I shall open my mouth in parables, I shall utter things

hidden since the foundation of the world,

3   Things we have heard and known, things that our fathers taught us.

4   They hid nothing from their children in the next generation, proclaiming the praises of the Lord and his mighty deeds and the wondrous works he has done.

5   He raised up a testimony in Jacob, he appointed the law in Israel, and he commanded our fathers to declare all the law to their sons,

6   So that the next generation would know, those sons yet to be born, and they in turn would arise to proclaim to their sons,

7   That they might set their hope in God and never forget the works of God and always seek his commandments,

8   That they not become like their fathers, a generation, twisted and rebellious, that did not keep its heart straight, whose spirit was not steadfast with God.

9   The armed sons of Ephraim carrying bows turned back in the day of battle.

10   They did not guard God's covenant, they failed to walk in his law,

11   And they forgot his gracious works and his wonders that he had shown them,

12   The wonders he had accomplished in the sight of their fathers, in Egypt in the plain of Tanis.

13   He split asunder the sea and led them all through, the waters standing straight up as if held in wineskins.

14   In a cloud, he guided them by day, all night in the radiance of fire.

15   He split the rock in the wilderness, having them drink from great depth

16 And making streams run from the rocks, making streams flow down in rivers.

17 Yet they kept sinning against him, in the desert they kept on rebelling against the Most High.

18 In their hearts they kept testing God, demanding he feed all their hungers.

19 And they spoke against God, saying: Why cannot God prepare a table in the wilderness?

20 Since he could smite the rock and make waters pour down in torrents, can he not also give bread or set a table for his people?

21 Hearing this, the Lord was enraged, and fire was kindled in Jacob, anger arose against Israel,

22 Because they did not believe in God nor put their hope in his salvation.

23 Yet he had commanded the clouds above and opened the doors of heaven,

24 Raining down on them manna to eat, giving them the heavenly food:

25 Men ate the very bread of angels, he sent them food to the full.

26 He brought the south wind down from the heavens and led in by his power a wind from the southwest.

27 He rained flesh down on them like dust, winged birds like sands of the sea,

28 Letting them fall amid their camps, falling all around their tents.

29 So they ate and were well filled, for he gave them their own desire.

30 They were not deprived of their desire, but even while the food was in their mouths

31 God's wrath rose up against them and cut down the stoutest of them, shackling the chosen of Israel.

32 In all these ways they kept sinning, not believing in his wondrous works,

33 And so all their days ended in emptiness, all their years in fear.

34 When he slew them they sought him and repented and rose up early in their prayers to God.

35 They remembered that God is their helper, the Most High God their redeemer.

36 So they loved him with their mouths but were lying to him with their tongues,

37 For their hearts were not straight with him, they were unfaithful to his covenant.

38 But he is compassionate and will be gracious to their sins and will not destroy them, again and again forgoing his wrath, never kindling all his anger.

39 For he remembered they are flesh, a breath that passes and never returns.

40 How many times, how many times did they provoke him in the wilderness, did they grieve him in the desert?

41 They turned away and tempted God, they provoked the Holy One of Israel.

42 They did not remember his hand in that day he freed them from the hand of the oppressor,

43 How he wrought his signs in Egypt, his wonders in the plain of Tanis,

44 And turned their rivers and rainfall into blood they could not drink.

45 He sent them swarms of devouring flies and frogs that destroyed them.

46 He gave their crops over to blight, their labor to the locust.

47 He destroyed their vines with hail, their mulberry trees with frost.

48 He also gave their cattle to the hail, all their substance up to fire.

49 He cast on them his anger's rage, anger and rage and affliction, as angels of destruction among them.

50 He made a path for his anger, not sparing their souls from death, and giving into death their cattle.

51 He struck down all the first-born in Egypt, the first-fruits of their labor in the tabernacles of Ham.

52 And he led out his people like sheep, he guided them like a flock out into the wilderness,

53 And he shepherded them in hope so that they never knew fear, and the sea covered up their enemies.

54 He brought them to the mountain of his holiness, this mountain his right hand had acquired.

55 He drove away the nations from before their face, apportioning them land by lots, and he settled in their tents all the tribes of Israel.

56 They tested God the Most High and they provoked him, not guarding his testimonies.

57 Like their fathers they turned back and acted faithlessly, changing direction like twisted bows.

58 They stirred him to anger with their sacrificial high places, they moved him to jealousy with their graven idols.

59 God heard them and disdained them, he rejected Israel utterly,

60 And he forsook the tabernacle of Shiloh, his dwelling

place and home amidst men.

61 He gave their strength into captivity, their beauty into the enemy's hand.

62 He gave his people over to the sword, disdaining his own inheritance.

63 The fire consumed their young men, their maidens were not even mourned.

64 Their priests fell by the sword, none ever wept for their widows.

65 Then the Lord awoke as from sleep, like a strong man besotted with wine,

66 And he drove his enemies out, giving them into lasting disgrace.

67 And he rejected the dwelling of Joseph, he chose against the tribe of Ephraim.

68 He chose the tribe of Judah, this Mount Zion that he loved.

69 And he built there his high holy place, like the very heavens above, he founded it forever on the earth.

70 He chose David for his servant and took him from the sheepfolds,

71 From tending ewes great with young, to shepherd Jacob his people and his inheritance Israel.

72 So he was shepherd to them in the integrity of his heart, he guided them with skillfulness of hand.

The Opening Eight Lines

Psalm 77 opens (lines 1–8) with a model of all acts of *learning*. In the first line—"Give heed, O my people, to my law, incline your ears to the words of my mouth"—the law, תּוֹרָה, *torah*, is something we can hear. For *YHWH* is a God who *speaks the words* of creation to us, the words that establish—in us, that is, in and as our heart—"the wondrous works he has done" (l. 4). The point of this establishing is plain: for us to remember the "works" in the keeping (i.e., keeping in the heart) of his commandments (l. 7). To do so is to set the heart straight (l. 8).

In the second line—"I shall open my mouth in parables, I shall utter things hidden since the foundation of the world"—these are things said from long ago to us, told us by our fathers.

The parallelism within line 1—"to my law" = "words of my mouth"—this equation leads into the powerful verbs of line 2: "open my mouth" = "utter things hidden" (or "sayings of old" in the AV). The model is emerging. To listen to what God is saying is (1) to keep in one's heart the things hidden from the foundation of the world; (2) to "walk in his law" (i.e., one's whole way of going is always into God); (3) to remember and to speak to one's children: "They hid nothing from their children in the next generation, proclaiming the praises of the Lord and his mighty deeds and the wondrous works he has done" (l. 6).

How is this the act of learning? How is holding in the heart, always turning toward and entering God, and speaking of God to one's children: how is this learning? It is so because this process is the process of learning the instruction given.

The *love* of the Psalms is possibly the key that releases salvation; for in *loving* them, one is loving Christ loving them.

Note, too, in the opening eight lines of Psalm 77: the "things hidden since the foundation of the world" (προβλήματα ἀπ' ἀρχῆς, *problēmata ap' archēs*)—this is knowledge taught us by the very fathers who were "twisted and rebellious" (77:8: σκολιὰ καὶ παραπικραί-νουσα, *skolia kai parapikrainousa*) in themselves: fathers who taught against the twistedness they could not themselves avoid, except

insofar as they did not "become like their fathers" (77:8: μὴ γένω-
νται ὡς οἱ πατέρες αὐτῶν, *mē genōntai ōs oi pateres autōn*). These eight
lines, which open the psalm at the Psalter's center, thus center that
psalm in the action of (in Ps. 77's title) "Instruction" (Συνέσεως,
Syneseōs)—and in so doing center the whole Psalter in this action.

To hide nothing from one's children is to set before them this
psalm and its fearsome depiction of their fathers' twisting; a depiction that, by psalm's end, presents the way out: to focus all one's life
on David and Christ as true shepherds who—in "integrity of heart"
(ἀκακία τῆς καρδίας, *akakia tēs kardias*)—guide and focus us "with
skillfulness of hand" (ἐν ταῖς συνέσεσι τῶν χειρῶν, *en tais synesesi
tōn cheirōn*, 77:72).

Note as well a divine fortuity: that Psalm 77 possesses the same
number of lines as the number of LXX translators (seventy-two).

The Deep Structure of History as Divine Presence (the Opening, Central, and Final Lines)

The eight lines at the center of Psalm 77 (33–40) "match" the opening eight. And both "match" the closing eight lines (65–72): To see
how these three sets of lines connect is to discern the deep structure
of history as divine Presence. What happens in these threefold sets
of eight lines is so continuously significant that the three sets, taken
in sequence, are themselves, taken together, a "psalm." For example,
the end of line 8 fits perfectly into the opening of line 33. That is,
line 8, "Whose spirit was not steadfast with God . . . ," fits with
line 33, "And so all their days ended in emptiness." And just so, the
grieving introspection of lines 39 and 40 "fits" (psalmically enough)
with the sudden awakening of line 65, "the Lord awoke as from
sleep." These "fittings-together" produce, in other words, a 24-line
psalm centering and framing the larger 72-line psalm.

1 Give heed, O my people, to my law, incline your ears to the words of my mouth.

2 I shall open my mouth in parables, I shall utter things hidden since the foundation of the world,

3 Things we have heard and known, things that our fathers taught us.

4 They hid nothing from their children in the next generation, proclaiming the praises of the Lord and his mighty deeds and the wondrous works he has done.

5 He raised up a testimony in Jacob, he appointed the law in Israel, and he commanded our fathers to declare all the law to their sons,

6 So that the next generation would know, those sons yet to be born, and they in turn would arise to proclaim to their sons,

7 That they might set their hope in God and never forget the works of God and always seek his commandments,

8 That they not become like their fathers, a generation, twisted and rebellious, that did not keep its heart straight, whose spirit was not steadfast with God.

33 And so all their days ended in emptiness, all their years in fear.

34 When he slew them they sought him and repented and rose up early in their prayers to God.

35 They remembered that God is their helper, the Most High God their redeemer.

36 So they loved him with their mouths but were lying to him with their tongues,

37 For their hearts were not straight with him, they were unfaithful to his covenant.

38 But he is compassionate and will be gracious to their

sins and will not destroy them, again and again forgoing his wrath, never kindling all his anger.

39 For he remembered they are flesh, a breath that passes and never returns.

40 How many times, how many times did they provoke him in the wilderness, did they grieve him in the desert?

65 Then the Lord awoke as from sleep, like a strong man besotted with wine,

66 And he drove his enemies out, giving them into lasting disgrace.

67 And he rejected the dwelling of Joseph, he chose against the tribe of Ephraim.

68 He chose the tribe of Judah, this Mount Zion that he loved.

69 And he built there his high holy place, like the very heavens above, he founded it forever on the earth.

70 He chose David for his servant and took him from the sheepfolds,

71 From tending ewes great with young, to shepherd Jacob his people and his inheritance Israel.

72 So he was shepherd to them in the integrity of his heart, he guided them with skillfulness of hand.

A Second Interior Psalm of Man's Twisting Away from God

This psalm-within-Psalm 77 also suggests another "fitting-together" of the two intervening passages (lines 9–32 with lines 41–64) to produce yet another psalm of 48 lines. Note, for example, the "fit" of line 32 to 41:

9   The armed sons of Ephraim carrying bows turned back in the day of battle.

10 They did not guard God's covenant, they failed to walk in his law,

11 And they forgot his gracious works and his wonders that he had shown them,

12 The wonders he had accomplished in the sight of their fathers, in Egypt in the plain of Tanis.

13 He split asunder the sea and led them all through, the waters standing straight up as if held in wineskins.

14 In a cloud, he guided them by day, all night in the radiance of fire.

15 He split the rock in the wilderness, having them drink from great depth

16 And making streams run from the rocks, making streams flow down in rivers.

17 Yet they kept sinning against him, in the desert they kept on rebelling against the Most High.

18 In their hearts they kept testing God, demanding he feed all their hungers.

19 And they spoke against God, saying: Why cannot God prepare a table in the wilderness?

20 Since he could smite the rock and make waters pour down in torrents, can he not also give bread or set a table for his people?

21 Hearing this, the Lord was enraged, and fire was kindled in Jacob, anger arose against Israel,

22 Because they did not believe in God nor put their hope in his salvation.

23 Yet he had commanded the clouds above and opened the doors of heaven,

24 Raining down on them manna to eat, giving them the heavenly food:

25 Men ate the very bread of angels, he sent them food to the full.

26 He brought the south wind down from the heavens and led in by his power a wind from the southwest.

27 He rained flesh down on them like dust, winged birds like sands of the sea,

28 Letting them fall amid their camps, falling all around their tents.

29 So they ate and were well filled, for he gave them their own desire.

30 They were not deprived of their desire, but even while the food was in their mouths

31 God's wrath rose up against them and cut down the stoutest of them, shackling the chosen of Israel.

32 In all these ways they kept sinning, not believing in his wondrous works,

41 They turned away and tempted God, they provoked the Holy One of Israel.

42 They did not remember his hand in that day he freed them from the hand of the oppressor,

43 How he wrought his signs in Egypt, his wonders in the plain of Tanis,

44 And turned their rivers and rainfall into blood they could not drink.

45 He sent them swarms of devouring flies and frogs that destroyed them.

46 He gave their crops over to blight, their labor to the locust.

47 He destroyed their vines with hail, their mulberry trees

with frost.

48 He also gave their cattle to the hail, all their substance up to fire.

49 He cast on them his anger's rage, anger and rage and affliction, as angels of destruction among them.

50 He made a path for his anger, not sparing their souls from death, and giving into death their cattle.

51 He struck down all the first-born in Egypt, the first-fruits of their labor in the tabernacles of Ham.

52 And he led out his people like sheep, he guided them like a flock out into the wilderness,

53 And he shepherded them in hope so that they never knew fear, and the sea covered up their enemies.

54 He brought them to the mountain of his holiness, this mountain his right hand had acquired.

55 He drove away the nations from before their face, apportioning them land by lots, and he settled in their tents all the tribes of Israel.

56 They tested God the Most High and they provoked him, not guarding his testimonies.

57 Like their fathers they turned back and acted faithlessly, changing direction like twisted bows.

58 They stirred him to anger with their sacrificial high places, they moved him to jealousy with their graven idols.

59 God heard them and disdained them, he rejected Israel utterly,

60 And he forsook the tabernacle of Shiloh, his dwelling place and home amidst men.

61 He gave their strength into captivity, their beauty into the enemy's hand.

62 He gave his people over to the sword, disdaining his
    own inheritance.

63 The fire consumed their young men, their maidens
    were not even mourned.

64 Their priests fell by the sword, none ever wept for their
    widows.

This second interior "psalm" is wholly *inside* the larger Psalm 77; and it is—read continuously—a psalm straightforwardly depicting human twisting away from God's wondrous works, a depiction ending in line 64 in total human destruction: "Their priests fell by the sword, none ever wept for their widows." There is no hope, all is wrecked; everything and everyone dies out; the holy city of Jerusalem is completely destroyed. As the opening lines of the next psalm reveal: "They have made Jerusalem into a gardener's hut. . . . They have made their blood flow throughout all Jerusalem, there was no one to bury them" (78:1–3).

But such a "psalm" as this one adduced from Psalm 77 *is not a Psalm*. Without the essential antinomic movement and character of Psalms, it misses entirely the Davidic—that is, Christic—redemption of the true 77th Psalm. For there indeed exists a way to unmake one's fathers' twistedness: that is, to choose, freely and wholly joyfully, David as shepherd; to choose Davidic "integrity of heart"—that is, the heart of Christ Himself. Thus, the three eight-liners at the heart of this psalm, which is the heart of the whole Psalter, reveal the way of psalmic resurrection. Without them, the twisting prevails.

And here is a source—an Asaphian source—for the eight-line stanzas of Psalm 118: the resurrection of true intimacy out of the darkness of violent intimacy.[3] The words of every psalm carry equally the power to cause resurrective intimacy with God—equally, in the sense of participatory power.

11

The Asymmetry of His Immeasurable Love

Psalm 118's Nine Words, the Lamed-Stanza, and the Defeat of Depression

The concept of asymmetricality is based on a model of medical decision-making that finds points of asymmetry in a pattern to be guides to the necessary healing response. The author views the highly patterned Psalm 118 as a model of healing in which the nine words for God's Law act as something like capillaries carrying lifeblood (spiritual energy) to all the parts of the psalm (and therefore to the one who prays the psalm). He looks at the points of greatest asymmetricality as foci of meaning guiding the process of noetic healing of the soul in its journey toward theosis, union with God: the ultimate healing. Constructing a Lexicon of the Nine Words, he shows how these words work in the psalm to enact healing—particularly the statutes, which generate the entire creation, everything about ourselves, every word and meaning of sacred text, and our comprehension of them; and they do this in such a way that we are directly nourished by those life-giving words and patterns. The chapter focuses

on the *Lamed*-stanza, the poem's asymmetric center, in which the way of
psalmic personhood is seen as the way of an incarnative relation between
the divine "Thou" and the human "I." The extreme asymmetry of this relationship requires a comparable humility (*tapeinōsis*, meaning also "affliction") on our part. The author offers the Mother of God as the model for
our humility and "an unceasingly perfect icon of perfect—indeed, perfective—humanity." He speaks of the demonic attack on our striving for perfection, in which the psalmic "I" loses all capacity for direct and intimate
contact with the divine "Thou"; and he concludes: "the Orthodox rhythm
of daily psalmic prayer perfectly engages the demonic rhythm of depression: an engagement wherein the attack is utterly defeated." The way the
two rhythms interlock is best characterized as an asymmetrical relationship in which the prayer vastly over-matches the depression. —*Ed.*

Grant
this,
oh Lord

C lassic literature in medical decision-making would have
you believe that everyone [practicing medicine] generates a
hypothesis and then follows a pathway with decision points. . . . But
no one really works that way."[1] What really occurs is this: a medical practitioner responds simultaneously—or fails to respond—to
a complex set of actual and potential disintegrations and traumas.
Hence, the healing response is one that is more spatial than temporal: that is, it is occurring on many fronts at once, each aspect (or
"plane") of the presenting disintegrative set touching—in ways that
are often dynamically shifting at every instant—every other aspect
in the set. Therefore, the healing response is best characterized as
asymmetrical, only faintly patterned at any given instant. That is, the
whole set never once assumes a fixed or symmetrical pattern. For
this reason, then, in order to be truly responsive to the asymmetrical disintegration that's taking place, the healing (or integrative)
response to this must itself always sustain a dynamically comparable
asymmetricality. Psalm 118—a poem of noetic healing, a poem,
indeed, of resurrection—takes a similar pathway.

Eg. a broken bone: It is out of place and can move around.
Response: Set it, and bind it with a
rigid cast

My point concerning asymmetricality in Psalm 118 is this. In this poem, the nine LXX words for "law" are very like the human body's nervous and capillary systems: for, taken together, these nine words are transmitting life-giving responsiveness and integrative energies to the psalm's whole body. Now, the Orthodox Christian emphatic placement of this psalm in the Matins of Holy Saturday thus possesses profound insight into the poem's whole meaning.[2] Consider this metaphor: the crucified Body of Christ has entered death; as He prays the psalm on Holy Saturday, the nine words together permeate His lifeless body as they do the psalm, restarting in Him its vast physical systems by infusing Him with a still vaster system of spiritual energies. And this "restarting" is the resurrection, brought about by God Himself, in and as the action of the Holy Trinity, while the psalm is, as it were, being composed in and as the mind of Christ. A reciprocal life-givingness. Our Lord may be thought of as entering and quickening the psalm that it may quicken Him—and all those by whom and for whom it is prayed.

It is therefore of highest interest to understand something of the nine words as an *entire system* of spiritual life-givingness. It is also of great moment to ask: Where in the poem does the greatest asymmetricality occur?

A Lexicon of the Nine Words

Let us begin by devising a kind of lexicon of the nine words for "law" in Psalm 118 (and throughout the Psalter, especially in Psalm 18), giving each a brief definition applicable to the poem. Using Hatch and Redpath,[3] I shall give the nine words in order of usage, the greatest first:

1. Commandment/s, *entolai* (ἐντολαί: 37 occurrences: 35 times in LXX plural, twice in LXX singular—with *logos*

appearing twice in Rahlfs' text at lines 57 and 139 with *entolai* given by Rahlfs both times in footnotes). *Entolai* translates MT *mitzvoth* (מִצְוֹת) twenty-one times and MT *piqqudim* (פִּקּוּדִים) sixteen times. A *mitzva* (מִצְוָה) is an act of self-emptying love for another, while a *piqqudah* (פְּקֻדָּה) is something left in trust as in grain stored against famine.[4] Using these Hebrew significances, we may say this: *a commandment is a loving action upon or toward another that becomes saving nourishment for both the agent and the recipient of that love.*

2. Statutes, *dikaiōmata* (δικαιώματα: 28 LXX occurrences, all plural), translating twenty-three times the MT plural *huqqim* (חֻקִּים) and five times the plural *piqqudim*. Related to the verb meaning "to cut into," "to inscribe deeply," a *hoq* (חֹק) is what God performs in all His acts of creating the world; hence, a *hoq* retains in the creation the *generative* power of the Creator.[5] Combined with *piqqudim*, the statutes (*dikaiōmata*) can thus be defined as: *the divine cuttings-into (or inscriptions) left by God in the creation to become the nourishment that powers our own true creativity.*

Two LXX words (3 and 4) occur twenty-two times each: *nomos* (νόμος, law) and *logos* (λόγος, word), translating (respectively) the two Hebrew singulars תּוֹרָה (*torah*) and דָּבָר (*davar*). (Note: the two words "rhyme" within both the Hebrew and the Greek.) Now, one distinction in usage: *torah/nomos* are always in singular forms in both Hebrew and Greek, while *davar/logos* occur in both plural and singular forms, with usage paralleling the Hebrew usage:

3. Law, *nomos/torah*. This is *the manifestation of God that is active in the present instant*—and is always (i.e., eternally) so active. *Nomos* is what the Apostles behold at the Transfiguration.

[Margin handwritten notes:]

ΕΝΤΟΛΩΝ ἄριστων

"Love one another"

Grant mercy and so store up treasures in heaven

Implication? God stored treasures in creation; "treasures in earthen vessels."

[Handwritten annotations in top margin: "perhaps: logoi are cohortative—they call for a response"; "Nomos is more intrinsic, unchanging but (from a human perspective) 'flowing'... because the logoi draw us into it."]

4. Word, *logos/davar*. This is *the spoken manifestation of God, the divine voice to which all creation responds because all creation arises from His logos.* "Let there be light," says God in creating the world (Gen. 1:3): here is *logos*. And we hear the same divine Word speaking at the Transfiguration: "This is My beloved Son" (Matt. 17:5).

Two LXX words (5 and 6) occur twenty-one times each: *martyriai* (μαρτυρίαι, testimonies) and *logion* (λόγιον, teaching), translating (respectively) עֵדוּת (*eduth*), plural; and אִמְרָה (*imrah*), singular:

5. Testimonies (*martyriai/eduth*) are *the witnesses (cf. "martyrs") in actual human history of the divine statutes; that is, the statutes as active in the historical record.*

6. Teaching (*logion/imrah*, sixteen singulars, five plurals) is the expressed voice of God, *the divine word (logos) become incarnate as a reality fully audible to human comprehension; hence, Scripture understood as the unceasingly living voice of Christ.*

7. Judgments (κρίματα, *krimata*; מִשְׁפָּטִים, *mishpatim*) occurs twenty times (mostly plural, four singulars). *These are revelations of God in judicial terms: that is, as specific applications of the "teaching" in situations of human dispute or conflict, applications that divinely resolve human conflict.* These "judgments" therefore involve a considerable dimension of *prophetic* functioning: that is, direct revelation of God's will for us.

8. Way (ὁδός, *hodos*; דֶּרֶךְ, *derekh*) occurs fifteen times. *This word signifies the human activity of moving toward union with God. The word's emphasis is on the actual practice of the movement; hence, it signifies ascetic practice.*

9. Path (τρίβος, *tribos*; נְתִיבָה, *nethivah*) occurs twice in Psalm 118 (ll. 35 and 105). In LXX Greek, the word is singular in line 35 and plural in line 105; in Hebrew, it is singular both

times. *Largely synonymous in meaning with* hodos *(see above),* tribos *differs in being a word of high literary antiquity—much the way the English word "abode" or "domicile" differs from "home" or "house."*

Now, as we have said, all nine of these words may be understood to work in the psalm the way the body's nervous and capillary systems work: to transmit divine (healing) energies to the human person. And this transmission of the energies has two closely related consequences. First, it fulfills every human potential for achieving blessedness; and second, this achievement of blessedness is what is signified by the word *theōsis* (θέωσις). And theosis is the system of the divine energies of Psalm 118's nine words—a system so deeply (i.e., divinely) patterned as to be—in our experience—dynamically asymmetrical in relation to us.

To best approach our question—Where in Psalm 118 does the greatest asymmetricality occur?—let us begin by noting this central fact of the poem: at every line, the poem is "over" in the sense of completely articulating everything about God's ways in the creation; yet, every line is *also* adding to continuously deeper and fuller revelation of God's ways in the creation. Thus, the psalm at every moment is at once perfectly complete and always entering into a still greater perfection: the perfection of achieving pure *perfectiveness*, that is, the purity of state wherein the poem brings about perfection in its reader. It is always over and always ongoing.

This central antinomy sustains, at every moment, the poem's asymmetricality—and, at every moment, it bestows upon the poem the dynamism of that asymmetricality. That is, the antinomy of being simultaneously complete and incomplete—an antinomy in which neither the poem's completeness nor the poem's incompleteness can ever diminish, abolish, or dominate the other—this antinomy is the engine that is being steadily fueled by the nine words.

Oh!. I didn't "get it" before.
That the Psalm doesn't progress the way others
do. no cadence. It IS 'Ison'

And the asymmetricality of the poem—that is, its ninefold healing response to the crisis of complex disintegration—establishes the poem's central stanza as a fulcrum of all its meaning.

The *Lamed*-Stanza

The twelfth or *Lamed* stanza (ll. 89–96) is the first stanza in the poem's second half. That is, the first eleven stanzas (ll. 1–88) employ, in successive stanzas, the first half of the Hebrew alphabet; the second eleven stanzas employ the alphabet's second half. This patterning therefore establishes the twelfth stanza as the poem's turning point. Thus, it is the poem's least symmetrical stanza in relation to the nine words in the sense that two of its lines (90 and 91) use none of the nine words; and one of its lines (96) uses the most frequently occurring word, *entolai* (commandments), in the singular form (a usage occurring only twice in the whole poem). The stanza is therefore worth our close attention.

89 Unto all eternity, O Lord,
     Thy word endures in heaven,
90 Thy truth unto generations of generations,
     Thou didst found the earth and it endures.
91 By thine ordering, each day endures,
     For all earthly things are thy servants.
92 If thy law had not been my meditation,
     I would have perished in my affliction.
93 I shall never forget thy statutes,
     In them thou hast quickened me to life.
94 I am thine, O Lord, save me,
     For I have sought thy statutes.
95 Sinners lurked for me to kill me,
     But I comprehended thy testimonies.

[handwritten annotation: Resurrection, with bracket spanning lines 92–93]

96 I have seen the limits of all achievements,
    But thy commandment is immensely spacious.

It is crucial to begin by noting that this stanza's fifth line (93) is
established in Orthodox Christendom as the psalm's exact center: "I
shall never forget thy statutes, / In them thou hast quickened me to
life." Since line 88, which concludes the previous stanza, is, in simple
fact, the psalm's arithmetical halfway point, why is line 93 called by
the Orthodox the *mese* or midpoint? Two related matters can help us
to respond to this crucial question. First, לֹ (*lamed*)—the letter of the
Hebrew alphabet that begins all eight lines of the Hebrew stanza—is
considered the heart of the alphabet both because the letter *lamed*
occurs midpoint in the alphabet and because the word *lamed* is considered cognate with both לָמַד (*lamad*; "study" [of Torah]) and לֵב
(*lev*; "heart"). Second, line 93 begins the second half of the *Lamed*-
stanza and therefore occupies the generative position in the whole
stanza: that is, the first four lines (89–92) prepare for line 93, while
the final three lines (94–96) can be seen as the heart of the stanza
that is itself the heart of the whole poem: everything in the entire
poem, we may say, flows into and out of this single line, 93.

Now, the key word in line 93—"statutes"—translates the LXX
word *dikaiōmata*, itself translating the Hebrew *piqqudim*, "precepts."
Here, then, is one of the seven cases in Psalm 118 wherein the
Hebrew "precepts" are being absorbed by the Greek "statutes." The
semantic significance of this absorption could not be plainer: the
specific act of Hebrew obedience to the divine Word (an obedience
prescribed by the "precepts") is, in the LXX, becoming incarnate as
and in the divine patterns of the whole creation (the "statutes"). For
you to "never forget" the statutes is to obey fully the divine patterns
in and as the way of your own life: an obedience that bestows God's
ongoing aliveness upon you. This incarnative significance is intensified by the grammatical modes of the Hebrew and the Greek verbs:

the iterative mode in Hebrew and the aorist mode in Greek. For the ongoingness in the Hebrew verb becomes the actualization in the Greek. Thus, the incarnative intensification of the statutes opens into the Orthodox experience of the resurrection: and life becomes forever ongoing. And the next three words of the LXX *Lamed*-stanza beautifully match the single Hebrew word: that is, σός εἰμι ἐγώ (*sos eimi egō*) translates לְךָ־אֲנִי (*lekha-'ani*), "I am thine"—a matching wherein the Hebraic semantic oneness becomes the LXX trinity, thereby underlining the line's entire incarnative meaning.

Here, then, is the key to the stanza: the way of psalmic person-hood is the way of an incarnative relation between the divine "Thou" and the human "I." As the "I" gives itself entirely to "Thee," *incarnatively* gives itself, two things happen at once: first, the eternally enduring logos of line 89 (Heb. *davar*)—that is, the divine voice to which all of the creation is a response—becomes the finite human voice responding; second, the human mind and heart become the fully able instruments of divine study. And the object of this divine study is the "enduring-ness" of the statutes. Thus, as the human heart moves always deeper into intimate contact with the divine logos, the human heart becomes "en-statute-ed"; that is, the instrument of human knowing becomes transfigured by—and *into*—the divine Intelligence.

And therefore the stanza's focus in the first three lines (89–91) is on what *remains*, what *persists*, what *endures* in this asymmetrical encounter. In line 89, God's word endures in heaven (Gk. διαμένει, *diamenei*; Heb. נִצָּב, *natsav*); in line 90, God's truth endures (Gk. *diamenei*; Heb. עָמַד, *'amad*) on the earth; and in line 91, each earthly day endures (Gk. *diamenei*; Heb. *'amad*). When we reflect a moment on this sequence, a startling question becomes plain: while we may understand (but exactly *what* do we understand?) how God's word endures in heaven, *how* exactly does God's truth on earth endure—and, still more puzzling, how can we say that "each day endures"? Similarly, how can we understand what Psalm 88 means by "forever" in its opening line: "O Lord I will sing thy mercies forever, with my mouth I will proclaim thy truth from generation to generation" (88:1)—especially when we note the emphatic phrasing of the LXX Greek rendering of this adverb (εἰς τὸν αἰῶνα, *eis ton aiōna*)—exactly the same phrasing used in 118:89 to mean "unto all eternity"? How can any earthly day be said to endure in the very way that God's word endures in heaven?

A response to this very crucial question can begin to be approached through the asymmetry of the *Lamed*-stanza: lines 90 and 91 are the only two lines in the entire 176-line poem *not* to use any of the nine LXX words. These two lines, then, interrupt the deep symmetry of the poem's otherwise unceasing use of the nine words; and they effect this interruption so as to emphasize the logically impossible fact that Psalm 118 is everywhere asserting: the earthly incarnation of the divine is raising all earthly things up, *and into direct participation in* God through the asymmetry of His immeasurable love for us. And it is this direct participation in God that divinizes the human action of devoutly studying God's *nomos*. As the human mind enters into unceasing meditation on God's law, it is slowly and deeply transfigured through its meditation into the very end of all its studies: the mind of God.

And this transfiguration of the human mind is radically—and unchangeably—asymmetrical in that the divine mind immensely exceeds every human action of comprehension. And yet (and here is the great point), the divine mind is always and forever "quickening" the human mind into an unceasing aliveness: a quickening that never obliterates the human mind but is, instead, always deepening it into being always more fully alive: for this is the foundational asymmetry of God's love for us.

The asymmetry continues in line 92:

If thy law had not been my meditation,
I would have perished in my affliction.

That the poem is, at every instant, simultaneously completely over and forever incomplete bears directly upon the central reality of the entire LXX: it is a *translation*. Thus, in the *Lamed*-stanza of Psalm 118, "each day endures" in the same way the Holy Mother's life endures: through the action of translation—translation to life.

It is worth noting that the three Hebrew verbs translated as "endure" in lines 89, 90, and 91 exhibit a significant variation: the first verb, in line 89, is נִצָּב (*natsav*), while the second and third verbs (in ll. 90 and 91) are both עָמַד (*amad*). The Hebrew psalmist thus registers a conceptual shift in moving from God's word *enduring* in heaven to the earth's and the day's *enduring*. But—and here's the point—the LXX translator uses the same Greek verb for all three occurrences, *diamenei*. In so doing, the LXX thereby *fulfills* the Hebrew by very alertly and very deeply emphasizing the Messiah's actual arrival on earth.

[handwritten note: ✴ עָמַד is personal - like standing in place נִצָּב hints at something at least very big, like a monument, erected]

Humility and the Defeat of Depression

These asymmetries of translation then, in line 92, become focused in a crucial LXX noun: *tapeinōsis* (ταπείνωσις). The word can mean (as it does here, in l. 92) "affliction"; it also—and equally—means "humility." The affliction that is genuine humility becomes the precondition for all psalmic meditative growling[6]—for, that is, every action of intimate contact with the divine *nomos* having become fully incarnate as earthly statute (l. 93). We can therefore perish in our humility if we forget—even for an instant—to seek our sole nourishment in God. For so to cease such seeking would be

[handwritten note: this is why we must never wish for the humiliation of others,]

to render drastically mute all our moanings of intense delight: and such muteness is the vivid psalmic icon of permanent death.

The realization of this intense psalmic delight is present in—*and as*—a life given wholly over to devout study of the Psalms: to, that is, that humility you can die of unless you ceaselessly seek God's law (l. 92). And, to Orthodox Christendom, the supreme model of such life-giving study is the Mother of God. Orthodox Holy Tradition remembers a signal fact about Mary: between the ages of three and fifteen, she dwelt in the Temple at Jerusalem as one of the holy virgins who give their lives to study and prayer.

In 1990, a few days before Sept. 8 (the Nativity of the Theotokos), I wrote this in my journal:

> To live in Psalms is my whole heart's desire: in Our Mother so to live, following her in the way of sacred study, wherein she (from age 3 to 15) studied in deepest devotion the Word of God, letting the sounds of each syllable fill her with deepest joy.
>
> I see her now, bent over her sacred Book as each word comes into her view and true ken; and the light of the text irradiates her face and shines back as her presence in the text: such that the prophecies come to embody her as she begins to fulfill them now. This moment is of highest meaning. Isaiah (e.g.), in the radiance of her study, begins *in the text itself* to take on her presence: the text "changes" as she shines her concentrated heart-in-mind into it; the text *becomes* her. And as this is going on she is fulfilling in her being all the meanings of prophecy (e.g., Lamentations before the Cross).
>
> The moment when Gabriel arrives at the Annunciation manifests fully this moment. She concentrates, in the discipline of obedience, the whole of herself before God: as she

did (and does) before the Holy Word. She hears; and she—in fullest obedience—interrogates the Presence: She asks, How can this be since I am vowed to chastity? And she wholly receives the divine response: *It is very chastity itself in you that shall bear fruit through you.* This is the model of how she follows the way of sacred study. Listen, interrogate especially concerning the limits of your holy vows; receive the sacred response and accept. In this way of study, light reciprocally acts such that the texts "change" and you bear fruit.

Such is psalmic life.

This reciprocal action of light is, I think, precisely what line 93 of Psalm 118 signifies by saying, here at the psalm's center: "In [thy statutes] thou hast quickened me to life." As she reflects back the light of the sacred text, beginning to take on in herself that very light itself, she is "quickened to life" in this light. The statutes are therefore generative at three levels simultaneously:

- they generate the entire creation and all things and actions occurring within it, including all of human history;
- they generate sacred text, every word—indeed, every least letter of every single word—and all the patterns those words assume;
- and they generate our comprehension of them in such a way that we become directly nourished by those life-giving words and patterns.

These generative powers of the statutes can begin to help account for the inescapable asymmetry in our relation to God's word. When, therefore, in the *Lamed*-stanza, the psalmist says, "I am thine, O Lord, save me," he is signaling this asymmetry by adding: "For I have sought thy statutes" (118:94). That is, you enter into salvific intimacy with God solely through seeking the "immensely spacious" light of His statutes (118:96). Psalm 35:9 expresses this reciprocity beautifully: "For with thee is the fountain of life, in thy light we shall see light." In this way, then, the asymmetry of the *Lamed*-stanza discloses the depths of divine intimacy.

Is there any true way to banish—nay: to defeat utterly—the demon of depression through psalmic prayer in Christ and the Holy Mother? Answer: there is no *other* way whatsoever. For the demons of depression seem to press upon me at every moment of my psalmic prayer, morning and evening: as *logismoi* (λογισμοί), as (that is) *intrusive thoughts* (chaotic feelings; endless terrors; swirls of mental busyness; profound tiredness; etc., etc.).[7]

The movement of psalms, in prayer, follows the curve of engagement with these enemies, seeking always their utter defeat. This experience of psalmic movement reveals the shape of the entire Psalter as well as the shape of Psalm 118's *Lamed*-stanza. Line 95 of the *Lamed*-stanza touches upon one of the constant subjects of the entire Psalter: "Sinners lurked for me to kill me"—that is, the subject of *enemies*. The LXX Greek word ἐχθρός (*echthros*; Heb. אֹיֵב, *'oyev*), meaning "enemy," occurs in 57 of the 150 psalms; and close synonyms occur in dozens more—as here in line 95: "sinners" (ἁμαρτολοί, *hamartoloi*). In psalms, the enemy has one overriding aim: to attack the psalmic reader with such ferocity that the speaker is not merely physically damaged but, more deeply, psychically wrecked. This inward wreckage is completed when the psalmic "I" loses all capacity for direct and intimate contact with the divine "Thou" (a capacity that *every* line in Psalm 118 fully affirms).

The Orthodox rhythm of daily psalmic prayer perfectly engages the demonic rhythm of depression: an engagement wherein the attack is utterly defeated. Again here is line 95 of the *Lamed*-stanza:

> Sinners lurked for me to kill me,
> But I comprehended thy testimonies.

Grant this, oh Lord!

MT:
אֶתְבּוֹנָן

1p. hitpael ≈ reflexive?
"I discern-myself
in your witness"
//d discerned them in me

The Asymmetry of His Immeasurable Love   **187**

The LXX verb that means "to comprehend" (LXX συνίημι, *syniēmi*[8]) contains, in its prefix (*syn-*), the relational reality that Psalm 118 everywhere affirms, a reality wherein the earthly witness to the divine statutes (the testimonies) is so fully comprehended by the human mind as to constitute a participation *in* those statutes. And the way these two rhythms interlock—the divine rhythm of truly psalmic prayer and the human rhythm of daily depression—is best characterized as an asymmetrical relationship: the prayer vastly (indeed, *immeasurably*) over-matches the depression.

Line 96 of the stanza then deepens this saving asymmetry:

I have seen the limits of all achievements,
But thy commandment is immensely spacious.

The exceedingly great (σφόδρα, *sphodra*) spaciousness (πλατεῖα, *plateia*) of the divine commandment (ἐντολή, *entolē*) is key to understanding God's immeasurable mercy and love. Used ten times in Psalm 118 (a dozen times in some well-attested manuscripts), *sphodra* is an intensifying adverb that, at every instance in Psalm 118, increases the velocity, depth, and power of the word it modifies. Here, in line 96, *sphodra* intensifies the *plateia* (spaciousness) of God's commandment—an intensification that so powerfully deepens and broadens the "space" the commandment occupies as to make that commandment *immeasurably* vaster than any merely human achievement (συντέλεια, *synteleia*[9]).

But what, then, *is* this spaciousness? Line 45 of the psalm points us toward the answer:

I kept on walking in spaciousness,
For I sought always thy commandments.

To seek God's commandments, as a way of actually moving in one's life, is to walk in this spaciousness. Note, however, that the LXX

Greek in line 45 is not *plateia* but *platysmos* (πλατυσμός)—a neologism coined by the LXX translators and employed only six times in the entire Bible, three of these in the Psalter. One of these three psalmic usages occurs in Psalm 17:

> 18 They overran me in the day of my affliction, but the
>   Lord became my support
> 19 And he led me into spaciousness, he will deliver me
>   because he delights in me.

The "day of affliction," when David's enemies overrun him, is indeed the depressive's daily rhythm of psychic catastrophe. Yet, as for David, so, too, for the depressive: the Lord leads him "into spaciousness" (*platysmos*) wherein God "delights" in him; and to inhabit God's divine delight is to enter immeasurably vast spaciousness.

And this experience of spacious delight occurs as the direct consequence of seeking God's commandments: seeking, that is, His *entolai*, His *mitzvot* (מִצְוֹת), His self-emptying acts of lovingly giving Himself for the life of the other. Note, too, that the LXX noun in Psalm 118:96 is in the singular, one of only two such usages in the thirty-seven occurrences of the word in Psalm 118—the other is two lines further on, in line 98:

> Thou hast made me wise in thy commandment
> Above my enemies, and forever it is mine.

In both instances, the LXX significance is plain: the singular commandment is to be understood as the perfect summation of countless acts of self-giving love. And the wisdom that results in the psalmist by these unceasing acts of love is a wisdom that is at once personal and eternal: it is given to him forever (*eis ton aiōna*), being simultaneously both fully *his* and fully God's gift *to him*. This wisdom thus "quickens" the depressive's daily rhythmic dying (what Saint John calls "general death") into the unceasing rhythm of psalmic prayer.

And at the Orthodox heart of this quickening wisdom is the Mother of God, whom we can—just—hear as she sings to her divine Son line 97 of Psalm 118:

> How I have loved, O Lord, thy law,
> It is my meditation all the day long.

The *nomos* of God is her unceasing nourishment in Him whom she herself has nourished. "All the day long" is, in LXX Greek, ἡ ὅλη ἡμέρα (*hē holē hēmera*): the day in its divinely given *wholeness*; therefore, the day in its capacity to perfect us wholly, "the day the Lord has made" (117:24). This reciprocal nourishment of Mother and Son begins in the asymmetry wherein the woman gives life to the child, then moves into the asymmetry wherein Christ ceaselessly loves Mary, an asymmetry whereby she becomes for us an unceasingly perfect icon of perfect—indeed, perfective—humanity. In this light, we may thus say that if Christ sings Psalm 118 on Holy Saturday, we can thereby hear her singing the entire poem at her Dormition, wherein the demon of depression is utterly defeated: "You were translated to life, O Mother of Life, and by your prayers, you deliver our souls from death." Thus we can say with Saint John Climacus: "He who has really gained [this victory] has become experienced in all good."[10]

The *Lamed*-stanza contains the way into such victorious experience.

12

The Making of Personhood

The Alphabetic Sequence and the
First Six Stanzas of Psalm 118

The Hebrew alphabetic sequence was understood to represent the stages of the incarnate creation, specifically the creation of Adam. An alphabetic poem, then (where each line begins with a particular letter in sequence throughout the poem), is a poem in which a generative process is unfolding. The LXX poet/translators retained Psalm 118's alphabetic character, not in the initial letters of lines, but in naming the psalm's 22 stanzas with the letters of the Greek alphabet. This chapter looks at the first six stanzas of the psalm (*Aleph* through *Waw*) with the understanding that Christ, as the second Adam, is here giving Himself into the process of incarnating the obedience in which the first Adam failed, and at the same time leading us who pray the psalm—to Him and with Him—into the fullness of our own personhood. When we do this, especially on Holy Saturday, we enter, with Him, into a fierce struggle against the "rulers of this present darkness," a struggle that will restore to us, by resurrection, not only the living Christ, the second Adam, but also the possibility of our living into the fullness of our own personhood in His likeness. The heart of the psalm reflects this quickening, this awakening of the signs of life, as in a mother's womb, in a way that suggests entry into the divine nature of God. This chapter opens by looking at the spiritual warfare of psalmic meditation, in and with Christ, as a way of restoring the fallen Adam within ourselves, against the "world rulers of the present darkness." It goes on to look at the first six stanzas of the Great Psalm as they contribute to this process. —*Ed.*

Christ the Second Adam

An alphabetic psalm in the Hebrew, Psalm 118 is divided into twenty-two eight-line stanzas, with each line in a given stanza beginning with one of the twenty-two letters of the Hebrew alphabet. That is, in stanza one, all eight lines begin with *aleph*, the first letter of the Hebrew alphabet; in stanza two, all eight lines begin with *beth*, the second letter of the alphabet; and so on, through all twenty-two letters in their Hebrew alphabetic sequence. Very perceptively, the LXX translators did *not* attempt to construct in their Greek anything resembling the Hebrew alphabetic "ignition" of every line in every stanza. Yet they did keep intact the eight-line stanza by "titling" each one with a Greek transliteration of the Hebrew letter used in the original. Hence, the first eight-line stanza of the LXX psalm is titled αλφ (for Hebrew *aleph*); the second stanza is called βηθ (for Hebrew *bēth*); and so on, to the final eight-line stanza, which is called, in Greek, θαυ (*tau*) for the final letter of the Hebrew alphabet.

The significance of these stanza-titles in the Greek is plain: the LXX translators saw that the Hebrew alphabetic sequence was ineradicably and profoundly meaningful to the whole Great Psalm. As learned Jews, these poet/translators, aware of the imminent arrival of Messiah, would assuredly have known that the sequence of the Hebrew alphabet is considered to be primarily a *generative* sequence: that is, the first letter, *aleph*, represents the first stage of the incarnate creation, while the twenty-second letter, *tau*, is the final stage. In Judaic devotional practice, this sequence of incarnation is held to refer specifically to pre-fallen Adam, to the *perfect man*. It is the sequence, that is, in which God the Father created Adam: perfect in humanity, yet able to fall and to repent from that fall through the act of remembering fully and truly who he (Adam) is: the created child of the Almighty Creator. The meaning of the alphabetic sequence in Psalm 118, then, is clear. Christ, the second Adam, who chooses the way of unswerving and whole-hearted obedience to the Father's will for Him, thereby going into death so as to enter and fulfill the promise made by God to Adam; Christ, the second Adam, who chooses and enters into eternal human aliveness in the heavenly God, the goal of all truly human desire: Christ Himself is therefore fully present in this immense and perfective psalm; and His presence has the power to make us perfect in Him as we pray the psalm. And thus we can see: to become truly a person is to be made perfect in Christ.

As we saw in chapter 11, the Matins of Holy Saturday is given over entirely to this psalm. On Holy Friday, Christ has been violently crucified and placed in the tomb; at Pascha, He will rise from the tomb, overthrowing the dominion of death. In between—and the way to get from crucifixion to resurrection—is Psalm 118. The Matins service can thus be understood as one wherein *we*, the witnesses and beholders of the crucifixion, now enter the Tomb ourselves, so as to be with Him; and what we find is that He, in the Tomb, is praying aloud this psalm in its entirety: praying so as to make crucifixion *become* the way of resurrection—to make violent death become the sole and perfect way into blessed aliveness that never ceases: *never.*

Thus, in using Psalm 118 as the primary text for the Matins of Holy Saturday, between Christ's death on the cross and His glorious resurrection, the Orthodox Church is calling the faithful to understand His passage from death to resurrection as actually occurring in and through this psalm. Here, then, is the fundamental significance of psalmic meditation: it is the way of resurrection. As we follow in prayer the movements of Psalm 118—from *aleph* to *tau*—we are following the way into resurrected life with Christ Himself.

Now, as we have seen, there are ten occurrences in the LXX Psalter of the noun μελέτη (*meletē*, meditation) and fifteen occurrences of the verb μελετάω (*meletaō*, to meditate). Seven of the ten nouns and five of the fifteen verbs—that is, twelve of the twenty-five occurrences—are found in Psalm 118. When the LXX translators rendered all these twenty-five Hebrew occurrences (10 nouns and 15 verbs throughout the Psalter), they chose one Greek verb and its one cognate noun (*meletaō* and *meletē*) for all of them. In my translation of the LXX psalms, I translate the verb *meletaō* ten times as "to meditate"; once each as "to plot," "to have . . . strength," and "to study."

It is of considerable interest to reflect for a moment on the predominant Hebrew verb: הָגָה, *hagah*. Brown-Driver-Briggs begins its presentation of this verb by noting that later Hebrew poets considered it *onomatopoeic*: that is, the word sounds to the ear very like the meaning it carries to the mind.[1] Its primary meaning is to *growl*, like a lion growling over its prey, while its Aramaic and Arabic cognates mean *to satirize, to insult, to scold* (ibid.). Its other, and closely related, meanings include *to moan* (like a dove in distress), *to groan, to utter sound, to speak*. In the first line of Psalm 2, the Hebrew *hagah* means *to imagine falsely, to devise deceitfully*: "Why do the nations rage and the people meditate [*meletaō*] vain things?" (Ps. 2:1). In Isaiah 8:19, *hagah* in its plural participial form signifies the "chirpings and mutterings [made by] necromancers and wizards."[2]

In this Hebrew verb, then, we can see the primary significance of psalmic meditation as spiritual warfare: it is an action wherein you overcome the enemy the way a lion brings down its prey. For spiritual warfare in psalmic meditation "quickens the pulse and shoots adrenalin into the bloodstream" precisely because we are "grappling with [in Saint Paul's words] 'the world rulers of this present darkness'" (Eph. 6:12).[3] We may approach Psalm 118, then, as a handbook for the practice of psalmic meditation if we approach it also as the way into this direct participation in Christ, and as the restoration *within ourselves* of the fallen Adam against these "rulers of the present darkness."

The Orthodox monastic tradition of psalmic prayer establishes the chiastic heart of Psalm 118, not at the numerically exact center point (which would be lines 88 and 89—or, rather, the space *between* these two lines); instead, it establishes the center (or *mesē* in Greek) at line 93, five lines into the psalm's central stanza, *Lamed*, which we have discussed in chapter 11: "I shall never forget thy statutes, in them thou hast quickened me to life."

There are two further things to note about this chiastic center of Psalm 118. The first is that the speaker of the line enters into eternal memory of God's statutes: of, that is, the divine patterns that shape all of creation, heavenly and earthly. Second, the speaker here experiences life-bearing "quickening," a verb that in both Greek and Hebrew is used to talk of the fetus's movements in the mother's womb. The center becomes even more vividly significant in the light of the psalm's next line: "I am thine, O Lord, save me, for I have sought thy statutes (118:94)." The LXX Greek words for "I am thine" in this line are the very same LXX words that God uses to name Himself to Moses (Exod. 3:14–15), as well as the very same words Christ uses seven times in the Gospel of John to indicate His divine nature: ἐγώ εἰμι (*egō eimi*); while the tense of the Greek verb for "I have sought" is the aorist of vivid specificity.[4] The meaning is clear: having now passed through the psalm's chiastic heart, the speaker enters into the Holy Name (hence, the divine nature) of God Himself.

Equally, the line immediately *preceding* the chiastic heart in line 93 carries vivid light; line 92 reads: "If thy law had not been my meditation, I would have perished in my affliction." The word "affliction," here just before the psalm's chiastic heart, is in Greek ταπείνωσις (*tapeinōsis*).[5] Very often this Greek word is accurately translated "humility" and thus, in the Patristic Fathers, is always conceived as a goal of all ascetic discipline. Yet the word *tapeinōsis* is also just as often rightly rendered as "affliction"—clearly the correct translation in line 92 of Psalm 118. The line therefore suggests that an ascetic can perish in his humility—and indeed *will* perish—unless he is practicing psalmic meditation upon God's Law. Unless, that is, one is actively engaged in the spiritual warfare with Christ in the tomb on Holy Saturday—one may well perish from the very thing that alone gives resurrectional life with and in Christ: from the humility of the Cross.

Let us look now at how the generative alphabetic process of resurrection and re-incarnation begins in the Great Psalm.

The *Aleph*-Stanza

In *Aleph* (signifying unity, power, stability and continuity), the terms are established as the generic human becomes a personal "I" and the impersonal divinity becomes "Thou." The dance of their relationship, walking in the law of the Lord, begins. The pairs of lines exhibit a partnership of reciprocity, a sort of two-way call and response moving toward deification as man learns to keep God's commandments and statutes. When the relationship falters, depression begins, and shame follows, but the stanza ends in praise, straightness, personal commitment, with humble prayer that the dance may continue. —*Ed.*

The *Aleph*-stanza can be understood as the one perfect—and perfective—starting point of the vast Psalm 118:

1   Blessed are the blameless in the way,
    Who walk in the law of the Lord.
2   Blessed be those searching his testimonies,
    Who seek him with the whole heart.
3   For the workers of iniquity
    Have never walked in his ways.
4   Thou hast charged that thy commandments
    Be kept most diligently.
5   O that my ways be all directed
    To the keeping of thy statutes.
6   Then I shall not be ashamed
    When I behold all thy commandments.
7   I shall praise thee with upright heart
    As I learn thy righteous judgments.
8   I shall keep thy statutes,
    Do not utterly forsake me. (118:1–8)

The first and second lines begin with the same LXX word: *makarios* (the word that begins the entire Psalter), "blessed" (plural form), signifying that we truly begin only in triumph. Note that the poem begins in the plural, the first three words being μακάριοι οἱ ἄμωμοι (*makarioi hoi amōmoi*); the human "I" is introduced in line 5 only after the divine "thou" in line 4. The point of this sequence is abundantly clear. The human person is—*can be*—manifested only *after* the divine Person becomes known. And once the plurality of the (not-yet-knowing-God) human has achieved the unity of the (knowing-God) person, then the divine "thou" can draw closer to the human "I."

From this perspective, we can therefore gain new light on the "affliction" encountered and asymmetrically overcome at the poem's center in the *Lamed*-stanza: the affliction of depression. Depression, we can now say, is the state wherein the human person turns away from an achieved-by-grace unity with God and into the disintegrations of desire, a turning-away that then becomes *a total state of being*. This totality of state is crucial. As Fr. Pavel Florensky puts it: "[T]he state of being devoured by sorrow or unrest is not an accidental state of the heart. The heart is constant desire, a ceaseless self-devouring flame that burns in the breast . . . so that . . . [the] one who is deprived of life is called ἀκήριος [*akērios*], heartless. . . . The desire to become 'for oneself' causes the soul to split into two."[6] Here is the key: the desire to become "for oneself" is the hunger to destroy the relational reality of the human "I" and the divine "thou"; and consequently, this desire of the human "I" for complete autonomy immediately becomes that reality of self-devouring known in the psalms as *akēdia*, depression.

Blessedness, by contrast, is the state wherein the human person chooses to "walk in the law of the Lord" (118:1: chooses, that is, to cease (μά, *ma*) devouring one's own heart (κῆρ, *kēr*). This choosing is an act of embracing the reality of the salvific relation existing between the human "I" and the divine "thou." To "walk in the law" is an actual practice of moving on the earth, in one's life, in a psalmic way—and it begins to happen to you when you begin to "search deeply [God's] law." To "meditate" (in the psalmic sense) is to walk in the law.[7] As you choose to embrace this reality, you are in turn embraced by God in such a way that you achieve the full reality of your own personhood as the direct gift of God's being in love with you. This making of personhood is the fundamental action of Psalm 118.

In this light, then, we can understand more fully this line from Psalm 141: "When my spirit fainted within me, then thou knewest my paths, for on the way I was going they had hidden a snare for me" (141:3). And, as we have seen already (in chapter 6), the next line ends this way: "no one saw deeply my soul" (141:4). The total devastation of all relational reality is, indeed, the "hidden snare" known as depression. And the psalmist is here very clear: this affliction constitutes a spiritual—and not a psychological—condition: the spirit (πνεῦμα, *pneuma*) collapses into death while the soul, or psyche, becomes hidden within that dungeon of autonomy called *Sheol*, the Pit.

The contrasting condition of blessedness is then disclosed in line 2 of Psalm 118's first stanza: "Blessed be those searching his testimonies, / Who seek him with the whole heart" (118:2). To search God's testimonies—that is, to investigate with one's whole heart those witnesses, in actual human history, of the divinely generative statutes—this searching establishes both the assured means and the glorious end of loving God: the means are those acts of cognition called prayer while the end is direct and loving contact with Him. Such searching and seeking together define the spiritual action of walking "in the law of the Lord" (118:1). Those who refuse such contact are thereby "workers of iniquity," workers of *anomia* (ἀνομία), best understood as being *a-nomic*, wholly absent from the *nomos* (or law) of God. For to become *a-nomic* is to have entered fully into the disintegrative condition of *akērios* (ἀκήριος, heartlessness): it is, as Psalms say, to go down into the Pit.

In the fourth and fifth lines of stanza 1 (*Aleph*), the divine "thou" and the human "I" are introduced in the poem. Here is the divine "thou" as second-person singular: "Thou hast charged that thy commandments be kept most diligently" (118:4). The divine "thou" is a unified Person, one whose unity is grammatically assured, in both Hebrew and LXX Greek, by the emphatic placement of the second-person singular pronoun as the first word—an emphasis then doubled in both languages by the possessive pronoun in "thy commandments." In the next line, the human "I" is introduced through the possessive pronoun "my": "O that my ways be all directed / To the keeping of thy statutes" (118:5). And both MT Hebrew and LXX Greek establish this decisive reality of the human "I" by the tiniest of verbal strokes (μου [*mou*] in LXX Greek; suffixed ׳ [*yod*] in MT Hebrew): tiny but hypostatically powerful.

Once these two hypostases are firmly created in the poem, they then begin their beautiful and surprising relationship with each other: poetically beautiful and spiritually surprising. The beauty of the poetics arises from this sustained esthetic fact: in both Hebrew and Greek, the connection in each half is a connection that *explains*—that is, expands, defines, opens up, deepens—the other half. Consequently, once the first half of the esthetic unit occurs (in MT Hebrew, the unit is the single line in two parts; in LXX Greek, the unit is the couplet or—on occasion—the triplet): once the first half happens, there are countless possibilities for the matching second half. For example, line 5 begins: "O that my ways be all directed" (118:5a)—and thousands of possibilities immediately open for a fully satisfying concluding second half. Yet only one conclusion expands and defines and deepens the first half: "To the keeping of thy statutes" (118:5b). The poetic beauty thus consists in (first) opening these myriad possibilities, and then (second) closing all possibilities so as to find the one conclusion that fully satisfies by fully sustaining the relational reality between the divine "thou" and the human "I."

And here is the spiritual surprise in each esthetic unit: the closing of artistic possibilities becomes the opening of spiritual relationality. In this opening, the divine "thou" draws near to the human

"I," God becoming always vaster and more immediate at the same instant the speaker of Psalm 118 is always falling more deeply in love with Him.[8]

Keeping Thy Statutes   *Shared harmony AND distinctiveness*   שׁוֹר

And crucial to this falling-in-love-with-God is the verb used in lines 4 and 5: the verb "to keep." The best approach to this important psalmic verb (φυλάσσω, *phylassō*) is through a passage from Saint Dionysius the Areopagite's "The Divine Names."[9] In discussing the divine attribute called the "Power" of God, Saint Dionysius says that God simultaneously *causes* all power in the entire creation and *exceeds* all power: "His power is infinite because all power comes from Him and because He transcends all power," adding: "The benefits of this inexhaustible Power reach out to humans, to animals, to plants, and indeed to all of nature." This power, he continues, enables all things "to achieve mutual harmony and communion," at once endowing all things to achieve their ends and distinguishing all things "without any confusion or intermingling of their characteristics."[10]

Upon reaching this point, Saint Dionysius then begins an astonishing sequence of eleven parallel assertions about divine Power, a sequence that begins with the verb "to keep":

1. It *keeps* the stars of heaven in their shining and unchanging orders.
2. It *gives* them the power to be eternal.
3. It *distinguishes* the circlings of time from its procession and duly brings them back to base.
4. It *fashions* the unquenchability of fire and the ceaseless moisture of water.
5. It *keeps* the atmosphere fluid, founds the earth upon the

void, making its labors endlessly fruitful.

6. It *preserves* the shared harmony and mixture of the linked elements in their distinctiveness and their separateness.

7. It *reinforces* the bonds of soul and body.

8. It *stirs* the powers which give nourishment and growth to plants.

9. It *guides* the powers which keep each creature in being.

10. It *establishes* the unshakable remaining of the world.

11. To those made godlike, it *grants* the power for deification itself.

In assertions 1, 5, and 6, Saint Dionysius uses the LXX verb *phylassō*; in the other eight, he provides a kind of conceptual lexicon to enrich, deepen, and clarify the primary meanings of "to keep": *to give, to distinguish, to fashion, to reinforce, to stir, to guide, to establish*, and *to grant*. What this lexicon plainly accomplishes is the deepest enrichment.

Perhaps less apparently—but nevertheless most significantly—this conceptual lexicon also *clarifies*. The motion of clarification is best described as a movement wherein the relation between God and man becomes always unceasingly richer by becoming always more beautifully *reciprocal*. This beautiful reciprocity culminates, for Saint Dionysius, in "deification itself" (θέωσις αὐτή, *theosis autē*).[11] Key to this reciprocity is Dionysius's sixth assertion in this paragraph: "It preserves the shared harmony . . . of the linked elements . . . in their distinctiveness and their separateness." Note well: the harmony of elements is fully shared at the very moment the harmonized elements sustain full separateness. And this condition of shared harmony and sustained separateness is the condition of *theosis*. That is, God fully bestows His glory upon man and thereby fully creates harmony between Himself and man *at the same moment* man remains fully distinct from God: here is *theosis*. And to sustain this antinomic reality is, for man, *to keep* God's commandments and statutes: here is the meaning of Psalm 118's first stanza. To "keep [God's] statutes" is therefore to enter fully into this antinomy of shared harmony and sustained separateness.

Line 6 of the *Aleph*-stanza then deepens this reality: "Then I shall not be ashamed / When I behold all thy commandments."

Defeating Psalmic Shame

Psalmic shame or disgrace can be defined this way: it is the condition that results when direct participation in shared harmony and distinctiveness is broken—either by oneself or by another. To be ashamed is, in LXX Greek, the action whereby shame (noun: αἰσχύνη, *aischynē*) comes fully upon (*epi-*) the verb's speaker (verb: ἐπαισχύνομαι, *epaiskynomai*). In line 6, this action is fully negated in and through the action of *beholding* God's commandments: ἐπιβλέπω (*epiblepō*)—the condition of seeing (*blepō)* the reality of shared harmony and sustained distinctiveness: a seeing so complete in the psalmist that it becomes fullest participation in God.

And this shame-defeating action of beholding (*epiblepō*) helps best to explain the vexing (but not at all itself vexed) issue of the relationship between the LXX Greek text of the Psalms and the Masoretic Hebrew text. The history of the relationship is indeed vexing: the loss of the Ur-Hebrew text in AD 70, at the Roman destruction of Jerusalem, begins the problem. For when the Masoretic text of the Psalms is established in the ninth century AD, the Hebrew differs in numerous details from the (now vanished) Ur-Hebrew text.[12] The vexing consequence emerges: one of the two texts (either Masoretic Hebrew or LXX Greek) shames the other.

Yet—and this is the immense point—the issue is not at all vexed *in itself.* That is, *both* texts point to the lost Ur-text insofar as *both* give themselves to one another in a reciprocal action of kenotic love. As Masoretic Hebrew gives itself in self-emptying love to LXX Greek, it comes into the presence of the (now-lost) original Psalter; and as LXX Greek, in turn, gives itself to Masoretic Hebrew, it achieves a divine beauty of shape that flows directly from the divine original. This LXX beauty of shape is seen most vividly in the *syntax* of the Greek psalms: a syntax always more steadily Hebraic than Hellenic—a clear sign of kenotic love at work in the LXX. And note well: as the LXX text of the second century BC is giving itself wholly to the (historically vanished) Hebrew original, it is *thereby*—in the range and depth of its self-giving—opening the door for the Masoretic Hebrew to give *itself* to the very divine original that is otherwise entirely lost to it.

In this way, then, psalmic LXX Greek and psalmic Masoretic Hebrew *together believed* "all [God's] commandments"—and thereby *together defeat* all psalmic shame. *Keeping* God's statutes (118:5) is this action of beholding; and this action brings all three texts (LXX Greek, Masoretic Hebrew, and the lost Ur-Hebrew) into fully loving relationship—a relationship wherein the reciprocal gaze of both LXX and Masoretic texts at one another is deepened and fulfilled in and through the gaze with which the Ur-Hebrew text directly beholds God. That LXX Greek *needs* the Ur-Hebrew text—and that Masoretic Hebrew *needs* LXX Greek—does not lessen in the slightest the ontological distinctions of both LXX Greek and Masoretic Hebrew. Instead, their reciprocal need for one another so as to sustain their (differing but complementary) relationships with the Ur-Hebrew beautifully harmonizes all three at the very moment the differing needs of the LXX and Masoretic texts serve to sustain distinctiveness.

In Praising God's Straightness the Psalmic "I" Emerges

A great light emerges. And this is the light wherein the seventh line can be seen. The Masoretic and LXX for the verb in the line's first half—"I shall praise"—carry in both texts a significant variety of meanings: including "confess" (in the sacramental sense[13]); "make grateful acknowledgment"[14]; and "give thanks."[15] The point of this powerful verb is clear: to the extent we, those who pray and love the psalms, can enter into truly beholding the sacred relationships of kenotic love between the three texts (LXX, Masoretic, Hebrew original), then each of us can emerge as a uniquely distinct "I" in the action of praising the *righteousness* of God's judgments: the δικαιο-σύνη (*dikaiosynē*), the יֹשֶׁר (*yosher*), of His judgments. The LXX Greek and Masoretic Hebrew usages concur: the *righteousness of God's judgments* (118:7) literally means their *straightness*. Once the psalmist can behold this *straightness*—this clarity of the relational gaze—then his, the psalmist's, own heart becomes fully straightened into comparable clarity.

The *Beth*-Stanza

In *Beth*, the power of *Aleph* comes to dwell in a "house," the house of psalmic prayer, as study begins to become understanding; where keeping God's words—the very acts of His creation—and ceasing one's own *logismoi* become a choosing of divine straightness over human twistedness. The place this occurs is "in my whole heart." There one hides the teachings, not just to keep them safe but so as to learn to do them. In the heart we find Christ, and David's song becomes our own. The stanza ends in line 16 in a fore-echo of the very heart of the psalm: "I shall never forget thy words." The author speaks of this as *expectatio*: a "leaning-forward" toward (and into) the God who is always "drawing nearer." —*Ed.*

The *Beth*-stanza then carries forth from this point:

9   How shall a young man make straight his way?
     In the keeping of thy words.

10 I have sought thee with my whole heart,
     Let me not stray from thy commandments.

11 In my heart I have hidden thy teachings,
     That I might not sin against thee.

12 Blessed art thou, O Lord,
     Teach me thy statutes.

13 With my lips I have declared
     All the judgments of thy mouth.

14 I delight in the way of thy testimonies
     As much as in every kind of wealth.

15 I shall deeply ponder thy commandments,
     I shall comprehend thy ways.

16 I shall meditate in thy statutes,
     I shall never forget thy words.

In the first line of this stanza an important point instantly emerges: the "commandments" (*entolai*) of line 4—where the verb "to keep" first is used in Psalm 118—become, in line 9, the "words" (*logoi*) of God. Used nine times in the plural (*logoi*) and thirteen times in the singular (*logos*), the term signifies the divine voice in the eternally present action of generative speech, speech that creates the worlds of heaven and earth. To keep God's *logoi* is to cease one's own *logismoi*,[16] choosing divine straightness over human twistedness.

It is also worth reflecting at this point on the significance of the first two Hebrew letters *in themselves* as archaic visual signs: א (*'aleph*) and ב (*beth*). The shape of *aleph* depicts an "ox,"[17] and indicates "unity" and "power, stability, and continuity."[18] As a visual sign, then, the *Aleph*-stanza yokes together all the powers of the poem and begins its progress.

Beth depicts a "house,"[19] and represents "the mouth of man, his dwelling, his interior."[20] The Talmud adds further meanings to these two letters: *aleph* represents the action of "studying" God's holy word while *beth* is the sustained action of "understanding"— that is, what results from *aleph*. *Aleph-beth* therefore constellate clear spiritual steps in a sequence moving always toward theosis. If you pray the Psalter continuously for years, you may (*just*) begin to glimpse something of the way the visual signs of the Hebrew letters in Psalm 118 are always becoming—in the blessed hands of the LXX poet/translator—the way into theosis in Christ.

If the *Aleph*-stanza describes the poem's guiding power, then *Beth* reveals the place where this power works in us: "in my whole heart" (118:10: ἐν ὅλῃ καρδίᾳ μου, *en holē kardia mou*). Line 2 first discloses this key psalmic understanding; and line 7 deepens it: the heart *in its wholeness, upright*. Saint John Climacus, in *The Ladder of Divine Ascent*, significantly refers to line 145 of Psalm 118—"I cried with my whole heart: / Hear me, O Lord, / I shall search deeply thy statutes"—adding, "that is, with body, soul, and spirit. For where the two last are gathered together, there God is in the midst of them."[21] Using this reference of Saint John's, the Glossary to the *Philokalia* further says: "'Heart' has thus an all-embracing significance: 'prayer of the heart' means prayer not just of the emotions and affections, but of the whole person, including the body."[22]

And, in *Beth*, we are given in line 11 the *way* this wholeness is sustained. To hide (LXX κρύπτω, *kryptō*) the teachings (LXX λόγια, *logia*) in one's heart is, first, to make them inaccessible to worldly assault and degradation; and, second, to plant them deeply in one's being in and as the very depth of one's personhood. This means (of course) the act of memorizing—of "knowing by heart." But more: it also means that God's *logion* (teaching)—His articulated words to us—is taken so deeply within us that we cannot merely *say* them: we must *do* them, the way our heart does all life in us. As I said in my lexicon (in chapter 11), the teachings are the expressed voice of God, incarnate and audible to human comprehension—that is, they are the speaking voice of Christ Incarnate. To hide this in the heart thus means that the source—the motive power, the force and pressure that makes things visibly occur—this source is out of our sight, at the very depth of the heart: better, in and as the very depth of the heart. If Christ's voice is planted deeply in our heart, it makes divinely straight every word of our lips, tongue, and mouth.

⟿

A few mornings ago (today is 11.26.05) I had a dream. I am part of a seminar on poetry, in which we are discerning the perfect— and perfective—poetry of an (unknown) contemporary master poet. The poetry's perfection consisted in its dynamic blending (without, in the least, confusing) of such disparate elements as massive solidity and lightness of touch; slenderness of movement and immensity of significance; finished shape and ongoing shaping. William Matthews is leading the seminar.[23] I awoke with the keenest certainty that we were talking about the Psalms. And that the poet was David himself, as the always-contemporary Master of Poetry.

⟿

The "house" wherein we dwell is therefore the very heart of David. And as we pray Psalm 118, David's heart becomes one with ours: insofar, that is, as we succeed in hiding God's teachings in our whole heart in our seeking His commandments.

Expectation

The sequence that ends, in line 16, with "I shall never forget thy words" points, in this final verb, to the poem's final line, 176: "I have never forgotten thy commandments." And both, in turn, point to—and are included in—the poem's verbal center; that is, point to and are included in the midpoint established in and by Orthodox Christendom (l. 93: "I shall never forget thy statutes, / In them thou hast quickened me to life."). And the noun in line 116b—"Do not disgrace my expectation"—brings to the poem's center the essential reality of all psalmic prayer: expectation (LXX Greek προσδοκία, *prosdokia*; MT שֵׂבֶר, *sever*). *Prosdokia* occurs often in the Fathers to signify the expectation of Christ by the Jews and the Greeks,[24] while *sever* in the MT Psalms carries much the same significance. Saint Jerome's Latin translation of the Greek sheds light on both the LXX text and the MT: *expectatio*—a key noun best defined as the always "leaning-forward" toward (and *into*) the God who is always "drawing nearer," the God who is always loving deeper and still deeper.

An Exhausted Awakeness of Spirit (Psalm 118:15)

A life in Psalms, for me, includes this experience: the "non-tiring tiredness" I experienced in the months of translating nonstop the whole LXX Psalter. In those long hours of every long day, I was deeply tired—but, strangely, I was not at all tired. Result: a kind of *tinyness of spirit*, a *smallness* of selfhood, that is, a poverty of spirit. Here is the key to a life, *a whole life*, in Psalms.

Here, too, is a key to Psalm 118's crucial verb: ἀδολεσχέω, *adolescheō* (Ps. 118:15). To "deeply ponder" God's commandments is to enter precisely this exhausted awakeness of spirit, this tinyness of poverty in the vast richness of God's presence. *Siah* (שִׂיחַ) in MT

Hebrew, the LXX verb is used five times in Psalm 118; and the first and fifth occurrences have, as their direct object, "commandments" (*entolai*), while the middle three have "statutes" (*dikaiōmata*) as the object of the verb "to ponder." We recall our lexicon of the nine words (in the previous chapter) defining "commandments" as the divinely created actions of our self-emptying love for the other, that is, a joyous blessing and a heavy burden: cf. Hebrew מִצְוָה (*mitzva*), and "statutes" as the divinely shaped patterns of the entire creation. To ponder the commandments of God is therefore to enter into the poverty of spirit that is (Christ tells us) the Kingdom of Heaven (Matt. 5:3): where we must dwell, or die.

To be broken, and in poverty, is to be at the starting point of dwelling in the house of psalmic prayer: broken by depression, poor in spirit, low in mind, heart, and soul. Here is the way of "making straight" one's way. The heart of all Scripture is the Psalms; and the heart of the Psalms is LXX Psalm 118. There is no other text that is—could ever possibly be—this heart that is LXX Psalm 118.

Such are some of the dynamics of the *Beth*-stanza.

The *Gimel*-Stanza

In *Gimel* (signifying boomerang/reversal, and camel/endurance), the psalmist seeks to see the wonders of God's law, to have the veil removed from his eyes so as to see as God sees the divine life that is streaming from Psalms and enlivening us. He seeks to have his desire transfigured so as to long for God's judgments, to be the homeless sojourner who knows the true home in heaven. The stanza then abruptly reverses, boomerangs, into God's angry rebuke of those who reject His gifts, and the psalmist prays to be one of the merciful ones, to escape the twisting and contempt. The author says that we must keep on carrying the burdens of ascetic practice and psalmic prayer in the fierce deserts of earthly contempt. He draws on a meaning of the word for "ponder" as entering into a genuine loving of the other—a loving fully matched by love that is approaching you—to conclude that the Gimel-stanza is establishing the dire context of all psalmic prayer—the toxicity of contempt—at the very instant it is overcoming all the toxins in the act of mutual loving. —*Ed.*

17 Give thy servant this reward:
    That I shall live and keep thy words.

18 Take away the veil from my eyes
    That I may see the wonders in thy law.

19 I am a stranger on the earth,
    Hide not thy commandments from me.

20 My soul has always longed to desire
    Thy judgments at every moment.

21 Thou didst rebuke the proudly arrogant,
    Cursed be they that reject thy commandments.

22 Take from me reproach and contempt
    For I have sought thy testimonies.

23 For princes sat and spoke against me,
    But thy servant pondered on thy statutes.

24 Thy testimonies are my meditation,
    Thy statutes my counselors.

Lyric Narrative and Lyric Intensification

The ancient symbology of this stanza's dominant Hebrew letter offers an interesting and significant variation: one meaning for ג (*gimel*) is the boomerang, the other is the camel. To approach an understanding of this variation—and of this stanza—we need to recall that Hebrew psalmic poetics may be said to employ two contrastive yet complementary phenomena: one, a lyric narrative in which unceasing terror and panic are followed by sudden reversals into highest joys; and two, a lyric intensification in which all assertions and images are constantly deepened. The skill with which the psalmic poet will employ intensification to advance the line of narrative moments while lyrically deepening every such moment: this poetic skill gives the Hebrew psalms their abiding aliveness. And it is this skill that the LXX psalmic poet perfectly translates—better: *transfigures*—at every moment.

For what the *Gimel*-stanza introduces into LXX Psalm 118 is dynamic transfiguration of Hebrew poetics into LXX spiritual experience. To approach this transfiguration I shall briefly sketch a recent experience of my own: Once, just before Nativity, midweek, I was walking the mile of road to our house and this image came to me: a square, maybe two feet in size, of beautiful wood, some half an inch in thickness—very beautiful, light-toned wood; and one side of the wooden square was covered tightly with a khaki-colored cloth remarkable for being neither rough nor smooth but *durably beautiful*. And from this square of clothed wood—if you touched anywhere on the cloth—came a heavenly light radiating everywhere from its surface and extending out maybe two or so inches on all four sides; and with this light also came forth a purest hum of heavenly sound. And I knew that I was beholding an image of the Psalms, that each and every psalm *is* this piece of clothed and illumined wood of durable beauty; and that each psalm possesses a perfectly unique light and tone at the same instant it is as perfectly beautiful as every other psalm.

I saw all this in a moment on my winter's walk—and then, a few moments later, I saw still more: that each name of the thousand or two names on my prayer list of those for whom I pray (living and deceased) is also held in and by this same image of clothed and beautiful wood, for each name is a whole life in Christ our magnificent Lord and Master.

A key to the *Gimel*-stanza can be found in line 18b: "That I may

✱ An ephod?

see the wonders [θαυμάσια, *thaumasia*] in thy law." For the LXX word *thauma* derives from the same root as the Sanskrit word *stabh*, meaning "to stiffen."[25] And C. S. Lewis brilliantly reminds us that the biblical Hebrew word אֱמֶת (*'emeth*; meaning "truth") "is that which does not deceive, does not 'give,' does not change, that which holds water."[26] Psalmic truth is that which—like my illumined and clothed square of wood—is stiffened wondrously so as never to give way. To use George Herbert's remarkable image in his poem "Vertue," wonder-making psalmic truth is like the virtuous soul:

> Onely a sweet and vertuous soul,
> Like season'd timber, never gives;
> But though the whole world turn to coal,
>   Then chiefly lives.

And to behold this wondrous truth is, says line 18b of the *Gimel*-stanza, to *katanoeticize*: to descend (*kata*) all the way into the *nous* wherein the transfigurative action is ceaselessly occurring, that action whereby the reality of our earthly sight is being filled—better: being *fulfilled*—by the divine reality of God's life-giving seeing of His creation. The veil is taken from one's eyes in this action; literally, in LXX Greek, one's eyes are "apocalypsed." And in this apocalypse, one then sees the essential and wondrous truth of all the psalms: divine life is streaming from them and enlivening us.

Here, then, is the "reward," *doulos* (LXX δοῦλος), given by God in this stanza: actually to live unceasingly in and through the *keeping* of God's life-creating words (*logoi*). As we noted above (*Aleph*-stanza), to *keep*—following Saint Dionysius—is to sustain shared harmony in such a way as to create deepest communion between God and man while at the same moment fully distinguishing them. As a result, all our human desire becomes transfigured into longing for God's judgments (Ps. 118:20): longing, that is, for the apocalypse wherein we shall behold all our earthly conflicts becoming fully resolved in God (see κρίματα, *krimata*, God's divine resolutions of human conflicts; chapter 11).

In this light, line 19 of the *Gimel*-stanza takes on vivid significance. To be an earthly stranger is to be the homeless sojourner who, in and by his homelessness here on earth, knows the true home there in heaven. Thus, to be homeless is to have the commandments not hidden from one (ἀποκρύπτω, *apokryptō*) but revealed (ἀποκαλύπτω, *apokalyptō*): a LXX "rhyme" that perfectly captures the Hebrew alphabetic rhyme between the imperatival form of the verb "to open," גַּל (*gal*), and the noun "sojourner," גֵּר (*ger*).

Rebuke, Contempt, and the "Reconciling Exchange"

Then line 21 opens the door into a new subject in the poem. What is new here is God's angry rebuke of those of us who reject His apocalyptic gifts to us. The point of the line is vividly clear: in the face of our arrogant rebuke of Him, God becomes to us a rebuker. This boomerang effect is made abundantly plain in this passage from Psalm 17:25–26:

25 With the merciful thou wilt be merciful, with the innocent man thou wilt be innocent;

26 With the elect thou wilt be elect, with the twisted thou wilt be twisted.

The psalmist in the *Gimel*-stanza then prays that he shall be himself merciful, innocent, and elect: and thereby escape becoming twisted in and by the central scourge of all psalmic spiritual life on earth: contempt (ὄνειδος, *oneidos*). For in becoming the object of contempt, one thereby becomes contemptible: "I have become their contempt" (Ps. 108:25).

The corrosive action of contempt is crucially disclosed at the conclusion of Psalm 88:

50 Remember the contempt, O Lord, I suffered in my
    heart, contempt all thy servants suffer from all the
    nations,
51 Contempt, O Lord, thine enemies have used to darken
    that reconciling exchange given by thy Christ.

The "reconciling exchange" (τὸ ἀντάλλαγμα, *to antallagma*[27]) is, in Orthodox terms, the experience of theosis: the deification of the human person that can take place through deepening into psalmic prayer so fully that one's earthly mind and heart begin to move solely in psalmic measures. This experience of deification is the goal of all psalmic prayer, and the constant destroyer of this experience is contempt: from others, in oneself—and, most terribly, *as oneself*: "I have become their contempt" (Ps. 108:25).[28]

The significance of the camel to this stanza thus emerges: to keep on carrying the burdens of ascetic practice and psalmic prayer in the fierce deserts of earthly contempt, as in line 23. The stream of toxic contempt can never be simply erased by psalmic prayer; but its hateful toxicity can be overcome—and the LXX verb is crucial here—through the act of "pondering": *adolescheō*.[29] Yielding our word "adolescent," the Greek LXX verb is best understood as the soul's act of sudden deepening in prayer. Lampe cites Origen's wonderful reference to Genesis 24:53, where Isaac approaches the "well of vision" at which his servant had beheld Rebecca—and had known instantly that she was to become the true wife of his master. Isaac goes forth at eventide to *adoleschein*, and Rebecca beholds Isaac—and knows him to be her true husband. To ponder, then, is for you to enter into a genuine loving of the other, a loving fully matched by the love that is approaching you. Here, in this depth of mutual loving, all the toxicity of contempt is overcome. And here, too, the *Gimel*-stanza articulates the right relation to God's statutes and testimonies. God's statutes—His life-generating patterns of the creation—become one's "counselors": in the LXX word they become one's *symboliai* (συμβουλίαι)—a word that Origen again beautifully understands as "indwelling spirit."[30] The love with which God so loves us that He gives it to dwell within us not only matches but magnificently exceeds our love for Him in the Psalms. The *Gimel*-stanza thus establishes the dire context of all psalmic prayer—the toxicity of contempt—at the very instant it overcomes all the toxins in the act of mutual loving.[31]

The *Daleth*-Stanza

Daleth (meaning "door") opens the door to the depths of our toxic depression and, in the same instant, the heights of God's healing and salvific love. The author says the instantaneity is crucial, for it means that, at the very instant the toxicity begins in us, God is opening for us the doorway (*daleth*) into that humble love called, in line 30, "the way of truth," which is God's eternal memory of me and mine of God: "I have never forgotten thy judgments." —*Ed.*

25 My soul lies prostrate on the earth,
    Quicken me according to thy word.
26 I declared my ways, and thou didst hear me,
    Teach me thy statutes.
27 Make me comprehend the way of thy statutes,
    I shall ponder thy wondrous works.
28 My soul has fainted from depression,
    Strengthen me with thy words.
29 Put the unjust way far from me,
    With thy law have mercy on me.

30 I have chosen the way of truth,
    I have never forgotten thy judgments.
31 I have clung to thy testimonies,
    O Lord, put me not to shame.
32 I have run the way of thy commandments
    When thou didst enlarge my heart.

The *Daleth*-stanza then opens the door into the depths of our toxicity and the heights of God's salvific love. Line 28 contains the only usage of the noun *akēdia* (depression) not only in Psalm 118 but in the entire Psalter—hence, its signal importance: "My soul has fainted from depression." The soul's depressive fainting is then fully healed, in line 28, in and by God's "strengthening." Saint Ignatius of Antioch uses this very verb "to strengthen" (βεβαιόω, *bebaioō*) in its adjectival form, βέβαιος, to describe the action of the eucharist upon the believer,[32] thereby revealing the incarnational power of God's love: a power that heals all depression. Thus, the two bracket experiences of the stanza—lying prostrate on earth (l. 25) and the heart's expanding capacity to love (l. 32)—are joined in the crucial contrast between human depressive weakness and divine psychic strength.

The Doorway into Toxic Depression Opens to God's Mercy and Love

Line 29 then opens yet another door in the psalm. The uniquely Septuagintal "rhyme" of ἀδικία (*adikia*, unjust) with ἀκηδία (*akēdia*, depression)—a rhyme achieved by reversing the two consonants of the two words—points to the significance: depression is an act in injustice. Fr. Adrian of New Diveyevo says: "Depression is an invitation to the devil."[33] For justice consists in holding fast to the "straightness of way" given by God, while injustice arises when the straight way is abandoned: an abandonment that is, first of all, and always ruthlessly, unmerciful. Depression causes psychic collapse ("My soul lies prostrate on the earth," l. 25) because the violence of ruthlessness is, first of all and deeply, self-hatred: as another psalm puts it, "he who loves violence hates his own soul" (Ps. 10:5).

The ancient symbolic meaning of the Hebrew letter ד (*daleth*) is "door." In fact, *daleth* means "door" in biblical Hebrew. We may thus say that the power of *aleph* takes up dwelling in *beth* so that the way of psalmic prayer can, in *gimel*, transform Hebrew poetics into that LXX spiritual experience best registered in the word *thaumasia* (wondrous deeds; see above), a transformation best understood in and as the double significance of complete reversal (the boomerang) and patient endurance (the camel). Then, in *daleth*, this transformation becomes the doorway into toxic depression and—in the same instant—into God's mercy and love. This instantaneity of the two ways (toxic human depression and God's redemptive love) is crucial: for it means that, at the very instant the toxicity begins in us, God is opening for us the doorway (*daleth*) into that humble love called, in line 30, "the way of truth" (ὁδὸς ἀληθείας, *hodos alētheias* in LXX Greek). The psalmic poet is here revealing that the way of humility is the overcoming of all our spiritual toxins, especially the toxin of depression. This way of truth—this way of *a–lētheia* (ἀ-λήθεία)—is the way of not-forgetting (ἀ-λήθη, *a–lēthē*): hence, to choose this way of truth is to enter into what Orthodoxy knows as Memory Eternal ("I have never forgotten thy judgments," 118:30b).

Fr. Pavel Florensky explains this crucial connection in this way: "Truth-*Aletheia* is Unforgetfulness, that which is not licked off by the streams of Time; it is Solid Ground not eaten away by corrosive Death; it is Essence most essential in which there is no Non-being at all."[34] He also beautifully connects truth and memory eternal to the moment when the Orthodox priest, preparing the eucharist before the start of the Liturgy, takes fragments from the prosphora breads given him by the believers, saying at each fragment: "Remember, O Lord, the servant/handmaiden [name] here commemorated, granting [him/her] Your peace." The point is vividly clear: to be remembered by God *by your unique name* is to come forever into that fullness of being wherein is nothing corruptible. Florensky adds: eternal memory "means both God's 'eternal memory' of me and my 'eternal memory' of God."[35] Here is the way of all truth.

Then line 31 opens yet another door. The verb "to cling" is the same verb used in line 25—there translated "to lie prostrate"—in both MT Hebrew and LXX Greek: דָּבֵק (*daveq*) in Hebrew, κολλᾶν (*kollan*) in Greek. This usage confirms a crucial meaning in the *Daleth*-stanza: the experience of depression opens into the experience of redemptive love. It is *not*, however, that depression *contains* in some fashion God's redemptive love; rather, the object to which one is cleaving—the earth in line 25 and God's testimonies in line 31—transfigures the toxicity into mercy.

The final line of the *Daleth*-stanza illumines the whole stanza. The concluding verb πλατύνω (*platynō*, to open, enlarge) in LXX Greek, רָחַב (*rahav*) in MT Hebrew—is powerfully significant: for the verb asserts that God directly acts upon our hearts to make us more fully loving. Psalm 4 puts it this way: "thou hast opened my heart when I was in distress" (Ps. 4:1); literally, "Thou hast enlarged me." These two psalmic images of this verb—in Psalm 4 and Psalm 118—together suggest the deification that (in the words of Saint Gregory of Nyssa) King David experienced as the singer of psalms: "the music which is in us [is] in accord with nature" and also "is a cure of nature."[36] To have one's heart become *larger*, Saint Gregory implies, is to have one's natural, divinely given music make direct and sustained concord with (in Saint Gregory's words) that "primal,

archetypal, true music" that governs God's actions in His creating
and sustaining all things.

Psalm 18:23 beautifully illumines this moment of the
Daleth-stanza:

> Day unto day utters speech and night unto night reveals
> knowledge.
> There is no speech nor language where their voice is not
> heard.

The "concord of all creation with itself," says Gregory, is "composed
through opposites," the primary opposition being perfect stillness
and unceasing movement. This concord of stillness and movement
produces, Gregory continues, "a blended and marvellous hymn of
the power which controls the universe."[37] Each day is uniquely itself
at the very instant it is speaking to all other days; each person's
speech is, at every instant, unrepeatably itself—and at one with the
divine voice of the "primal, archetypal, true music"[38] wherein day
and night—forever distinct—nevertheless speak together to *reveal
knowledge*: such is the action of that musical concord arising when
God directly enlarges one's heart.

Psalm 18 is also crucial to Psalm 118 because it, too, sings praises
to multiple words for God's act of speaking: law (LXX *nomos*), testimony (LXX *martyria*), statutes (LXX *dikaiōmata*), commandments
(LXX *entolai*), and judgments (LXX *krimata*). Indeed the whole of
Psalm 118 may be seen as a symphonic elaboration of these three
lines in Psalm 18:

> 7 The law of the Lord is perfect, converting the soul; the
>   testimony of the Lord is sure, making children wise,
> 8 The statutes of the Lord are right, rejoicing the heart;
>   the commandment of the Lord is pure, enlightening
>   the eyes,

9   The fear of the Lord is clean, enduring forever;
the judgments of the Lord are true and righteous
altogether.

Saint Gregory of Nyssa says this:

> Whence the narrative attributes the accomplishment of this
> divine music to David. Once when he came to Saul, who
> was frenzied and out of his right mind, he healed him by
> soothing his passions with song [1 Kings 16:23 LXX], so
> that Saul's understanding returned to him again in accor-
> dance with nature. The goal, then, of the symbolism of the
> singing is clear from these words. It recommends that we
> achieve the subjugation of those passions which arise in us
> in various ways from the circumstances of life.[39]

What coheres these five words—and what also coheres the nine
words in Psalm 118—is what Saint Gregory of Nyssa calls "musical harmony"[40]: the five (Ps. 18) and the nine (Ps. 118) strike the
same *tone*.

When I visited Mount Athos at the end of 2003, I asked an
American monk at Vatopaidi Monastery, "What should a pilgrim to
Mount Athos take back to the world?" Fr. Matthew thought a long
minute. "Take back the *tone* of Mt. Athos, the *savor*." The words Fr.
Matthew used carry great significance. And they returned to me
a few days ago when, serving as subdeacon at the Liturgy to Saint
Mark of Ephesus on January 19, 2006, as I stood at the altar, the air
and light and sound of the service seemed to me entirely Athonite:
a calm January morning sunlight, air illumined by the sounds of
the few singers and fewer faithful, the priest—Fr. Mark—celebrat-
ing both his name day and the day of his ordination twenty-one
years ago: the music and air, in other words, of Memory Eternal—here is the tone of Mount Athos. And in this tone, the soul is

transfigured, children achieve wisdom, the heart rejoices, the eyes are enlightened—and you then begin to see the way into psalmic theosis. Psalm 18 concludes: "The words of my mouth and my heart's meditation will be continually pleasing in thy presence, O Lord, my strength and my redeemer" (18:14).

"Continually": the LXX is διὰ παντός (*dia pantos*), "throughout everything," while "in thy presence" is literally, in the LXX, "before thee." Here is theosis in the Psalms, the experience of being cleansed of immense wickedness ("I shall be cleansed of great transgression," Ps. 18:13), both one's own sins and those of others, the experience wherein one's words become entirely shaped by God's words and one's heart begins to move solely in the rhythmic measures of God's love. Such is the Athonite tone and savor.

And such is the doorway that the *Daleth*-stanza opens in Psalm 118.

The *He*-Stanza

The *He*-stanza is a window that opens to an essential psalmic experience: fear of God. The author draws on a George Eliot novel for an understanding of this fear as a form of wisdom that acts as a safeguard, "like quickness of hearing," "a faculty, like vision," and is, in this sense, very like love of God, producing both humility and joy. He sees in this "an entire transfiguration of all human desirings," expressed in line 36. He discusses *pleonexia*: endless desiring, the Adamic fall, the uprooting from the heart of all the divinely implanted patternings. *Pleonexia* is an emotional turning away from the historical dimension where death and resurrection occur, for the pressures of historical actualities are what give concrete form to the statutes. And he discusses contempt: the central toxin of all spiritual life on earth. The transfiguration offered in this stanza offers release from contempt-generated dread, opening a window to see God's judgments as gracious and not terrifying. Line 40 speaks of "quickening in righteousness"; the psalmist's desire has become salvific. With this clarification of the psalmist's experience of prayer as movement toward God, the window opens to the *Waw*-stanza. —*Ed.*

33 Give me as law, O Lord, the way of thy statutes,
     And I shall seek it out always.

34 Give me wisdom to search deeply thy law,
     I shall keep it with my whole heart.

35 Guide me on the path of thy commandments
     For I have desired this.

36 Incline my heart to thy testimonies
     And not to endless desirings.

37 Turn away my eyes from empty things,
     Quicken me to live in thy way.

38 Establish thy teaching in thy servant
     That I may be rooted in fear of thee.

39 Take away my scorn, which I dread,
     For thy judgments are gracious.

40 Behold, I have longed for thy commandments,
     Quicken me in thy righteousness.

If *Daleth* opens doors (and it does), then the fifth stanza, ה (*He*), opens a window through which flows an experience essential to the whole psalm. The LXX Greek is here (in l. 38) extremely stark so as to fit the starkness of the Hebrew: στῆσον τῷ δούλῳ σου τὸ λόγιον σου εἰς τὸν φόβον σου (*stēson tō doulō sou to logion sou eis ton phobon sou*; literally, "make to stand . . . the teaching . . . into fear of thee"). The LXX poet here employs the usual classical verb ἵστημι (*histēmi*) to achieve an unusual significance, a significance best registered by using two English verbs for the Greek verb: "establish" and "be rooted in."[41] For—and here is the significance—the LXX verb sees God's acting upon the psalmist ("establish") as *the very same action* whereby the psalmist is becoming "rooted in fear of" God.

Fear of God

What is this psalmic "fear of God"? Of course, this question applies not only to the *He*-stanza of Psalm 118 but also to the entire Psalter—indeed, to all of Scripture, to both Old and New Testaments. Fear of God: why does the psalmist pray so fervently for it?

The title character in George Eliot's magnificent novel *Daniel Deronda* says this at one point to a young woman who has sought his counsel:

> Turn your fear into a safeguard. Keep your dread fixed on the idea of increasing that remorse which is so bitter to you. Fixed meditation may do a great deal towards defining our longing or dread. We are not always in a state of strong emotion, and when we are calm we can use our memories and gradually change the bias of our fear, as we do our tastes. Take your fear as a safeguard. It is like quickness of hearing. It may make consequences passionately present to you. Try to take hold of your sensibility, and use it as if it were a faculty, like vision.[42]

This astonishing speech sheds considerable light on our important question. Our earthly fears are like sharpness of eye and ear: we behold terrifying consequences everywhere—and are plunged into "a state of strong emotion." But (Deronda is saying) we can "gradually change the bias [or directionality] of our fear" and, instead, fix the fears on "increasing that remorse which is so bitter to you"—that is, upon increasing the action of repentance, of μετάνοια (*metanoia*), that 180-degree change of our total being. In the deliberately chosen calmness of such meditation, we can change the whole direction of our fears from earth to heaven—and all earthly fears fall completely away: "Though an army come round about me, my heart shall not fear" (Ps. 26:3a); "On God I have set my hope, I will not be afraid what man can do to me" (Ps. 55:11); "The Lord is my helper, I shall never fear what someone could do to me" (Ps. 117:6). Fear then becomes what Deronda calls it: "a safeguard," divinely given protective armor. And this God-focused fear can then become a faculty, "like vision," a faculty with which one can see and hear—and smell and touch and taste—more fully, deeply, and accurately the reality of God.

Towards the conclusion of *Ecclesiastes*, a verse appears that is here pertinent: "The words of the wise are as goads, and as nails firmly planted, which have been given by one shepherd by agreement" (Eccl. 12:11 LXX). A midrashic commentary reflects on this text:

> Note that the text does not say "as nails set," but as planted. Why? In describing the words of the wise as nails, Scripture is pointing up the fact that since a nail has a head it is easy to pull out. Hence the phrase *as nails planted* implies the following: The roots of a tree deep-planted are hard to pull out, yet they do not have strength like the strength of iron; a nail of iron, on the other hand, though it has strength [can easily be pulled out]. Therefore both the strength of iron and the tenacity of a tree's deep-planted roots are given to the words of Torah.[43]

The midrash then adds another comment: "As the roots of a tree spread in all directions, so words of Torah enter and spread throughout the whole body of a man."[44]

When the psalmist prays to God that He establish His teaching so that he may become "rooted in fear of thee," we may rightly understand the midrashic emphasis on the roots of the tree of Scripture. Hence, in line 34 of the *He*-stanza, the psalmist prays: "Give me wisdom to search deeply thy law" (Ps. 118:34a). These are two LXX verbs that variously translate two MT verbs: LXX Greek ἐξε-ρευνάω (*exereunaō*) and ἐκζητέω (*ekzēteō*) for MT Hebrew נָצַר (*natsar*) and (*darash*).[45] The two Greek verbs mean approximately what the two Hebrew ones signify: to seek, to search deeply, to preserve and guard closely—and this is the meaning plainly at work in line 34 of the *He*-stanza. As such, fear of God is a form of wisdom that (in Daniel Deronda's important phrases) acts as a safeguard, "like quickness of hearing," "a faculty, like vision." And in this sense, fear of God is very like love of God.

Saint Isaac the Syrian has an extraordinary passage in Homily 51 that sheds light on the point:

> There is a humility that comes from fear of God, and there is a humility that comes from the fervent love of God. One man is humbled because of his fear of God; another is humbled because of his joy. The man humbled from fear of God is possessed of modesty in his members, a right ordering of his senses, and a heart contrite at all times. But the man humbled because of joy is possessed of great exuberance and an open and insuppressible heart.[46]

Clearly, for all the crucial differences between them, the two fears are one humility; and it does no violence to Abba Isaac to understand that the "contrite heart" is—or must inevitably become—also the "open and insuppressible heart"—and vice versa: open exuberance must join measured contrition in the act of humble love. The window that the *He*-stanza opens, then, provides an entire transfiguration of all human desirings. And this transfiguration of desire is expressed in line 36: "Incline my heart to thy testimonies / And not to endless desirings" (Ps. 118:36).

Pleonexia: Endless Desiring

The phrase "endless desirings" translates the LXX Greek word *pleonexia* (πλεονεξία)—the only use of this word in the entire LXX Psalter. There is, however, a usage in the *Wisdom of Solomon* that sheds some light on line 36 of the *He*-stanza. In Chapter 10, the narrator tells us that Wisdom "kept guard [διεφύλαξεν, *diephylaxen*] over the first father [Adam] of the human race; she saved him after his fall, and gave him the strength [ἰσχύν, *ischyn*] to master [κρατῆσαι, *kratēsai*] all things" (Wisdom 10:1). The narrative continues in chapter 10, recounting Wisdom's decisive presence throughout patriarchal history, saying this about Jacob: "When men in their rapacity [*pleonexia*] tried to exploit him [i.e., Jacob], she [Wisdom] stood by him and made him rich" (Wisdom 10:11); above all, teaching Jacob "that godliness is the greatest power of all" (ὅτι παντός δυνατωτέρα ἐστὶν εὐσέβεια, *hoti pantos dynatōtera estin eusebeia*, Wisdom 10:12).

The strength to master all things—especially the mastery over *pleonexia*—is a power arising solely from godliness. And godliness, in the *He*-stanza, occurs solely when all desire becomes an inclination of the heart to be rooted in God's testimonies (*martyriai*)—in, that is, the actual human historical witnesses to the divinely incarnate statutes. Why? Why are the ways of the statutes, *in historical actualities*, the focus of the heart that will open the way out of *pleonexia*? The answer is that the pressures of historical actualities give concrete form to the statutes. For history (as *martyria*) is the dimension where death/resurrection occurs: the sole and full and salvific dimension. And the key to the statutes—to those patterns of God's dynamic creativity—is precisely in Christ's death and resurrection.

Thus, *pleonexia* is the emotional turning-away from this dimension: and *pleonexia* is precisely the Adamic fall; hence, the testimonies are precisely the Adamic resurrection of Holy Saturday Matins. In this Adamic resurrection, the fifth stanza (*He*) is

By stepping into antinomy (both-at-once)
one may experience dispassion

where emotional life is given its perfect and perfective shape: the way (*hodos*) of thy statutes (*dikaiōmata sou*). Note, too, the verb in line 33, νομοθέτησόν με, Κύριε, *nomothetēson me, Kyrie*; literally: "statutes-implant-in-me," "em-place in me thy statutes, Lord." *Pleonexia* therefore uproots from one's heart all the divinely implanted patternings in—and of—the heart.

The transfiguration of human desire, then, is (following Abba Isaac) the psalmic experience wherein one's heart becomes, at one and the same instant, both fully contrite and endlessly exuberant. And all your fear of God then becomes love of God: just as, reciprocally, all love becomes fear.

Then line 39 opens the window still further. As noted both above and below, scorn, or contempt (ὄνειδος, *oneidos*), is the central toxin of all spiritual life on earth: both the scorn one is dealt by others and the scorn one deals out to others. Either way, psalmic scorn produces the act of *dreading*—and the LXX poet uses a remarkable Greek verb, one used in line 39 for the only time in Scripture (with one crucial exception): ὑποπτεύω (*hypopteuō*), a verb that Lust defines as "to view with apprehension or anxiety."[47] This dreading that arises from scorn is the *pleonexia* that is at once endless and empty, and this dread can never have any content because it is always rooted in the haunting fear of another person's power—and never in the salvific fear of God.

Release from Dread and Quickening into God

The one other use of *hypopteuō* in Scripture occurs in *Ecclesiasticus*, or the *Wisdom of Sirach*:

> Keep clear [μακράν ἄπεχε, *makran apeche*] of a man who
> has the power to kill,
> And you will not be haunted by the fear of death. (*Sirach* 9:13)

To "keep clear" of such power—both in oneself and in others—is to begin transfiguring all one's heart's inclinations. And the result, in the *He*-stanza, is the release from all contempt-generated dread, a release that opens the window through which one can thereby behold God's judgments as entirely "gracious" (χρηστός, *chrēstos*) and not at all terrifying.

Twice in the stanza (ll. 37 and 40) the LXX verb "to quicken" is used (ζάω, *zaō*).[48] The verb means "to give life, to cause to be alive, to enliven," "to live," and the purport is clear in both line 37 and 40. In line 37, God's "way" signifies the actual human movement toward union with God. To turn toward such movement—and thus to turn away from emptiness—is to experience the end of scorn and the beginning of joy: that joy wherein God's judgments become entirely "gracious"—become, that is, *chrēstos*, "anointed, messianic," the divine become humanly incarnate. It is also pertinent here to note that *chrēstos* is LXX Greek for MT Hebrew טוב (*tov*), which (says d'Olivet) is "the sign of resistance united to that of interior action . . . the symbol of healthy fructification, used of a force capable of setting aside every corruption."[49] To be quickened in God's way is to experience this inward power whereby every corruption is set aside so that every fruitfulness can occur: here is the joy of psalmic ascetic practice. In line 37, to be quickened by God is to enter this joy.

In line 40, the psalmist asks God to be quickened in His righteousness (LXX δικαιοσύνη, *dikaiosynē*; MT צֶדֶק, *tsedeq*). Driver defines the masculine noun as "what is right, just, normal," and the feminine noun this way: "God's attribute as sovereign."[50] Along with Fabre d'Olivet, he construes this word as the impulsion to divide actuality with sharpness, a *process of clarifying*, a way of justice in the same fashion that a sculptor chipping stone into form is acting justly. Now, *dikaiosynē* in LXX Greek, says Lampe, means "justice" or "righteousness," a divine attribute that finds its likeness in human persons.[51] Taken as the LXX Greek for MT *tsedeq, dikaiosynē* is the quickening of the human into movement toward *and into* God; and the actualization of the movement occurs as the spiritual sword of divine clarification, a shaping of the human that is simultaneously the giving birth of the divine.

Thus, by line 40, desire has become wholly salvific: for the testimonies as focus for the heart's longings have the *mitzvot* of actual practice: self-emptying loving of the other. Result (ll. 37 and 40): quicken me—cause me to be born anew—in thy way (ὁδός, *hodos*) and in thy righteousness (*dikaiosynē*), where the divine way chosen by the human is the righteousness of the heavenly Father who is God.

The window of the *He*-stanza opens in this way: onto the full clarity of the psalmic experience of prayer as the movement toward—then *into*—God. And thereby the window of *He* opens perfectly onto the next stanza, the *Waw*-stanza.

The *Waw*-Stanza

In *Waw* ("hook" or "anchor") the word "mercy" appears for the first time in this psalm. It is God's love that never gives up on you at the very instant it is your unswerving and steadfast love for Him; and it is thus the unceasing fruitfulness born of those acts of love. We are "hooked" by God. To walk in spaciousness is to have one's mouth completely filled with the "hook" of God's truthful word—and not with toxic contempt. While lines 42 and 46 explicitly engage the fact of contemptuous speech, line 45 presents the one spiritual antidote to its toxicity: "I kept on walking in spaciousness, / For I sought always thy commandments." The eternality of deification opens up in the *Waw*-stanza. —Ed.

41 Let thy mercy, O Lord, come upon me,
      Thy salvation according to thy teaching.
42 I shall answer those who taunt me,

For I have hoped on thy words.

43 Take not the word of truth
Completely from my mouth
For I have hoped in thy judgments.

44 So I shall keep forever thy law,
Always and unto ages of ages.

45 I kept on walking in spaciousness,
For I sought always thy commandments.

46 I kept on speaking of thy testimonies
Even to kings, never once ashamed.

47 I kept on meditating in thy commandments
For I have deeply loved them.

48 With upraised hands, I loved thy commandments,
And I kept on pondering thy statutes.

In line 41, there occurs—for the first time of seven LXX usages in Psalm 118—a word used nearly ninety times in the LXX Psalter to describe an essential attribute of God: ἔλεος (*eleos*, mercy). As here, and as throughout the Psalter, LXX *eleos* translates a single Hebrew word, חֶסֶד (*hesed*), a word of immense spiritual and scriptural significance: therefore, it behooves us to acquire some knowledge of it.

D'Olivet characterizes the three consonants of *hesed* in this fashion:

ח (*heth*)—intermediate between *abundant* existence and *relative* assimilated existence; hence, an equilibrium achieved by the illumined labor of normal, legislative action;

ס (*samekh*)—circumscribed and circular movement that connects the center of a circle to its circumference; and

ד (*daleth*)—the abundance born of division.

Pious, tender love – by which the transcendental infinite can bend down to the infinitessimal dying speck – and say "I love you" and by these words transmute it to light and life

Hence, following d'Olivet, we may say that the work which gathers all things into the center through the ceaselessly dividing abundance of specificity: this work of ingathering fruitfulness is *hesed*, mercy, love. Eugene Peterson rightly says that, to translate accurately the Hebrew word, we must employ "adjectives to bring out the distinctive quality and broad reach of this love: steadfast love, loyal love, covenantal love."[52] *Hesed* is love, Peterson continues, joined "with stability, dependability, unswerving commitment, and steady reliability."[53] The key to *hesed* is this joining of eternal abundance and relative existence—a joining, we may say, that incarnates the fruitfulness of God in the work of ascetic practice. *Hesed* is God's love that never gives up on you at the very instant it is your unswerving and steadfast love for Him; and *hesed* is thus the unceasing fruitfulness born of those acts of love.

And in this context, we can best approach the ancient meaning of the Hebrew letter that dominates this stanza: ו (*waw*): "hook" or "anchor." God's *hesed* anchors us in such a way that His words can become incarnate as our salvific hope: and we are thus "hooked" by God. In Saint Matthew's account describing the calling into discipleship of Peter and Andrew, Jesus tells these first two disciples to leave their fishing nets and "I will make you fishers of men" (Matt. 4:19). To be caught by such a fisher is, plainly, to be pulled from the "shadow of death" up into where "Light has sprung up" (Matt. 4:16). The Hebrew letter *waw* signifies this dynamic action.

Line 43 intensifies these stanzaic meanings. To have "the word of truth" so anchored in your mouth that only God Himself could remove the hook (which the psalmist prays will never happen) is to have the saving hope in God's judgments: in, that is, the specific applications of God's teaching in situations of human dispute or conflict.[54] Mercy (*hesed*) brings us God's teaching (*logion*), while our salvation opens in our becoming truly anchored—or "hooked"—in and by the hope in His incarnative presence in all our earthly conflicts.

Thus, the issues of contemptuous human speech now take new focus in Psalm 118. As noted above, contempt is conceived by the Psalter as the central toxin of all spiritual life on earth. While lines 42 and 46 explicitly engage the fact of contemptuous speech, line 45 presents the one spiritual antidote to its toxicity: "I kept on walking in spaciousness, / For I sought always thy commandments." I have earlier defined a "commandment" as the divinely inscribed self-emptying action of loving another that at once nourishes both lover and beloved.[55] To walk in "spaciousness" (πλατυσμός, *platysmos*) is to keep on experiencing that reciprocal nourishment which heals spiritual toxicity in both the contemptuous and the contemptible; to walk in spaciousness is to have one's mouth completely filled with the "hook" of God's truthful word—and *not* with toxic contempt. For then one can speak even to kings and never once be ashamed (l. 46): *and keep on speaking.*

As a result, the eternality of deification opens up in the *Waw*-stanza. The LXX Greek for this line's second half matches nicely the intensifications of the Hebrew. The Greek here translated "forever" is *dia pantos* (διὰ παντός), literally "moving into and through all things." The MT Hebrew behind the LXX Greek is תָּמִיד (*thamid*),[56] an interesting instance of which occurs in Numbers: "continual loaves [of consecrated bread] shall be put on the table of the tabernacle" (4:7)—where "continual" is MT *thamid* and LXX *dia pantos*. These continual loaves are, plainly, the instrumentality of deification here in Psalm 118:44; and the constancy of such nourishment arises from the healing of one's mouth from the toxicity of contempt: from, that is, having the divine "hook" firmly in one's mouth.

Line 47 adds still another dimension. Rather than bringing you *out of* the dark swirl of human history and anxiety, psalmic meditation plunges you directly into that fearful churning—never smoothing out the anxieties but, instead, always deepening them into God. The waning of mental focus, a lessening of every conceptual power: here is the experience that is overcome by the intensities of line 47: "I have deeply loved [thy commandments]"—ἠγάπησα σφόδρα (*ēgapēsa sphodra*).

The intensity is then increased in line 48. What increases the LXX intensity is the use of the adverb *pros*: literally, "I have raised my hands *toward* [*pros*] thy commandments, which I've loved." The effect of *pros* centered in the line (five LXX words on each side of *pros*) is to increase the *dynamism* of the line by giving the sense of a very vivid directionality.

Saint Gregory of Nyssa writes:

For just as in a fragment of insignificant glass it is possible to see the whole circle of the sun reflected in the gleaming part, as in a mirror, as though the smallness of what is gleaming contains it, so also all the music perceived in the universe is seen in the miniature cosmos, I mean in human nature, the music in the part being analogous to that in the whole, since the whole is contained by the part.[57]

Gregory's insight works powerfully on two levels at once: the spiritual and the esthetic. In terms of LXX psalmic poetics, Psalm 118 uses luminous details to contain and reveal the music of the whole. For example, the first line of the *Waw*-stanza is a tiny masterpiece of rhythmic shape:

καὶ ἔλθοι ἐπ᾽ἐμὲ τὸ ἔλεός σου, Κύριε,
τὸ σωτήριόν σου κατὰ τὸ λόγιόν σου.

(*kai elthoi ep'eme to eleos sou, Kyrie,*
to sōtērion sou kata to logion sou.)

Let thy mercy, O Lord, come upon me,
Thy salvation according to thy teaching. (Ps. 118:41)

The second half of this line achieves balance at the exact rhythmic midpoint while this midpoint [*kata*] also expresses the element of incarnational "downward mobility" so crucial to the line's assertion about *hesed* (*eleos*, mercy): salvation (*sōtērion*) becomes incarnate as teaching (*logion*). Just so, in the first half, "upon me" (*ep'eme*) focuses the sounds of both the verb (*elthoi*) and the subject (*eleos*) by *modulating* the sound of *elthoi* through *ep'eme* into *eleos*: a modulation untranslatably perfect. The musical details of the single line thus incarnate, we may say, the music of the whole poem.

What, then, is this music of the whole? Again, Saint Gregory is crucial: "For the concord of all creation with itself, which has been composed through opposites, is truly a hymn of the glory of the inaccessible and inexpressible God produced by such a rhythm."[58] "This," says Gregory, "is also how the great David was listening when he heard the heavens describing the glory of God."[59] The "concord of all creation with itself" *is* the great music of Psalm 118, a concord at once vastly complex and singly focused, the whole contained in every tiniest detail. Such music forms the "spaciousness" in which the psalmist keeps on walking. And this music—in part and in whole—forms the incarnational "hook" or "anchor" of the *Waw*-stanza.

EPILOGUE

Love at the Boundary:
An Orthodox Poetics

XENIA SHEEHAN

Two years after Don Sheehan's repose, I found two pages of handwritten notes hidden in plain sight in a top drawer I frequently opened. When they were written, or how they got into the drawer, or why we had not seen them before remains a mystery, and I have since lost track of the original after several moves. The notes appear to be a sketch for an entire volume, or several, on Orthodox poetics, Don's consuming interest in his last years. Because they make a fitting ending to this book by focusing so many of its significant concerns and conclusions, I include the notes here and go on to develop them as I am able, using his words where I have them. But I want to be clear that he should not be held accountable for any of what follows that is not actually attributed to him. It is I who have collected and connected his thoughts here, possibly in ways that would surprise him. I believe, though—from our long (though to my mind not long enough!) years in conversation together, in which

I learned so much from him—that he would be entirely content with this unenvisioned result.

My hope is that some readers may connect with the ideas in these eleven points and be intrigued to follow them up, and that this may begin a wider conversation on Orthodox poetics. In the spirit of conversation, I include also a few comments from others who have read the notes: my son Benedict, his wife, Maria, and our old friend (now my priest) Fr. John Konkle, whose homilies so often offer perspectives I am in need of just at that moment.

Notes Toward an Orthodox Poetics

Donald Sheehan

1. Orthodox poetics is rooted in the "moment" the Hebrew word incarnates in LXX Greek—at the boundary [where] YHWH (*Yahweh*) becomes θεός (*theos*). Κυριος

2. Orthodox poetics is unique: not borrowing from either Classical Greek or Biblical Hebrew.

3. Without Orthodox poetics, the Orthodox Liturgy would crumble, losing word and music (chant and song).

4. What happens in (1) above is that the LXX translators take their Greek and bend it into obedience and love of Hebrew; at the same moment, their Greek rules and loves the Hebrew. Thus, *Orthodox poetics is love at the boundary where heaven and earth meet and co-inhere without confusion.*

5. The key is syntax: the way wherein Biblical Hebrew holds the sentence pattern is the way God creates the world and everything (and everyone) in and of it; and the way wherein LXX Greek conceives (and reconceives) that syntax is knowing wherein the λόγος (*logos*) becomes σάρξ (*sarx*): that is,

knowing of the incarnate God; and the Hebrew [*YHWH? Ruach?*] released by LXX Greek syntax is the Person of the Holy Spirit. Here is the meaning of the Holy Spirit's "proceeds from the Father": the joy of syntactic [creation?].[1]

6. St. Paul's Hebrew outwardly bears witness to Christ's discoursing with the rabbis in the Temple: bears witness to the fact of Christ's heavenly command of Biblical Hebrew at the same moment St. Paul's Greek bears witness to the incarnate word in Biblical Greek. For our Lord's command of Greek incarnates the LXX as the spoken words of actual speech.

7. Thus, the relation between New Testament *koine* and LXX Greek repeats the relation between LXX Greek and Biblical Hebrew: i.e., both NT *koine* and LXX Greek are incarnations of heavenly speech in and as earthly language.

8. LXX Greek : NT *koine* :: Bib. Hebrew : LXX Greek. That is, LXX Greek binds Biblical Hebrew and NT *koine*. "We correct the Hebrew from the [LXX] Greek."[2]

9. St. Paul's Hebrew gives deep shape to his *koine* Greek—especially the way wherein the *koine* syntax of the Epistles shapes the urgencies of creating the Church on earth as the Book of Christ: or, that is, the incarnate Body.

10. Thus: Biblical Hebrew, LXX Greek, *koine* Greek, the Church—all exhibit the deep syntax of an Orthodox poetics. (Connect: Church architecture and Pauline syntax.)

11. Concerning (9) and (10): Matthew, Mark, Luke, and John each use a syntax unique to them. St. Paul—in the urgency of creating the Church—employs yet another syntax. The four Gospels are *why* we need a Church; St. Paul is the making of that Church.

Reflections on the Way of Orthodox Poetics

To be clear: though I have studied both literature and Orthodox theology at the graduate level, I am neither a poet nor a student of poetics, nor in any sense a theologian. To those readers who do have such knowledge, with respect to any art (for it is not limited to poetry, and perhaps not even to art), and especially to those among you who practice the Orthodox faith with understanding, I extend a heartfelt invitation to enter the conversation. Don would surely have welcomed that. Alhough he felt his faith to be essential to his literary study and spent the twenty years after his conversion revising his understanding in the light of Eastern Orthodox Christianity,[3] he never, ever, pushed it on anyone or saw their different faith, or lack of it, as diminishing or limiting the value of the gifts they had to offer.

Our younger son, Benedict, who composes music, instructs and leads Orthodox seminarians and Church choirs in liturgical hymnography, and conducts a large professional Orthodox choir (many of whom are practicing Orthodox believers), adds here that what Don calls "Orthodox poetics" might better be thought of as a "divine poetics" or "true poetics":

> *Benedict Sheehan:* What he is speaking of is more universal than, not limited to, "Orthodox," which is a polemical term. The Church only started using it in exclusion of heretical teachings, and even for a great part of the history of the Church that wasn't how people thought of themselves: as Orthodox. I think if we lean into the term too much we make it too limited. The kinds of things he's speaking about can be found in beautiful art and beautiful creation all over the map. That's because he's speaking of an organic process of discovering what is real and true: all that comes from the one true God, who is personal and creates and reveals

Himself according to certain patterns. Anything beautiful is in some way a revelation of this truth and these patterns. I think he's trying to get at a sense of fundamental patterns that govern the whole act of creation. It's bigger than what we mean polemically by Orthodox. It's not Orthodox as opposed to Roman Catholic or anything else. It's just simply true. That being said, I think his point is about the ascetic. *Psalmic poetics is the way of ascetic beauty.*

The Way of Psalmic Poetics

What Don means by psalmic poetics is a poetics that reflects and enacts patterns instilled in God's creation from before time; or, to use Benedict's phrasing, it follows "fundamental patterns that govern the whole act of creation." Some of these patterns are revealed in certain qualities of Psalms that Don points to in these chapters (especially chapter 8):

- Psalms abound in what Don calls "noetic swiftness" leading to "noetic inebriation," which gives rise to a "state of unending significance, that state in which meaning ecstatically never ceases its increasing." The deeper you enter a Psalm, the more this is true, as you begin to touch on the fecundity and depth of God's creativity, and the unity and relatedness of the whole.
- The psalmist, discovering himself to be a beast before God, is taken by the hand by the Father so as to "make present to him, in the warm touch of coursing blood, the fact that . . . the father is continually with him."[4] This fundamental reality of Psalms is never absent.
- Supplication and gratitude, freely offered, are our right relation to God, always.

[margin handwritten note] Psalm 73: 21-22

[bottom handwritten note] I've seen it with Psalm 114/115, Psalms 109, 119, 120 (120/121) (116)

- Psalmic meditation or contemplation (aspects emphasized by (St. Diadochos) is an "action of memory wherein God incarnates in the human mind as the human mind becomes deified." And thus our very entrance into the depths of Psalms moves us closer to Him.
- Psalms' foundation in Scripture, in which the "fundamental patterns that govern the whole act of creation" are revealed to us, "yields an entire way of life, a way that we are now calling the way of psalmic poetics."

That such patterns of God's involvement in His creation arise from before time and are not changed by time does not at all place the psalmic engagement with Him *outside history*. Indeed, one of the Psalms' strongest (and most challenging) characteristics is that they seem to be mired *in* history. On the other hand, it is also key to psalmic poetics that their miring in history is in no way a being *ruled by* history. This is the point. Psalms rather *hold* history, and in doing so they pattern and repattern it. Perhaps it could even be said that Psalms, words of God not limited by time, are where God, who has taken on our history as His own, meets us and shows us the way through, which is the way to Him. For, as Don tells us in chapter 2, Christ, "both prophetically through the poets of Psalms[5] and in His own earthly life and prayer," "infused into Psalms His own presence," wholly filling them "with the *goodness of what is*: that is with . . . Himself." Don had no doubt, ever, that "Christ is *present* in the whole of Psalms." Reciprocally, he says, Psalms "formed in Him the consciousness that was always latent in them" (chapter 1).

Both this reciprocity between Christ in Psalms and Psalms in Christ and the miring and ruling/patterning nature of Psalms in relation to history make clear the need for their chiastic structure. To repeat a passage quoted earlier from St. Isaac of Syria:

The trials that are inflicted by the paternal rod for the soul's progress and growth, and wherein she may be trained, are the following: sloth, oppressiveness of the body; enfeeblement of the limbs; despondency [or depression]; bodily pains—or suspicion of bodily illness; temporary loss of hope; darkening of thoughts; absence of help from men; scarcity of bodily necessities; and the like. By these temptations a man's soul feels herself lonely and defenceless, his heart is deadened and filled with humility, and he is trained thereby to come to yearn for his Creator. Yet divine providence proportions these trials to the strength and needs of those who suffer them. In them are mingled both consolation and griefs, light and darkness, wars and aid. In short, they straiten and enlarge. This is the sign of the increase of God's help. (Homily 42:209–10)

This is the psalmic experience: fierce trials straitening the soul, crying out to God for help, joyous praise and heartfelt thanksgiving when He does—and consequent enlargement of the soul. It calls for a chiastic poetics that clearly foreshadows and prepares for the cross of Christ. It is "a *spatial* art primarily," Don writes; "not governed by the narrative forward movement alone but also the chiastic center [i.e., the crossing at the center, where the opposing narrative movements meet, and from which they may also be seen to proceed]: each psalm thus sounds a *single complex sound* that possesses 'shape,' in which the aesthetic pattern and the theological significance converge in *one shape*." The central shape is the cross, present in Psalms from the beginning. Governed by this shape, psalmic poetics gives way to a "lyric narrative in which unceasing terror and panic are followed by sudden reversals into highest joys, and to a lyric intensification in which all assertions and images are constantly deepened" (chapter 12). "[W]hat begins as an attack upon God" may, at the very edge of the precipice to which it has led you, turn to become a divinely given gift of psalmic inspiration and composition" (see chapter 8).

Don proposes a three-step process for entering into the way of psalmic poetics:

1. Psalmic poetics is *penitential*: that is, in turning away from the flames of transgressive desire, the sons of Korah are turning toward the beauty of the divine King. "Thus, when we fervently remember God, we feel divine longing well up within us from the depths of our heart" (chapter 8). This transformation of the heart, he says, "constitutes the first step in the way of psalmic poetics."

2. The second step is "the distinct and exact practice" in biblical meditation of *"staying in the historically present and real* until the truly Real, or the entirely and ceaselessly Present One, is met finally and fully" (chapter 3). This is work that he characterizes as "slow, patient, undramatic" work like that of the ox plowing the field, which in the end bears great fruit. He writes of the "steadiness that holds . . . catastrophes and . . . exultations (the nightmare of actual historic disaster and the undying vision of Lord God's redemptive love) in perfect composure." This yields what he calls an "aching beauty: the power to make whole in God all of human historic experience" (chapter 1).

Benedict says this point jumps out at him from his own experience as a composer:

Benedict Sheehan: One of the things I've realized is the need for there to be routine, sameness, dryness, things that on the surface are not immediately interesting, in order for real beauty to emerge. As a conductor I'll tell a choir not to make everything an event, not to make everything sweet, but to allow moments of great sweetness to emerge gradually over time—they're that much more powerful and intense. Or, as a composer, I'll deliberately restrain myself in musical passages, to deny the realization of sweetness or fulfillment or ecstasy deliberately even when it could be achieved sooner. The moments of arrival are that much more climactic. That's the ascetical spirit—it's not a rejection of beauty but actually rather an affirmation of beauty. . . . This staying in the historically present is very important. A creation is not an abstract schema, nor is it a fantasizing about what *could* be. As an artist you start with your tools and your materials. You can choose them arbitrarily, but you have to start from the concrete and from the experience of really inhabiting a context.

This is what God does. He inhabits the context of *us*, stays with us, works with us, waits for us, affirms our beauty, so that we may bear fruit in season. And from our vocation to become *like* Him in these things spring all the "rules" of an Orthodox life and poetics.

3.   The third step in entering psalmic poetics is an "inward process: *searching*, . . . in memory, . . . in the night, . . . noetically, in the darkness in the heart," where the actual God is:

"In the valley of death's shadow within, we search the holy words of Psalms: and their life bursts upon us, flooding us with depth of connection, with intensities of meanings. Meditation is the process of this search within complaint-song, a search at once suffused with the stillness of sacred study and churning with the heart's darknesses—and the stillness and the churning are one complex event within us." (Chapter 3)

What moves every Hebrew line of psalmic poetry is best comprehended as the "growl" of unceasing nourishment: a rhythmic growl
that is softly audible and deeply pleasurable—a pleasure, Don
claims, that is not lost in the sounds of the LXX Greek. The way of
psalmic poetics is thus entirely the way of Orthodox ascetic beauty.

It is also a beauty of relationship and what Don calls *connectiveness*. "The beauty of the poetics [of Psalm 118, for instance] arises
from this sustained esthetic fact: in both Hebrew and Greek, the connection in each half is a connection that *explains*—that is, it expands,
defines, opens up, deepens—the other half" (chapter 12). It is always
conversational, not as between "equals" but rather instructive (as the
chiastic center of the Psalter, Psalm 77, is a psalm of "instruction").
The goal is what Orthodox theology calls *theosis*, the human partner
becoming divinized, *like* the Divine, *as God*, each bending toward,
"leaning into" the other, and in the end, yes, becoming His equal in
an equality wholly and eternally given by Him.

Benedict and Maria offer the following observations about the
relationship Don points to:

> *Maria Sheehan:* This describes a *true* relationship. Using the
> model of Christopher Alexander's "pattern language,"[6] Don
> is ultimately relating the quality of the relationship with
> the matrix out of which the work is born to the quality of
> the work itself. It's interesting to me that he describes this
> relationship as the fundamental prerequisite for the work.
> It's not only the relationship of man with God, but that of
> translator and language [see chapter 2], language and con-
> tent. One of the things that made Don happiest, I think,
> was to make unusual descriptive, analogous connections
> between things you wouldn't think were related. He uses
> relationship language to talk about how words show up in a
> writer's mind. That's kind of an unusual idea.

Benedict Sheehan: In some ways he's describing *unequal* relationships: so it's also partly the relationship of the greater to the
lesser, the giver to receiver. In a relationship of translation,
for instance, there's an implicit hierarchy—there's the original and then there's the attempt to express it in the new
language.

Maria: But that's not a static relationship. It's more that thing
where you're having to exercise either conservatism or lib-
eralism [as in a literal vs. a "free" or noetic translation as
described in chapter 2]; it's in the choice about the degree
to which you apply one or the other that the relationship
shows up in its qualitative form. And the sensitivity to the
thing that's being altered has to be expressed in a fluid way
so as not to create a dead thing.

Benedict: It's still a hierarchical relationship. Beauty arises out
of a particular way of approaching that relationship. Translating the Hebrew into the Greek of the LXX is an act of
incarnation, or analogous to that. It's the act of making a
thing that's distant and inaccessible immediate and accessible. It's always conversation, not as between equals but as
instructive.

Xenia: I think this may be the essence of what you've described
as an ascetic practice. In ascesis or self-emptying (*kenosis*),
the "other" is always the instructor. Or, in God's case, He
gives us autonomy and equality to the extent we can handle
them, because He is raising us up to be His equals. And
I would be ignoring the obvious if I didn't add here that
the Orthodox liturgy would indeed crumble without its
numerous sung or chanted litanies. Not only do these form
an ongoing dialogue of prayer and supplication between the
people and God, making each of us a crucial participant in

this "work for the people," but the liturgy cannot be performed at all without the people. We enact it in relationship
with God.

Don offers a fitting conclusion to this discussion of psalmic
relationship in chapter 8, where he says that "The way of psalmic
beauty is . . . the way of consummated union, the marriage of the
heavenly King with the earthly Queen, Christ with the Church, a
relationality that is therefore ontological in its nature: the very being
of both Bridegroom and Bride is rooted in this union. The way of
psalmic poetics lies in entering into this union."

To repeat, psalmic poetics is deeply relational. It is a poetics of

> unceasing *connectiveness*, a praying without ceasing wherein
> each sound and syllabic shape connects once, twice, or more
> to surrounding sounds and shapes. This connectiveness is,
> first of all, a local "breathing," a kind of capillary or synaptic
> flow or humming, that awakens us wholly; and the further
> we probe this connectiveness the wider—and deeper—run
> the patterns of it. These patterns are plainest in the Hebrew
> but they are held almost entirely in LXX Greek. (Chapter 3)

The Septuagint: Love at the Boundary

A further instance of this kind of relationality is found in the process that Don believed governed the Septuagint translation. In
Point 4 of his list, he speaks of the translators bending their Greek
into obedience and love of Hebrew, while at the same moment their
Greek rules and loves the Hebrew. Benedict offers this reflection on
their process:

> *Benedict Sheehan:* In showing an enduring respect for the
> Hebrew in their translation, the LXX translators *served* the

original rather than being enslaved by it. God allowed this change and extension of His message to take place because it was not about simply reproducing the original. It's interesting that neither Judaism nor Islam has historically been comfortable with the idea of translating Scripture, at least not as something normative. Even Christians have sometimes had misgivings about translation. But translation shows a willingness to work together with someone else, to allow yourself to be altered. We each have a part to play, and our God allows us to play it. A student mentioned in class recently the apocryphal quote from Martin Luther: "Even if I knew that tomorrow the world would go to pieces, I would still plant my apple tree." Its meaning was taken to be that we always have to be building on the tradition and looking to grow, even if there's no apparent hope or no immediate reason in sight.

Xenia: I would even say that it is our vocation as faithful servants to play our part *with* God, as in Matthew 25:14–29, where we are shown the risks of being unprofitable servants by hiding our talents. God means for us to grow into our inheritance—to grow into our relationship with *Him* in *theosis*.

In chapter 3 Don suggests, with supporting linguistic evidence, that it is in the LXX Greek of Psalms and the translations that proceed from it (made in kenotic obedience, in love, at the boundary between the languages) that the path to *theosis*, our union with God, is most fully opened to us.

As the first point in the list makes clear, the Septuagint marked a critical watershed, for it came into being during the prolonged historical moment leading to Christ's incarnation. It's no small thing that tradition holds the translation to have been written by six

members from each of the twelve tribes of Israel. They are said to
have worked separately, but in noetic concert. Thus it was the work
of a "people," God's people, a people devoted to listening to God, to
deeply pondering His prophecies, and to practicing His teaching,
a people whom He had been leading to this point at least since the
time of Abraham. It may have been the most significant historical
moment since the world was created. At a time when the history
and prophetic knowledge given to God's people were threatened
by numerous historical upheavals, the Greek translation preserved
these by committing them to a language with an ultimate reach
far beyond those to whom the faith had first been given. It further
opened crucial doors of understanding, paving the way toward the
Lord's incarnation. And it provided a transmissible scriptural foundation for generations to come for understanding and honoring—
for *receiving*—the incarnation that was about to take place and that
was, on some level accessible to the Seventy, already taking place.

In the translation itself, what is true of the Hebrew is perfectly
re-created, Don says. It is *translated to Life* in the movement and
sound of LXX psalmic Greek. It is a re-creation always deferential
to Hebrew and yet completely nourishing all who attend to LXX
psalmic music. Key to the process is the *kenotic obedience* of the LXX
translators, whose love for the Hebrew makes it possible at the same
moment for their Greek to love and to "rule" the Hebrew. And
because of this "love at the boundary," the shift from a "psalmic"
poetics to a poetics that was to become "Orthodox" was a fulfillment, not a discontinuity.

Don has pointed out in chapter 3 some of the numerous small
but significant linguistic changes that took place from the Hebrew
text to the LXX, such as:

- clarifying the hypostatic reality of the two "partners" (the
  human I and the divine Thou) in the human-divine coming

together in an intimacy of instruction, obedience, praise, and thanksgiving;

- opening the way to the actual union of man and God in what Orthodox Christianity understands as *theosis*;

- and preparing for a wonder even beyond this (or made possible by it): "the earthly incarnation of the divine . . . raising all earthly things up, *and into direct participation in* God through the asymmetry of His immeasurable love for us" (chapter 11).

And this involves, perhaps, a rereading of Psalms in that new light, but it does not essentially change them or their poetics, for they knew that Messiah was coming and they followed faithfully the patterns, the syntax, that led to His coming. The LXX seems rather to make translucent and present—in the sense of *Presence*—what, or *Who*, had previously been more opaque and hidden as expectation and promise.

Thus it seems possible that the actual "poetics" of the two texts are one and the same. Indeed, read rightly, they are necessarily so if we understand the "syntax" of Psalms to derive from their reflection—their incarnation even, in language and song—of God's "statutes," "His life-generating patterns of the creation." For "the way wherein Biblical Hebrew holds the sentence pattern is the way God creates the world and everything (and everyone) in and of it" (Point 5 above).

History, Statutes, and Syntax

To review Don's understanding of history, as he describes it in these chapters, it is "the arena wherein the divine and the human fruitfully interact" (chapter 9). God's *statutes* are what "generate the entire creation and all things and actions occurring within it, including all of human history"; they are *"the divine cuttings-into (or inscriptions) left by God in the creation to become the nourishment that powers our own true creativity"* (chapter 11). They are "the patterns that we cannot fully comprehend with our minds, containing (among other things) (1) linear human history; (2) angelic interventions in that linearity; and (3) the shaping hand of God Himself" (chapter 6). "[T]he pressures of historical actualities" give "concrete form to the statutes. For history (as *martyria* [witness]) is the dimension where death/resurrection occurs: the sole and full and salvific dimension. And the key to the statutes—to those patterns of God's dynamic creativity—is precisely in Christ's death and resurrection" (chapter 12): His giving of Himself to death so that we may have life. This is no ransom to the devil, no bargain or exchange, but rather *Who* He essentially is: the one who gives Himself that others may live, because that's how Life occurs, it's the deep pattern. And that's what we must do to follow Him so that we may unite with Him in *theosis*, God-becoming.

Would it be too simple to say, then, that the poetics we are talking about is the generative or creative process of entering into life only when we are willing to die to ourselves? One of Don's favorite quotes was the one from John 12:24 (AV) that Dostoevsky used as the epigraph for *The Brothers Karamazov*: "Verily, verily, I say unto you, except a corn of wheat fall into the ground and die, it abideth alone: but if it die, it bringeth forth much fruit. He that loveth his life shall lose it; and he that hateth his life in this world shall keep it unto life eternal." This sort of *kenosis* (self-emptying) is what Don means when he speaks about the noetic action of translation in chapter 2: "That is, our noetic seeing is primarily a fact about the thing, or the face, we are beholding—rather than about ourselves. And we are always being surprised by the reality of others: such is noetic seeing." Defining *noetic*, he explains: "The *nous* is the directly ontological organ of our personhood, disclosing who we are in and

through the actions wherein we comprehend—swiftly and completely—the divinely given reality of *someone other than ourselves.*"
This seems to be the crux of all creative process, no matter what the
scale. This is love at the boundary: seeing and entering into the reality of the "other"—the one outside our self-defined and self-defining
boundaries—in order to raise the other up and give it/him/her new
life, even when this means reshaping or relinquishing our own life
and self-appointed aims.

My daughter-in-law Maria, also a musician, formulates this
process in a more modern language:

> *Maria Sheehan*: The architect and philosopher Christopher
> Alexander observed that, for objects or spaces, which can
> include everything from the smallest tool all the way up to a
> city, to have the characteristics that he refers to as *life*, it has
> to be created according to what he calls the *generative pro-
> cess*. The fundamental precept of generative process is that
> the creator must inhabit the space or the object somehow.
> From the creator's habitation in the thing, the steps of its
> creation can unfold in a way that preserves its life until its
> generation is complete. . . . The basic idea is that, if you want
> to create the thing he calls "life" you have to put yourself *in*
> the thing. You have to judge it or make decisions about how
> it's going to be made from that position of inhabiting it. It's
> an incarnative action that is the baseline for any creative
> process. It's intensely experiential, not at all abstract.

It's not much of a stretch to see in this a reflection of what we
understand about God's manner of creation. For instance, Don tells
us that "In making His own life whole in and through the Psalms,
our Lord made comparably whole the entire course of Israelite history, the history of God-loss and God-gain over and over" (chapter

4). That is, He *inhabited* that history and by so doing gave it His life, translated it to Life, and finally gave even Himself, on the Cross, in the death that ended death forever. Orthodox Christians sing joyously at His Pascha (the Feast of His Resurrection): "Christ is risen from the dead, trampling down death by death, and upon those in the tombs bestowing life!"

I would like us also to consider in this context the lovely meditation that Don wrote in his journal (quoted in chapter 11) about the Mother of God at her study:

> I see her now, bent over her sacred Book as each word comes into her view and true ken; and the light of the text irradiates her face and shines back as her presence in the text: such that the prophecies come to embody her as she begins to fulfill them now. This moment is of highest meaning. Isaiah (e.g.), in the radiance of her study, begins *in the text itself* to take on her presence: the text "changes" as she shines her concentrated heart-in-mind into it; the text *becomes* her. And as this is going on she is fulfilling in her being all the meanings of prophecy (e.g., Lamentations before the Cross).

Again we are seeing "the arena wherein the divine and the human fruitfully interact." Though neither she nor the prophet is divine, the divine is clearly present and open here to both; both might in this sense be called birthgivers of God. And both would appear to be in antiphonal, even chiastic, conversation with history through her deep engagement with Scripture, by which she infuses herself into the prophecies and the prophecies into herself in their working out in time. Like a psalm, then, even history may be considered chiastic. Its narrative may be read both "forward" and "backward," the earlier and later lines speak to one another, and their meaning is fulfilled at the center, at the point of the cross, toward which the Lord's incarnation and birth could be seen as the first step.

"To the AD 70 nonbelieving Jew," Don says in chapter 1, "the destruction of the Temple was a cessation of historic actuality. To cease history is to experience the end of God's active presence in time. To the Christian Jew, the holy figure on the Cross was defeat-become-triumph: a break from the literalized deathtrap of history into the spiritual freedom of true history: the ceaseless Presence that is *never* lost."

In the same chapter we are told that "History is a process of idolatry: the making by us of self-idols and the smashing of them by God. So in one's own life, as historical process. The Psalms, only (and Scripture as a whole), know this; and they alone show the whole process. For God is in our darkness, that is, in what we are withholding from Him of ourselves in our (violent, crazed) attempt to make ourselves holy *in our own eyes*, not in His." And "once we begin to glorify ourselves, and no longer glorify God, we enter into a history in which God no longer acts, and history therefore becomes merely an extension of empirical tangibilities and no longer the arena wherein the divine and the human fruitfully interact" (chapter 9).

In his fifth point, Don tells us that "The key is syntax." This is the *way* (*hodos*) and the *path* (*tribos*) by which the *pattern* of His statutes (*dikaiōmata)*—themselves the patterns of His creation—lead us through our following of His *precepts* fully to embrace His *statutes* and enact his *commandments*, translating them into Life (see chapter 11 for full definitions of the "nine words")—translating them, that is, into our own life, in Him, not in ourselves, not sacralized with temples to ourselves filled with our own glorified self-images. And when this happens, the *precepts* (the many once-prescribed small and homely acts of ascesis that held God's people together for so long), now no longer necessary, are themselves absorbed into the statutes as we move closer to God Himself, who is moving closer to us. By this path and way, following His own patterns, Christ is incarnated in human flesh both as Himself and, through and by Him, in us (if we consent) in *theosis*, and the Spirit proceeds from the Father to guide us on our (His) way. It is a way that we can follow when we love Him, if we engage in and with Him in spiritual warfare against the "world powers of the present darkness" (which seek to deform us, both within and without). This warfare—most often waged against our temptations to glorify ourselves and disregard or denigrate the other—is our ascesis. The Psalms, especially Psalm 118, show us how.

Orthodox Poetics and the Way of Ascetic Beauty

The first point in Don's list is this: "Orthodox poetics is rooted at the boundary where *YHWH* becomes *theos*. The LXX Greek, rooted in Hebrew, bending in obedience and love to the Hebrew, and yet ruling it, is in itself an act of love at the boundary where heaven and earth meet and co-inhere without confusion." His fifth point includes this: "the way wherein Biblical Hebrew holds the sentence pattern is the way God creates the world and everything (and everyone) in and of it," while "the way LXX Greek conceives (and reconceives) that syntax is knowing wherein the *logos* becomes *sarx*: that is, knowing of the incarnate God." This is an important difference. Biblical Hebrew, syntactically, is embedded in the process of God's creation, while the LXX moves in the knowledge of His incarnation. Both are stages of His creative work—His poetics if you will. Both reveal the process of God entering into relation with the created world—His creation—first by creating it, then by entering into it Himself. Or, as we have just considered, first by entering into it—we might say *noetically*, though I don't know if this can be said of God—and from there creating it incarnatively, in some sort of unimaginable conversation between the two ends, if ends there are. However we try to look at it, it is a continuous, not a sudden, process, and it is probably more spatial than temporal. Temporally, however, one grows into the other over a long period of time. But He doesn't change, His statutes don't change, His teachings and commandments don't change, His laws don't change.

Rather He is making, ruling, changing (and at every boundary loving) the world—and us—in order that He may unite Himself with us, or in order that we may unite ourselves with Him. He waits, perhaps, for the translation of Scripture to open wider to Him, and to reach more people so as to prepare them for Him. He waits, perhaps, for His mother to be born and to immerse her whole being in His holy writings so that she may know Him, watch for Him, and receive Him when the archangel is sent to her. And He waits for those to be born who will become His apostles and make His Church so that His Word (*logos*) may have a fitting Body (*sarx*, literally "flesh"), a permanent place to dwell on earth. But what Benedict has called "the fundamental patterns that govern the whole act of creation" don't change. And this must be understood as the syntax or poetics of both Psalms and the Church.

What becomes possible following the incarnation, and especially following Christ's death and resurrection, is that we may look back at Psalms and discover that He has become closer and more visible to us in them; our relationship with Him has become deeper and more personal; our prayers for deliverance from "the pressures of historical actualities"—terrible pressures—have been answered, and therefore *will be* answered. For He has come among us, as one of us, to take them upon Himself for our sake. If we are to look for a change in psalmic poetics, this, it seems to me, is where we should look. Even though the psalmist found over and over that, in answer to his cry for help, God would enter into his suffering and deliver him and His people from it—this being the pattern, the syntax, the statute that informs Psalms—it seems evident to me that, following the Lord's death and resurrection, we look for a far greater deliverance, though no lessening of the trials (which may, however, have become more internal); and the deliverance is less material, far more deeply joyous, and permanent.

Father John Konkle spoke on 2 Corinthians (in a homily I paraphrase here considerably), beginning with 3:7–8, where "the children of Israel could not look steadily at the face of Moses because of the glory of his countenance, which glory was passing away." St. Paul asks, "how will the ministry of the Spirit not be more glorious?" Moses, not wanting the people to see that the glory was dissipating, had covered his face with a veil, says Fr. John, and St. Paul uses this to contrast Old Testament life with the life available to us:

> *Fr. John (in paraphrase):* We are the tabernacle of God now. When we look into the mirror of our hearts, we are seeing the same thing Moses saw when he would go into the tabernacle. We don't have to keep going back to the filling station. Insofar as we think of our lives as going to church or to our prayer corner to be filled up, we enter back into the Old Testament way of thinking. Sure, Jesus goes away to be alone and pray, but this was part of the continuing awareness that God is with us at every moment, to teach us to look into that mirror of our heart. We need such times to help us remember that God is with us. We live in constant communion with Him. We are being transformed from glory to glory, nothing is taken away but all is expanding and growing. We are able to have God with us wherever we are.

At the same time, this text from 2 Corinthians emphasizes a continuity between Old Testament, or at least psalmic, and New Testament life. Fr. John went on to refer to St. Paul's long digression (from the end of chapter 2 through chapter 6) about the fragility of our lives, which are not in our control; about St. Paul's own inability to do what God has put right in front of him (to preach without Titus); and about his need to be reminded that we live in constant communion with God and that this is our only hope, a hope not available under the law but available to us at every moment.

> *Fr. John (in paraphrase):* And then God comforted St. Paul by the coming of Titus, a gift given only after he had been thrown into the position of having to realize his constant dependence on God. Only in learning that his life is totally connected to his savior can he be comforted by the coming of Titus. To experience another person coming to you as a comfort is a gift from God—from which we learn that our lives need to be constantly lived in the tabernacle of our heart. God loves St. Paul so much that he won't give Titus to him until Paul has learned that God is living in us, though we keep wanting to go elsewhere to find him.

And this, as we have seen, is entirely psalmic. It is a trial in the desert necessary to bring us to the remembrance of God, without whom the desired end cannot be achieved. At the same time, as the historical, patristic tradition of the Orthodox Church makes clear, it is much more than a going back to the Temple for renewal, but a learning to enter the Tabernacle in the Heart that is always with us, where God Himself resides. A deeper and more personal work of ascesis has become necessary to make fast our intimacy with God and our entrance into His holy Joy: "His *euphrosynē*." Don would hold, I think, that, in countless small ways, the LXX opened the way to this clarity. It was and is a further stage in the creation of ascetic beauty.

A Place to Dwell

Following the Septuagint translation, the next defining historical moment came when one Hebrew woman, whose birth had been prophetically yet hiddenly prepared for many generations, was—seeking nothing for herself—given everything, and became able to receive into her body the fullness of her people's God and bring their Messiah to birth in loving maternity. Once again, love at the boundary. The infinite universe came to be held within the compass of a human womb, and this changed everything, except of course the "fundamental patterns."

Orthodox poetics is clearly incarnational. It begins, we must suppose, with God's creation of a people He knew would betray Him. It continues in the Old Testament saints and prophets who suffered and bent themselves in love to receive and proclaim His will against terrible odds. It approaches fulfillment when the LXX translators, in kenotic love, learn to bend their Greek to receive Hebrew into it, "transforming Hebrew poetics into spiritual experience" (chapter 12). It is brought to birth in Christ's incarnation by means of the holy virgin, who gave her life to the study of all the faithful believers who preceded her and who offers all of herself to God when He asks. It is then fulfilled in Christ's life—and dare I say in His praying of Himself into Psalms for the sake of all of those His servants who came before and would thereby come to foreknow Him? It "ends," in a sense, in His crucifixion and resurrection—though this was another and greater beginning rather than an ending.

Recently, I attended a funeral where Father John Konkle said this:

Fr. John: The body is the true temple of God. The creation story as recorded in Genesis says that God created things and kept saying, "This is beautiful!" But after five and a half days He looked around and said, "This is beautiful, but where do *I* live? I haven't created a place for me yet." Well, of course He could live anywhere because He fills all of His creation. But there was no place for Him to live in a way that was appropriate for God to inhabit, where creation could respond to His love in the way that God Himself loves all of creation; that is, in a way appropriate to the way in which it was created. Time and again in Psalms, we see all of creation praising God, but none from freedom.

So He created Adam and Eve in His image to have a place to live in His creation, a place to dwell. As St. Paul tells us, God is love. There needed to be a vessel, a receptacle appropriate for holding love, one that can love back, respond, return freely. And so he created Adam and Eve and said, "Behold, look! Exceedingly beautiful!"

. . . The human body was created to be God's home; He's not going to simply throw it out when we die, He's going to wake it up so that for all eternity it can be His habitation, His home. The way our lives come to be God's home is by denying ourselves, taking up our cross and following Him, dying to our attachment to things of this world, letting go of everything that's a substitute for God. That's what it means to let go of the things of this world. The world God created is beautiful, we don't have to deny that. We can love its materiality, but we can't love the creation in place of the creator. So we have to die constantly to our desires to protect ourselves, to secure ourselves, to make ourselves feel good or important in this world in ways that are substitutes for God as our provider, our protector, our source of security, our source of intimacy. So we die daily, as St. Paul says, we take up our cross daily. That's how we become His temple.

The infinite God constricted Himself by coming to dwell in a *place*, a place contained within His own creation; and where He dwells, whether we call it life or death, His life is present, always. He enters this place through the Virgin's womb—what could be more constrictive? And what meeting at the boundary could be more filled with love? Obedient to the rules He Himself has made—all the rules of physics and biology, all the religious laws and restrictions of His culture—He grows to become a young child, then a young man. And finally He allows Himself to be nailed to a cross and placed in a tomb, where we find Him at Holy Saturday Matins, at the center of all the violence; praying—even, as Don imagines, composing—the Great Psalm of resurrection that will lead us also, one by one, to become places for Him to dwell, to be his very temple, as we learn from Him to diminish our self-inflation through ascesis and take up our cross to follow Him. Love at the boundary.

And so in our own time, in the services of Holy Church, His sacrifice of love continues to be enacted—not symbolically but actually, at each Liturgy, on each consecrated altar, by a priest ordained within an unbroken lineage proceeding from the Lord Himself. And it goes out from there in the many sacrifices of love reflected in all our own acts of ascesis and our own continuations of His creative action in the world, performed in His image.

Don loved the photograph of a monk paddling his tiny craft to shore through ocean waves. He wrote this of it:

Bands and cords: this is how religion is felt—as restriction, as being tied down, tied up. The earth's powerful,

especially, experience God as this terrible constriction, for
He invalidates—makes sick—their power. What is religious constriction? It is the deliberate construction of a
place to be. There is a photograph of an Athonite monk in
a small boat, standing as he rows a single oar/rudder and
guides his small craft shoreward, while behind him the
whole vast ocean opens up. The image is this: a frail tiny
craft with a lone man who, nevertheless, is in control, upon
the sea. Religion is the tiny craft, the ocean is God. One
can rail against the craft's tinyness in comparison to the
ocean's vastness; one can even see the craft as restriction
and bondage—and plunge, instead, directly into the ocean.
But the craft of religious discipline allows one to negoti-
ate the ocean in ways superior to mere swimming, for row-
ing the boat strikes the right relation between human skill/
strength and oceanic power. Swimming quickly exhausts
human strength; the craft allows one's strength to guide a
lifetime of being with God.

And this brings us, if only briefly, to the final points on Don's
list, concerning the construction of a seaworthy craft, a place to
dwell, a house for the Lord on earth, His very Body—that is, the
Church. I can offer only this summary of his points, for I lack the
knowlege to do more: In the years following the Lord's incarnation,
Matthew, Mark, Luke, and John, in their various ways, made His
words their own and infused the common speech with them, translating it into Life (see chapter 2). St. Paul, immersed in the patterns of Hebrew, then "shapes the urgencies of creating the Church
on earth as the Body[7] of Christ: or, that is, the incarnate Body."
The Church *is* this, His Body. This *is* the "poetics" of Orthodoxy:
the God-given patterns; the loving and humble bending to and of
those patterns in order to translate them from Hebrew into Greek

and beyond; the passing of those patterns into the languages of the people; the making of the Church in the knowledge that it is the very Body of Christ, in and through which we may all participate and ourselves incarnate His divine energies through Holy Communion and spiritual ascesis—and through our own God-given creative works.

To summarize: As I understand all this, Orthodox poetics is the incarnative process of the Divine becoming human, the Word working its way through specific human languages and artistic media and lives—in all their joys and disasters—bending to us in love as we bend to Him, until we become, in the end, persons in His likeness—and thus ourselves creators and saviors of His creation. The source is *YHWH*, the Father; the medium is the Word. As we bend in loving obedience to His Word(s) we—ourselves a beloved boundary—(along with our ascetically enacted works of beauty?) ultimately become the substance wherein heaven and earth may meet and coinhere. The making of the Church on earth follows such a syntax and has, or is, an Orthodox poetics that includes all of this. I don't see that it differs in substance or shape from psalmic poetics; certainly it would have no life without the God-given foundation of Psalms. The divine syntax, however, is both more visible in it, and, I suspect, simultaneously more ascetic and more joyously beautiful.

I see an hourglass shape, no doubt both a chiasm and a chalice: an infinite divinity narrowing to the small space of the Virgin's womb, the tomb of Holy Saturday, the even smaller common cup and eucharistic spoon, the constrictive ascesis of our spiritual practice, and opening again, through the liturgical communicants, to the whole world so that He may incarnate in and through all of us in the midst of our joys and terrors, our inspirations and confusions, our loves and our works—of which, who knows? He may someday say, "Behold, look! Exceedingly beautiful!"

How is such a poetics to be defined? How far and how deeply does it penetrate? It cannot proceed by rules, but only, as we have seen, by learning to *inhabit the other*, who is ultimately God Himself. There are no hard and fast prescriptions for it, though there is much patristic writing to guide us in the ascesis of how to do it. In our time, few read those guides, and pretty much everything is up for grabs. Local churches—Orthodox or those going by some other name—create and define their own versions of tradition. Or, sadly, bombarded by a seemingly infinite variety of images and practices of "good living," we give it all over to the pundits and the professionals and the advertisers to decide for us what is "healthy" and "good." Is there not therefore a high value to be assigned to understanding the poetics—the patterns and syntax—of a genuinely Orthodox or "true," "ascetic" life and art and practice? Which versions of tradition are essential and which are inspired by the spirits of some present age? What makes something genuinely Orthodox or true? Where and how do we go astray? Where and how do we hit the mark? These haven't changed; we simply forget, perhaps never having really understood.

A monk of Athos once spoke to Don of taking with him as the fruit of his pilgrimage the "savor" of the Holy Mountain—to my knowledge the oldest continuous Orthodox Christian monastic community on earth. I think it not wrong to extend this sense of *savor* to the "poetics" of the Church as a whole. Certain qualities of it come to my mind: undramatic, ascetic, sober, patient, deep, dark and bright at the same time, antiphonal, chiastic, supplicating, thankful and praise-giving, humble and kenotic, joyous. There is little artistic *self*-expressiveness, little emotionally inspired or stimulating decorativeness, and few artists' signatures on the icons. The human countenance prevails, but individual features and personalities of depicted saints are restrained in order to allow the presence of

God in them to shine through; for what makes a saint is that he or she has taken on something of Christ's countenance. All church art and architecture and music follows patterns and traditions designed to focus the holy and allow it to show through, rather than engaging and following emotional impulses to express the "self" or the spirits of the present age (often one and the same). Even the gorgeous decoration of much Orthodox art, when it's present, seems generally to depict the variety and beauty of God's creation and to organize it in clear patterns that serve to glorify, hold, and focus our attention toward what is holy. It is seldom, in my experience, present for its own sake. For we are being trained, carefully, over many ages, to express God rather than our accidental selves—*who* rather than *how* we are.

Such "straitening and enlarging," to use St. Isaac's language, is the way of ascetic beauty. Borrowing Don's language, it is an aching, delicate, golden, durable, divine beauty, an oil of gladness, a beauty enjoyed by the very angels—a beauty that shines plainly in the bareness of a mid-October Vermont hillside in the rain, "the very dreariness the strength of the beauty."

For our God is a deeply ascetic God, Creator and Lover of the exceeding beauty released by His sword of ascetic clarification. To meet the sharpness of this sword by which "our eyes and hearts are opened" so we may learn to become one with His beauty, He gives us the shield of psalmic prayer: "not poems merely, but sacred sounds taking (for our joy) the outward shape of poems."

"Blessed the people who know the joyful sound" (Ps. 88:15).

APPENDIX

On Numbering of Psalms and Praying the Kathismata

Numbering of Psalms

Septuagint Psalm Numbers	Hebrew Psalm Numbers
1–8	1–8
9	9–10
10–112	11–113 (*add 1 to the number of each psalm*)
113	114–115
114	116:1–9
115	116:10–19
116–145	117–146 (*add 1 to the number of each psalm*)
146	147:1–11
147	147:12–20
148–150	148–150

Order of Reading the Kathismata in
Daily Prayer (outside Great Lent)

Day	Morning	Evening
Sunday	II, III	
Monday	IV, V	VI
Tuesday	VII, VIII	IX
Wednesday	X, XI	XII
Thursday	XIII, XIV	XV
Friday	XIX, XX	XVIII
Saturday	XVI, XVII	I

NOTES

Despite the fact that so much of the material in this book is from journals or rough notes for lectures, the author generally took remarkable care to reference his sources. As editor, I have elaborated on these where necessary, occasionally corrected them, and added cross-references, but I have added "Ed." to discursive or explanatory notes of my own and to citations I have added but am not certain of. I have also added *JWC* or *JTC* to notes provided by two extraordinary men, John Wayne Coatney and John Taylor Carr, who substantially assisted me with the Hebrew and Greek, respectively. —*Ed.*

A Life in Psalms: Editor's Introduction

1. *Ascetical Homilies of St. Isaac the Syrian* (Boston, MA: Holy Transfiguration Monastery, 1984), Homily 1 (hereafter St. Isaac). This book is available in a revised second edition (2011) with different pagination. Page references herein are to the 1984 edition, cited by homily:page. For more on this passage from Homily 1, see chapter 8. —*Ed.*
2. See glossary for *nous*; also throughout, especially chapters 2 and 8.
3. See Pavel Florensky, *The Pillar and Ground of the Truth* (Princeton, NJ: Princeton Univ. Press, 1997), 238.
4. Quoted in Hilary Mullins' article on "The Transfiguration of Don Sheehan" at http://numerocinqmagazine.com/2013/08/06/the-transfiguration-of-don-sheehan-essay-hilary-mullins/. —*Ed.*
5. *The Grace of Incorruption: The Selected Essays of Donald Sheehan on*

Orthodox Faith and Poetics, ed. Xenia Sheehan (Orleans, MA: Paraclete, 2015). —*Ed.*

6. This prayer is most notably discussed in *The Way of a Pilgrim*, trans. R. M. French (Seabury Press, 1970; numerous more contemporary editions are available), a book that the author came across some weeks after the prayer began for him. From it he learned that his prayer, known as the Prayer of the Heart, had long been central to the Eastern Orthodox Church, which he subsequently learned to be the Church as it had developed according to the Great Commission in the eastern part of the Roman Empire following Christ's Resurrection and Ascension and the coming of the Holy Spirit at Pentecost. See glossary entry on Orthodox Church. —*Ed.*

7. Masoretic Hebrew refers to the ninth- or tenth-century reconstructed Hebrew text of the Old Testament Scriptures, of which much was lost in the destruction of Jerusalem in AD 70 (see glossary for more on the dating of this text, about which there is scholarly debate). Most English-language Bibles today are based on the Masoretic text (abbrev. MT), the most noted being the 1611 King James Authorized Version (AV). The Greek Septuagint, or Translation of the Seventy (LXX), was made in Alexandria from the much older Hebrew text in the second and third centuries BC. See glossary entries for Septuagint and Masoretic Text. —*Ed.*

8. The author's translation of the LXX Psalter was commissioned by and eventually published in the *Orthodox Study Bible* (Nashville, TN: Thomas Nelson, 2008), with some editorial changes. Over the next several years, he continued to make revisions in his own version, re-lineating the verses in the Coverdale style (except in Psalm 118[119], where he chose to preserve something closer to the "trim and shapely half-lines" of the Hebrew). He also changed the text to use the second-person singular (thee/thou—not used at all in the OSB). He demonstrates the necessity for this in chapter 12 herein, showing the human "I" to be introduced in line 5 of Psalm 118 only after the divine "thou" in line 4. "The point of this sequence is abundantly clear," he says. "The human person is—*can be*—manifested only *after* the divine Person becomes known. And once the plurality of the (not-yet-knowing-God) human has achieved the unity of the (knowing-God) person, then the divine 'thou' can draw closer to the human 'I.'" And this is the prerequisite for the intimate, incarnative,

and salvific relationship that then grows throughout the psalm between God and the psalmist. In 2006 he wrote, quoting George Steiner, *After Babel: Aspects of Language and Translation* (Oxford, England: Oxford University Press, 2nd ed. 1998), 97: "No language has been found to lack a first- and second-personal singular pronoun," adding in his own words: "For all languages on earth are in this sense foundationally psalmic: all are capable of deepest intimacy, truly capable as each one's foundational drama." His final version of the Psalter, *The Psalms of David: Translated from the Septuagint Greek,* was published posthumously by Wipf & Stock in 2013. —*Ed.*

9. See glossary entry on *chiasm/chiastic structure*, and chapter 5.

10. Mother Maria [Lydia Gysi], *The Psalms: An Exploratory Translation* (North Yorkshire, England: Greek Orthodox Monastery of the Assumption, 1973).

11. Mullins, "Transfiguration."

Chapter 1. Reflections on Psalms and Psalmic Prayer

1. The author attributes this to Origen. —*Ed.*

2. The author's notes clearly contain the word אוּר (*ur*), which is an obscure word for firelight, or fire. The far more common term for light is אוֹר (*or*). —*JWC*

3. Abba Philemon (or Philimon), in *The Philokalia*, comp. St. Nikodimos of the Holy Mountain and St. Makarios of Corinth; trans. and ed. G. E. H. Palmer, Philip Sherrard, Kallistos Ware, vols. 1, 2, and 4 (London, Boston: Faber and Faber, 1981), 2:343–57; also included in Igumen Chariton's anthology, *The Art of Prayer: An Orthodox Anthology* (New York, NY: Farrar, Straus and Giroux, rev. ed. 1997).

4. Theophan the Recluse, in Chariton, *Art of Prayer.*

5. At the point of Orthodox baptism, one is given the protection and name of a patron saint (which may be one's own name; or one may then take the saint's name as one's own, though it is not required). Thus, Carol was given and decided to keep (following her Russian godmother's preference) the name Xenia at her baptism on Holy Saturday of 1989, after St. Xenia of Petersburg: an eighteenth-century Russian noblewoman, widowed young, who gave away all her property and lived on the streets of St. Petersburg as a "fool for Christ," devoting herself to prayer, repentance, and giving aid to others. For

her life, see https://oca.org/saints/lives/2019/01/24/100297-blessed-xenia-of-st-petersburg. Blessed St. Xenia, pray to God for us! —*Ed.*

6. A Dartmouth friend and colleague, now Rev. John Konkle, serving for the past decade as Resident Priest at the Orthodox Monastery of the Dormition of the Mother of God in Rives Jct., Michigan, where the Editor now resides. —*Ed.*

7. Francis Brown, *The New Brown–Driver–Briggs–Gesenius Hebrew and English Lexicon* (Peabody, MA: Hendrickson, 1979), 211b; hereafter BDB.

8. Its other, and closely related, meanings include *to moan* (like a dove in distress), *to groan, to utter sound, to speak*. In the first line of Psalm 2, the Hebrew *hagah* means *to imagine falsely, to devise deceitfully:* "Why do the nations rage and the people meditate [*meletaō*] vain things?" (Ps. 2:1). In Isaiah 8:19, *hagah* in its plural participial form signifies the "chirpings and mutterings [made by] necromancers and wizards" (BDB, ibid.).

9. On *chiastic*, see glossary and throughout, especially chapter 5.

10. BDB, 1044a.

11. Eugene Peterson, *Answering God: The Psalms as Tools for Prayer* (HarperOne rprt ed., 1991), 95; hereafter cited as *Answering God*.

12. Sophrony [Sakharov] (Archimandrite; now Saint), *St. Silouan the Athonite*, trans. Rosemary Edmonds (Crestwood, NY: St. Vladimir's Seminary Press, 1991), 209–10.

13. Ibid., 423.

14. St. Isaac, 37:182.

15. St. Isaac, 50:241.

16. Exod. 3:14a: "Then God said to Moses, 'I AM the Existing One.'"

17. See also ch. 12, p. 231, for the full meaning of *hesed*.

18. St. Isaac, 54:269.

19. See *Philokalia*. In the *Philokalia* glossary this word is translated as "watchfulness," though it is related in the glossary to the concept of "attentiveness." —*JTC*

20. Robert Alter and Frank Kermode, *Literary Guide to the Bible* (Cambridge, MA: Belknap Press of Harvard University Press, 1990), 255.

21. Kathleen Norris, *The Psalms* (New York, NY: Riverhead, 1997), 352.

Chapter 2. Translated to Life

1. A troparion is a short hymn of one stanza, or one of a series of stanzas, sung in the Orthodox Church. The Feast of the Dormition celebrates the "translation" of the Mother of God to life at the end of her earthly life. It is a dogmatic tenet of the Orthodox Church that she was fully mortal, truly died as all people die, and was taken up bodily into eternal life by her Son. The clear point here is that "translation" is able to—even must—carry the fullness of a text's life, its body and soul, across a language barrier into fullness of life in a new language. It need in no way be a loss or a thing to be grieved, but rather a fulfillment. —*Ed.*

2. Twentieth-century Orthodox theologians Alexander Schmemann and Thomas Hopko (in *The Winter Pascha*, SVS Press, 1984) held that "Mary is the Great Example, not the great exception" (as Western Christianity views her). She is the entirely human model of humility, faith, obedience, prayer, study, and forgiveness whom every Christian may and should follow. —*Ed.*

3. This gives us a further—though perhaps not altogether different—layer of meaning and form to translate. As at her Dormition, the full personhood of the Mother of God, body and soul, passed through death and was translated to the fullness of unending life, in translating Psalms it is not simply a meaning that must be extracted somehow from the form that first communicated it, and then communicated in a new way. Rather, the poem itself is a living entity that, in being translated, must find new, resurrected life, body and soul, in a new language. —*Ed.*

4. Baron Wormser, former Poet Laureate of Maine, has authored many books of and concerning poetry. This explanation was contributed at the editor's request. —*Ed.*

5. This quality of *resistance* could be considered as an essential component of the ascetic poetics of Psalms, as discussed in the book's Epilogue. —*Ed.*

6. On *chiasmus* and *chiastic form*, see glossary entry and throughout, especially chapter 5. —*Ed.*

7. *Philokalia*, 1:362–63.

8. See glossary for *ontological*.

9. E. R. Dodds, *Journal and Letters of Stephen MacKenna* (MacMillan,

1936), 155, 114. I am not certain this was the edition the author used. —*Ed.*

10. Ibid., 116, 147.

11. Loeb, *Plotinus*, 3:161 (exact source uncertain).

12. Dodds, *Journal and Letters of Stephen MacKenna*, 155.

13. Ibid., 107.

14. Mother Maria, *The Psalms*, preface.

15. Ibid.

16. BDB, 970b.

17. Here and throughout, the Tetragrammaton is transliterated without vowels (יהוה, *YHWH*), indicating that it is not to be pronounced. Most will pronounce it "Yahweh." However, in Hebrew, the Name is never given these vowels; it is usually given the vowels for the word Adonai (which is why some thought the Name was pronounced Jehovah), and occasionally the vowels for Elohim. It is widely agreed that the Name (יהוה, YHWH) is etymologically connected to the onto-logical verb ("to be") and its imperfect first person ("I am"). Also, "life" and "to live" are from the root verb חוה, which is very close to the verb "to be": הוה, but the connection between the two is in their inherent meaning rather than etymology, for to live is to be and to die is to cease to be. —*JWC*

Chapter 3. Five Conundrums of Translatability

1. The author noted here: "Smyth 1872 ref. on Greek participles." I assume this to be Herbert Weir Smyth, *A Greek Grammar for Colleges*, ed. Gordon M. Messing (Martino Fine Books, 1956 edition, reprinted in 2013), chap. 1872 on Participles. This chapter can be accessed online at http://www.perseus.tufts.edu/hopper/text?doc=Perseus%3Atext%3A1999.04.0007%3Asmythp%3D1872 —*Ed.*

2. BDB, 328.

3. The author notes here: "[more on contrastive participle usages]—door closes with indicatives." —*Ed.*

4. The transliteration of Hebrew letters used by Dr. John Coatney (and recommended by the Society of Biblical Literature) would transliterate *Aleph* as *Alef.* Because in *The Psalms of David* the author used the Greek transliterations of the letters and labeled the stanzas of Psalm 118 accordingly, we have retained that spelling here to avoid

confusion. —*Ed.*

5. See chapter 12 for discussion of this point.
6. See chapter 11 for a fuller exposition of this.
7. See also chapters 6 and 11.
8. *Biblia Hebraica Stuttgartensia: SESB Version.* Electronic ed. (Stuttgart, Germany: German Bible Society, 2003).
9. Francis Hare, *Liber Psalmorum Hebraïca* (Forgotten Books, 2018), 301.
10. Quoted from the *Seper-ha-Yihud*, a late thirteenth-century kabbalistic text, in G. H. Hartman, ed., *Midrash and Literature* (New Haven, CT: Yale University Press, 1986), 145.
11. *The Psalter According to the Seventy* (Boston, MA: Holy Transfiguration Monastery, 1997).
12. BDB, 967a.
13. *Deuterosemia* is the process whereby we enter into the depths of sacred words *so as to enter our own depths*: for we cannot do the first *unless* we do the second. And when we enter the word's depths, we find in our own heart *these very words*: they *are* our heart's depths. This seems similar to what Stephen MacKenna (in chapter 2) says about seeing through a good or "free" translation to the original. It also seems this may be a synonym for *noetic seeing*, or perhaps the mirror or match of it: we enter our own noetic depths, our heart, in order to enter the depths of sacred words. See glossary for the author's comments on *deuterosemia*. —*Ed.*
14. In this context, I refer the reader to the author's introductory essay on "The Mind of David and the Mind of Christ" in *The Psalms of David: Translated from the Septuagint Greek by Donald Sheehan*, ed. Xenia Sheehan and Hieromonk Herman Majkrzak (Eugene, OR: Wipf and Stock, 2013). —*Ed.*

Chapter 4. The Angels Sing: Reflections on a Rule of Prayer

1. Introduction to Mother Maria, *The Psalms*.
2. See glossary on *theosis*. This journal entry is dated January 1987. —*Ed.*
3. Chariton, *The Art of Prayer*, 405.
4. Abba Philemon (or Philimon), in *The Philokalia*, 2:347.
5. *The Psalter According to the Seventy*, 10.

6. St. Isaac, 75:365–66.

7. See appendix for a weekly pattern of reading Psalms.

8. For an extended development of this subject, see "Introduction: The Mind of David and the Mind of Christ" in *The Psalms of David*, xxv. —*Ed.*

9. This half-line (Ps. 1:3) was not included in the published version, *The Psalms of David*. Whether this was inadvertent (on our part) or deliberate (on his) we are at this point unable to determine. —*Ed.*

10. See glossary entry on *nous*.

11. See glossary entry and bibliography for *Philokalia*.

12. Mother Maria [Lydia Gysi], *Orthodox Potential* (North Yorkshire, England: Greek Orthodox Monastery of the Assumption, 1973).

13. St. Innocent, Metropolitan of Moscow, in Chariton, *Art of Prayer*, 232.

Chapter 5. Chiastic and Temporal Movement in Psalms

1. Ronald E. Heine, *Gregory of Nyssa's Treatise on the Inscriptions of the Psalms* (New York, NY: Oxford University Press, 1995), 110; I:80. All quotations of St. Gregory herein are from this work. The first number is Heine's page, the second Gregory's reference where there is one.

2. Heine, 164; II:134.

3. Heine, 121–23.

4. See glossary on *antinomy*.

5. St. Isaac, 52:261.

6. Heine, 121; I:117.

7. St. Isaac, 52:261.

8. St. Isaac, 52:261–62.

9. See glossary entry on *theoria*.

10. St. Isaac, 52:261.

11. Unless noted otherwise, all Psalms quotations are from Sheehan, *The Psalms of David*.

12. Florensky, *The Pillar and Ground of the Truth*, 138–40.

13. See chapter 1 and elsewhere on this understanding of psalmic meditation.

14. See the author's development of this idea in chapter 10.

15. St. John Climacus, *The Ladder of Divine Ascent* (Boston, MA: Holy

Transfiguration Monastery, rev. ed. 2001), 7:7. Cited hereafter as *Ladder*, followed by step and paragraph numbers.

16. Sophrony, *Saint Silouan the Athonite*, 143.

17. Alter and Kermode, *The Literary Guide to the Bible*, 260 (Alter's translation).

18. Ibid., 255.

19. Ibid.

20. Heine, 121; I:117.

21. *Philokalia*, 4:428.

22. *Philokalia*, 4:314.

23. Bp. J. D. Zizioulas, *Being as Communion* (Crestwood, NY: St. Vladimir's Seminary Press, 1997), 59.

24. Heine, 122–23; I:122.

25. Fyodor Dostoevsky, *The Brothers Karamazov*, trans. and annot. Richard Pevear and Larissa Volokhonsky (San Francisco, CA: North Point Press, 1990; repr. New York, NY: Vintage, 1991).

Chapter 6. Psalmic Enemies: Absalom

1. Lancelot Brenton, *The Interlineary Hebrew and English Psalter* (Grand Rapids, MI: Zondervan, 1979).

2. The author made a marginal note here to expand this point, but I do not find any record of his having done so, at least in writing. It is entirely consistent, though, with his understanding of depression, discussed elsewhere in the book—even with his own arrival (see editor's introduction) at a rock-bottom sense of his life being broken, and understanding this as a starting point; or with Mother Maria's description of the End-Point (see ibid.); or with the psalmic pit as a way to psychic resurrection, "for every power is taken away so completely from the person in the pit that God can thus directly work His redemptive will for him." —*Ed.*

3. Robert Alter, *The Art of Biblical Narrative* (New York: Basic Books, 1981), 306.

4. Ibid., slightly paraphrased.

5. On *statutes*, see also chapter 11 and the glossary. —*Ed.*

6. See glossary and throughout, especially chapter 5, for discussion of *chiasmus*. —*Ed.*

7. *Tehillim*, 1:77. (See bibliography for full reference.) Rabbi Shlomo

Ritzchaki, known by the acronym Rashi, was a medieval (1040–1105) French rabbi and commentator on the Talmud and Tanakh; RaDak, or David Kimchi (1160–1235), was a noted rabbi, biblical commentator, scholar, and grammarian. —*Ed.*

8. See G.W.H. Lampe, *A Patristic Greek Lexicon* (Oxford, England: Clarendon Press, 1969), 150a.

9. St. Isaac, 4:33.

10. BDB, 92a/b.

11. Lampe, 222b.

12. BDB, 2a.

13. Lampe, 222b. The citation in Lampe, says John Carr, is to a collection called the "Clementine Homilies"—homilies attributed to St. Clement but considered by scholars to be authored by other unknowns. —*JTC*

14. *Tehillim*, 2:1096.

15. Kurt Aland, Matthew Black, Carlo Martini, et al., *Greek New Testament* (Stuttgart: Wuerttemberg Bible Society, 2nd ed. 1968).

16. The author is here following Florensky's discussion of the word *makarios*, based on Schelling (*Einleitung in die Philos. d. Mythologie* [Samtl. W., 2-te Abth. Bd. I. SS. 469–77, 2 Buch, 20 Vorles]), where he refers to "*kardia, kear, kēr* (genitive=*kēros*, 'heart' . . . the most sincere part of a man, his proper selfhood, the place of 'passions' in general, and, among them, of love in particular." Florensky, *The Pillar and Ground of the Truth*, 138. —*Ed.*

Chapter 7. The Sword of Depression and the Shield of Psalmic Prayer

1. Heine, 84–85; I:4–8.

2. Heine, 85; I:8.

3. Cf. Lampe, 1206b. St. Gregory of Nyssa, however, also sees the "poor man" as a figure of Christ Himself.

4. See Lampe, 61b.

5. *Ladder*, 13:11.

6. *Ladder*, 13:5.

7. *Tehillim*, 2:1228.

8. Ibid.

9. Florensky, 151.

10. Lampe, 443a.

Chapter 8. The Sons of Korah and the Way of Psalmic Poetics

1. Heine, 59.
2. Numbers 16:13–16, with some paraphrasing.
3. *Tehillim*, 1:523.
4. Rahlfs gives the "I" of line 17 in a well-attested footnote to the third-person plural verb he prints.
5. *Philokalia*, 1:361.
6. Fabre d'Olivet, *The Hebraic Tongue Restored*, 1815, trans. Nayán Louise Redfield (New York, NY: G. P. Putnam's Sons, 1921), 328.
7. Ibid., 377–78.
8. *Ladder*, 28:61.
9. *Philokalia*, 1:361.
10. *Tehillim*, 1:561.
11. Ibid.
12. Shocher Tov, ibid.
13. Ibid.
14. See Lev. 11:20–21 and 22:5.
15. *Tehillim*, 1:562.
16. Greek *kallas* (Johan Lust, et al., *Greek English Lexicon of the Septuagint*, Part 2 [Stuttgart, Germany: Deutsche Bibelgesellschaft, 1996], 225b); Hebrew יָפָה, *yafah* (BDB, 421b).
17. *Tehillim*, 1:486–87. Unable to locate this source, John Wayne Coatney found the parable in William G. Braude, trans., *The Midrash on Psalms* (New Haven, CT: Yale University Press, 1959), 428–30. —*Ed.*
18. *Philokalia*, St. Diadochos, 1:280.
19. Ibid.; I give the translation of the line from Psalm 44 in my version, not in the one used in the English *Philokalia*.
20. Alshich, *Tehillim*, 1:568.
21. Ibid.
22. See Job 42:14.
23. BDB, 1032c.
24. BDB, 169.
25. BDB, 189–90.
26. 3 Kings 3:5–8; slightly paraphrased.
27. St. Isaac, 1:6.
28. Ibid., 2:12; the single bracket is the translator's and the double one mine.
29. Ibid.

30. Ibid., 1:6 #25.
31. Ibid., 37:179.
32. Ibid., 37:181.
33. BDB, 555a; see Ezra 7:6; Prov. 22:29; Isa. 16:5.
34. D'Olivet, 393.
35. Heine, 98; I:41.
36. D'Olivet, 295.
37. BDB, 776b.
38. Edwin Hatch and Henry A. Redpath, *A Concordance to the Septuagint*, 2nd ed. (Grand Rapids, MI: Baker Books, 1998), 939a; BDB 228a.
39. See Lampe, 578b.
40. [Pseudo-]Dionysius, *The Complete Works*, "The Mystical Theology" and "The Divine Names," trans. Paul Rorem, Classics of Western Spirituality (Mahwah, NJ: Paulist Press, 1987), 190; see Heil and Ritter, *Corpus Dionysiacum* (Berlin, Germany: DeGruyter, 1990), 2:58–59.
41. See Lampe, 4a.
42. 3 Kings 3:10–11; very slightly paraphrased.
43. *Tehillim*, 1:559.
44. Don cites here BDB, 1116b. I am told that the lexical form of the word found in this psalm's superscription is actually *shoshan* (שׁוֹשַׁן), which has no direct connection with the verb *shanah* (שָׁנָה). It is entirely possible, however, that the translators of the LXX perceived a connection between them and that this is why the Greek translation is ἀλλοιωθησομένων, as suggested by Johan Lust in his *Greek-English Lexicon of the Septuagint*. Based on the LXX's otherwise unexplained translation, I would argue that there is enough warrant for the connection to share Don's imaginative understanding here. —Ed. with the help of JWC, JTC, and JJ.
45. See *Tehillim*, 1:560.
46. See Lampe, 76a.
47. This word, ἠλλοίωσαν (*ēlloiōsan*), is found in Daniel 3:28 in the Lancelot Brenton text with translation, *The Septuagint with Apocrypha: Greek and English* (Grand Rapids, MI: Zondervan, 1982), though not at this location in Rahlfs'. —JTC
48. Martin Buber, *Right and Wrong: An Interpretation of Some Psalms*, trans. Ronald Gregor Smith (Norwich, England: SCM Press, 1952), 45.

Chapter 9. "In Their Very Midst He Judged among the Judges"

1. *Tehillim*, 2:1038.
2. The Trisagion (meaning "thrice-holy") is an Orthodox Prayer—"Holy God, Holy Mighty, Holy Immortal, have mercy on us"—sung in the Divine Liturgy and chanted or sung in other services and private prayers, especially Hours, Vespers, and Matins. —*Ed.*
3. Buber, *Right and Wrong.*
4. Martin Buber, *Good and Evil: Two Interpretations* (New York, NY: Charles Scribner's Sons, 1953).

Chapter 10. The Chiastic Heart of the Psalter

1. Heine, 12.
2. Cf. the author's essay on "The Mind of David and the Mind of Christ," Introduction to *The Psalms of David*, xxv.
3. Cf. Sheehan, *The Grace of Incorruption*, part 2, chapter 6, p. 195, on "The Drama of Intimacy."

Chapter 11. The Asymmetry of His Immeasurable Love

1. Jerome Groopman, "A Model Patient: How Simulators are Changing the Way a Doctor Is Trained," *The New Yorker*, May 2, 2005. Material was drawn from the author's journal entry citing this article in creating the introduction to Part 2 ("Orthodox Poetics and the Great Psalm: Introduction to Psalmic Poetics") in *The Grace of Incorruption*, 126. —*Ed.*
2. Fr. John Konkle notes that, in confirmation of the resurrectional meaning of the Great Psalm, church rubrics for all Orthodox call for it to be sung or read every Saturday at Matins or at home in private prayer, since this is the day for remembering the departed, especially the martyrs. Most Orthodox outside of monasteries, however, don't experience the centrality of this psalm in their regular parish life, either because the Saturday Divine Liturgy is not served or, if it is, the presence of Psalm 118 is far less emphatic than it is on the Saturdays before Pascha that are so focused on the impending celebration of the Resurrection. The author nonetheless prayed it regularly in his Saturday morning prayers. —*Ed.*
3. Hatch and Redpath, *Concordance.*

4. BDB, 824a and b.
5. *Hoq* is the nominal form of *chuqqah*.
6. See chapters 2, 5, 8, and 12.
7. See glossary entries on *demons* and *logismoi*.
8. Lampe, 1332a.
9. Lust, II:460b.
10. *Ladder*, Step 13:15.

Chapter 12. The Making of Personhood

1. BDB, 211b.
2. Ibid.
3. Peterson, *Answering God*, 423.
4. Bernard A. Taylor, *The Analytical Lexicon to the Septuagint* (Grand Rapids, MI: Zondervan, 1994), 159a.
5. Taylor, 417a; cf. Lampe, 1375a; as well as Hatch and Redpath, 1335c.
6. Florensky, *Pillar and Ground*, 138–39.
7. Not to be considered here as different from the fierce energy and pleasure of attacking and devouring one's own sins discussed above and in previous chapters. —*Ed.*
8. The author notes marginally at this point: "Contrast: modern 'I' as autonomous self-expressive 'creativity.' Florensky: icon as canonic." —*Ed.*
9. [Pseudo-]Dionysius, *The Divine Names*.
10. Ibid., 8:2–8:5.
11. Ibid., 893A, 112.
12. See *Masoretic Text* in glossary for a guide to other information about dating of this text.
13. See Lampe, 499a.
14. See Lust, 1:162a.
15. Ibid.
16. See glossary. The *logos* is God's Word to us; our *logismoi* are generally our fallen thoughts. —*Ed.*
17. H. F. W. Gesenius, *Gesenius' Hebrew Grammar*, ed. E. Kautzsch and A. E. Cowley (Oxford, England: Oxford University Press), 23; hereafter Gesenius.
18. D'Olivet, 287.
19. Gesenius, 23.

20. D'Olivet, 300.
21. *Ladder*, 28:61.
22. *Philokalia*, 1:362.
23. William Matthews, an American poet (1942–97) whom the author deeply admired. —*Ed.*
24. See Lampe, 1166b.
25. E. R. Wharton, *Etyma Graeca: An Etymological Lexicon of Classical Greek* (London, England: Percival and Co., 1890), 56.
26. C. S. Lewis, *The Abolition of Man* (San Francisco, CA: HarperOne, 2001), 28.
27. Lampe, 150a.
28. The author notes in his journal to link this to Ps. 68:29b: "the salvation of thy face has taken hold of me."—*Ed.*
29. Lampe, 36b.
30. See Lampe, 1282b.
31. The author appears to have considered this explication unfinished and asks marginally in his journal: "What does *Gimel do*—as act—that furthers *Aleph* and *Beth*?" —*Ed.*
32. See Lampe, 294b.
33. In St. Herman of Alaska Brotherhood, *Conquering Depression: Heavenly Wisdom from God-Illumined Teachers* (Platina, CA: St. Herman Press, 1996), 80, #117.
34. Florensky, *Pillar and Ground*, 143.
35. Ibid., 144.
36. Heine 90; I:23.
37. Heine 90; I:20.
38. Heine 90; I:21.
39. Heine 91–92; I:24.
40. Heine 90; I:20.
41. The classical meaning of this word *histēmi* is "to stand"; the author here shows how the meaning is deepened in the LXX. —*JTC*
42. George Eliot, *Daniel Deronda* (New York: Lovell, Coryell, & Co., 1876), 2:58.
43. Alter and Kermode, 631.
44. Ibid.
45. *Exereunaō* has the meaning "to search out," to "examine" in Ps. 118:34; *ekzēteō* means "to search" in Ps. 118:3. —*JTC*
46. St. Isaac, 51:244–45.

47. Lust, 494b.
48. The author includes two notations here: (a) connect "quickening" to "gracious"; (b) connect "gracious" to fear of God. —*Ed.*
49. Dr. John Coatney adds: "I'm fairly sure that he's making word-play between χρηστός (good) and χριστός (anointed); that's the only way that טוֹב (*tov*) fits."
50. BDB, 841b, 842a.
51. See Lampe, 369b.
52. Eugene Peterson, *Leap Over a Wall* (San Francisco, CA: HarperOne, 1998), 173.
53. Ibid., 173.
54. See chapter 11, Lexicon of the Nine Words.
55. See ibid.
56. BDB, 556a.
57. Heine 91; I:22.
58. Heine 89; I:20.
59. Ibid.

Epilogue: Love at the Boundary

1. Bracketed words were not legible in the author's handwriting. These are best guesses. —*Ed.*
2. The author was told this by his Israeli Hebrew teacher at Dartmouth College. —*Ed.*
3. Much of this is recorded in *The Grace of Incorruption*.
4. Buber, *Good and Evil*, 45.
5. In chapter 3 he says: "Psalmic tradition affirms ten authors of Psalms. All are David. The logic of this is *prophecy*: David is prophetically the author of all the psalms. We do not have the category of prophecy." —*Ed.*
6. Christopher Alexander, *A Pattern Language* (Oxford Univ. Press, Center for Environmental Structure Series, 1977).
7. Not having the Notes to refer to, I am uncertain whether he wrote "Book" or "Body" here. I first thought it was "Book," but "Body" makes more sense. A case could also be made for "Book," however. —*Ed.*

GLOSSARY

The foundation for this glossary was prepared by Fr. Moses Hibbard and Mark Montague, with the editor, for publication in *The Grace of Incorruption: The Selected Esssays of Donald Sheehan on Orthodox Faith and Poetics*, ed. Xenia Sheehan (Paraclete, 2015). Many entries not relevant to this book have been deleted; others unique to this volume have been added by the editor, based on the author's various mentions or discussions of the term in question (see, e.g., "Blessedness" or "Cadence").

Abba Philemon—One of the greatest desert dwellers of all, according to the *Philokalia*. No historical date is available as to when exactly he lived, but he was said to be a great man of prayer, experiencing constant tears of repentance and practicing extreme asceticism.

Angels—The angels are one part of a threefold created order: angels, humankind, and the rest of material creation. Saint John of Damascus (eighth-century Syrian priest monk and polymath) tells us, "Compared with us, the angel is said to be incorporeal and immaterial, although in comparison with God . . . everything proves to be gross and material" (*Exact Exposition of the Orthodox Faith*, II, 3; 37:205; in *Writings: Fathers of the Church*). There are nine ranks of angels, of which the ones that concern us most are those who serve as God's messengers to humankind (Greek *angelos*) and watch over peoples, nations, and each person to assist in the working out of God's Providence (see Makarios, *Synaxarion*, II, 63–66). The Orthodox Church understands the goal of this Providence to be the raising of humankind to be even higher than the angels. For we are told, "Therefore you shall be perfect, just as your Father in heaven is perfect" (Matt. 5:48). See also Demons.

Antinomy/Antinomical—"The affirmation of two contrasting or opposed truths, which cannot be reconciled on the level of the discursive reason although a reconciliation is possible on the higher level of contemplative experience" (Ware, "Debate about Palamism," 46). Their reconciliation, however, requires that neither pole of the apparent opposition be rejected. See especially chapters 5, 9, 10, and 11 herein.

For theological clarification concerning human reason and antinomy, I refer the reader to the following comment kindly provided to me by Fr. Matthew Baker in connection with the publication of the author's *Psalms* volume (*The Psalms of David*, n. 10, p. xxxiv): Fr. Georges Florovsky has written that "the divine Logos is no antinomy which undermines the 'logical'; rather, here is the full measure of Logos. Antinomy is removed in 'contemplation': *theoria—henosis* [union] . . . That is, while knowledge of God may be, according to a certain definition, supra-rational, it is not irrational, and may (according to a wider definition of reason) be rightly called 'rational'." G. Florovsky to S. Sakharov, May 15, 1958, in Arkhimandrit Sofronii [Sakharov], *Perepiska s Protoiereem Georgiem Florovskim* (Essex/Moscow: Svyato-Ioanno-Predtechenskii Monastyr'/Svyato-Troitskaya Sergieva Lavra, 2008). —*Ed.*

Antiphonal Singing/Antiphony—The word *antiphony* literally means "one voice against another." When practiced in church singing, this is done when one choir (or person) responds to another choir (or person). The goal is not to create two distinct realities against one another, but rather to integrate the two realities into one, thereby emphasizing unity, especially with regard to true worship of the Triune Godhead. Prof. Sheehan often uses *antiphony* in the context of the psalmist's (or our) dialogue with God as we move toward deeper relationship with Him.

Ascesis—A Greek term originally referring to athletic training, an analogy that Saint Paul was wont to use (Phil. 3:12–16; 2 Tim. 4:7). The practice of asceticism within the Orthodox Christian tradition is not merely a physical exercise, although it has this as one component, but rather a setting aside of earthly pursuits and concerns to come to full actualization of the person in the life of God in the Church.

Athonite—See Mt. Athos.

Blessedness/Beatitude—Psalmic blessedness is, first, a choice, a decision: the decision to *be* "unity moving into renewal." Thus, blessedness arises in the activity of negating *as a way to* God's activity; it is a *walking*, an actual putting down of first one foot, then another, a way of going somewhere that is "not in the counsel of the ungodly." And it takes root in choosing the delight that arises when one becomes rooted *in the Law*, in the great Torah, or Teaching, of God. Blessedness thus begins in not perpetuating the disaster that is the world; it is a deliberate turning away from this world-disaster, leaving the Egypt of our settled, enslaved lives, at every moment choosing to risk the encounter—as *direct a contact as we can stand*—with the growling, the weeping, the thunderous shock that are our God and our history. This is the "exodus" basis of Psalms—for all of psalmic blessedness is, precisely, the enactment of God's historic incarnation in and as Israel.

Cadence/Cadential Shape—Rhythmic flow of a sequence of words or sounds; poetic form governed by cadence rather than a fixed metrical pattern. Also, in Psalms, the convergence of the aesthetic pattern and the theological significance into *one shape*. In Psalm 118, the author identifies two kinds of cadence that give shape to the poem: (1) fixed (the alphabetic sequence of stanzas; by extension, God's presence in the poem and His statutes, the poem's chiastic structure); (2) flowing, which partakes of the incarnate and is driven by many different factors, such as: the particular nature at any given point of the encounter between the angelic and the human, the nature and interaction of voices, the nine words, as well as metric and sonic qualities inherent in Hebrew and the language of translation. Cadential shape is additionally, if not primarily, given by the interaction or "fit" between the two types of cadence.

Cappadocian Fathers—This term usually refers to Saint Gregory of Nyssa, Saint Gregory Nazianzus, and Saint Basil the Great. The theology espoused in the fourth century by these three men, and others in their company, was instrumental in articulating the Church's understanding of personhood in the context of early conciliar discussions regarding the two natures of Christ and the Three Persons of the Holy Trinity.

Chiasm/Chiasmus/Chiastic—A rhetorical form based on concentric parallelism, by which the first line of a poem in some way parallels the last, the second the penultimate, and so on, creating, in addition to the normal linear progression, a centripetal flow of meaning. That is, "meaning is developed from the beginning and end of the passage toward the middle. Accordingly, the ultimate meaning of a chiastically structured passage is expressed not at the *end*, in what we understand to be the 'conclusion.' The real meaning or essential message of the text is to be found rather at its *center*" (Breck, *Scripture in Tradition*, 93). See also Breck, *The Shape of Biblical Language*.

Church Fathers—A title given to the collective body of saints in the Orthodox Church that has helped to bequeath and pass on the Orthodox Christian tradition through the ages. Note that in Orthodox tradition this title is not reserved for a select group that ceased to exist after an arbitrary date in the third or fourth century, but still serves to describe those who facilitate the life and witness of the Church in our own day.

Commandments (*entolai*)—One of the "nine words" of Psalm 118 (see chapter 11). A loving action upon or toward another that becomes saving nourishment for both the agent and the recipient of that love. This word, in LXX Psalms, has absorbed many instances of the word (Heb. פִּקּוּדִים, *piqqudim*) translated "precepts" in texts based on the Hebrew MT.

Compunction—Deep repentance that combines consciousness of one's sinfulness with the tenderness and joy of knowing God's forgiveness. See *Philokalia* 4:314.

Deification—Also known as theosis or divinization, deification is the underlying goal of all Orthodox Christian spirituality. It is the process of participating in the Life of God by sharing in His Divine Energy. The Orthodox do not espouse the possibility of sharing in the Divine Essence of the Holy Trinity, which is shared only among the Persons of the Uncreated Godhead. See also *Blessedness*; *Theoria*; *Theosis*.

Demons—The Orthodox understanding of demons is that, in the first moments of the creation of the invisible world, Lucifer, highest and brightest of the angels, thought to rival God's power and immediately fell into the depths of hell, bringing down with him a multitude of angels of every rank. These once free angelic spirits became what we know as demons. They were confined to the earthly sphere of existence with a limited power to disturb and try the souls of humankind. The Orthodox Church teaches that Christ, in accepting death for our sake, ended forever, for all who follow Him, this demonic power that would lead us to share in their eternal death. For the Orthodox, this following of Christ is a lifelong incarnative practice leading through repentance to theosis and a glorification beyond even that of the angels. For further information, see Seraphim Rose, *Soul After Death*, St. Herman of Alaska Brotherhood, 2009. See also Angels.

Deuterosemia—A word for which the only source we can find is the author. It is the process whereby we enter into the depths of sacred words *so as to enter our own depths*. For we cannot do the first *unless* we do the second. And when we enter the word's depths, we find in our own heart *these very words*: they *are* our heart's depths. It is the *friction* set up by opening the hidden inwardness of Hebrew words—that is, the discontinuity, or *apartness*, that results from having a word [such as *rahav*] *turn in upon itself* by reflecting its own semantic surface at its kabbalistic depth. This friction creates the circumstance wherein meanings-at-depth *break through* the semantic surface: not as the *result* of our examination but as the provocation and cause of it. As we open the word we must open ourselves: such is the law of *deuterosemia*. "And you shall remember that the Lord your God led you all the way these forty years in the wilderness, to humble you and test you, to know what was in your heart, whether you would keep His commandments or not" (Deut. 8:2). The way God knows what is in our hearts (i.e., in the hiddenness of us) is through deuterosemia. Thus: "man lives by every word that proceeds from the mouth of the Lord" (Deut. 8:3). And we know this only (says Deuteronomy) when we experience the humilities of the wilderness; for there, alone, we get it that our lives depend not upon the material arrangements we manage to pull together for ourselves (i.e., not on "bread alone") but rather upon the word of God that is at our heart's hidden depths.

Dionysius the Areopagite—Originally mentioned in the Acts of the Apostles as a companion of the Apostle Paul, he is the purported author of some of the most well-known mystical works in the body of Christian literature; these include *The Celestial Hierarchy, The Ecclesiastical Hierarchy, On the Divine Names,* and *The Mystical Theology*. According to modern scholarship, the name is a pseudonym for someone who was writing in the sixth century, but many Orthodox believers (including the author) hold Saint Dionysius to be identical with the figure mentioned in the New Testament. His feastday is celebrated in the Orthodox Church on October 3. No matter who actually composed the works attributed to him, it is undeniable that these works have been profoundly influential in both the East and the West.

Divinization—See *Deification*.

Dormition—The falling-asleep-in-the-Lord of the Mother of God, or Virgin Mary, called Panagia (All-Holy) or Theotokos (Birth-giver of God). An ancient hymn sings: "He whom the entire universe could not contain was contained within your womb, O Theotokos." Her dying and ascending into Heaven is celebrated on August 15 (August 28 on the Julian calendar). In the Orthodox Church, Mary is considered the Great Example, the one whom we may emulate and follow to salvation; she leads the way. See also Theotokos.

Fathers, Orthodox—See *Church Fathers*.

Heart—The *Philokalia* defines this as "not simply the physical organ, but the spiritual center of man's being, man as made in the image of God, his deepest and truest self, or the inner shrine, to be entered only through sacrifice and death, in which the mystery of the union between the divine and the human is consummated" (*Philokalia* I:361). Within the Orthodox Tradition, the heart (usually the translation for the Greek word *nous*, though "intellect" is also misleadingly used) is properly understood to be the instrument or faculty by which the human person experiences God. In secular philosophy it has become commonplace to view the human person as a duality: mind and body. However, in Orthodox teaching, it is important to note that the heart is not the same as the mind, thereby reflecting the Orthodox Christian understanding of the human person as tripartite: body, soul, and *spirit*. The existence of the spiritual aspect of the human person reflects the placement of the heart (*nous*; the highest faculty in the human person) within that makeup and allows for the workings of the One, Holy Spirit: the third Person of the Holy Trinity. At the same time, drawing on Hebrew understanding, d'Olivet (378) describes the heart this way: the Hebrew word לֵב (*lev*) "constitutes a root whence emanate all ideas of vitality, passion, vigour, courage, audacity: literally, it is *the heart*, and figuratively, all things which pertain to that centre of life; every quality, every faculty resulting from the unfolding of the vital principle." Thus the heart is also the seat of passions and, if turned in self-glorification away from unity, hungering to become "for oneself," will fall into the disintegrations of desire. And St. John Climacus, in *The Ladder of Divine Ascent*, says that the "'Heart' has . . . an all-embracing significance: 'prayer of the heart' means prayer not just of the emotions and affections, but of the whole person, including the body" (*Philokalia*, Step 1:362). See also *Nous*.

Hesychia/Hesychast—A Greek word meaning "stillness." In practice, hesychia is the repetitive recitation of the Jesus Prayer (see below) in order to achieve inner stillness. The goal of achieving inner stillness, or hesychia, is to participate in the Uncreated Energy of God, which is manifest in the vision of the Uncreated Light, experienced especially among the Saints. The practice of hesychia is rooted in the ancient Eastern Orthodox tradition dating from the third, fourth, and fifth centuries and today is most commonly associated with the monks of Mt. Athos, although there are many other monasteries throughout the world devoted to its practice.

Holy Saturday—The Saturday that ends Holy Week, preparatory to Pascha (Western Easter). It is on this day that Christ, after His death and burial, descended into Hades to release from the bondage of sin and death all those who had died prior to this time. A resurrectional joy is already present in the Liturgy of this day, to which the change to white vestments and many of the Scripture readings give witness.

Holy Spirit—The Third Person of the Holy Trinity, who, as the Nicene-Constantinopolitan Creed states, "proceeds from the Father, who with the Father and the Son is worshipped and glorified, who spoke by the prophets." The Holy Spirit is of the same Uncreated Essence as the Father and the Son, yet was shared *energetically* with the Church on the first Pentecost (see Acts of the Apostles I).

Holy Trinity—See *Trinity*.

Humility—Also, following the Greek, *tapeinōsis*. The greatest of all the Christian virtues, because without humility it is impossible to attain any other virtue. The greatest example of humility in the Christian tradition is Christ Himself, whose supreme act of self-emptying love on the Cross fuels the ability for anyone who follows Him to attain to a humble spirit. The author also speaks of the Mother of God as the model of humility. Humility is the antidote for the initial sin of humanity in the Garden of Eden: pride.

Hypostasis—A Greek term denoting a unique realization of a nature, and often translated into English as "personhood." Throughout the writings of the Orthodox Church Fathers, hypostasis is utilized to distinguish between the three Persons (hypostases) of the Holy Trinity: Father, Son, and Holy Spirit, distinct in personhood, yet united in Divine nature. In patristic theology, all human beings have a distinct, unique hypostasis. In this volume, the author most often uses the phrase "hypostatic unity" to refer to an ontologically separate person (in the grammatical first person), as, for instance, opposed to a member of humanity spoken of in the third-person plural. Most crucially, he speaks of and values the intimate and free coming together of this essential human personhood, the "I," with God in His distinct divine personhood, as "Thou." See also *Ontological, Theosis, Deification*.

Icon—Greek for *image*. Within the Orthodox Church, *icon* is used to describe both the creation of humankind in the *image of God* (Gen. 1:26) and the painted icons of the incarnate Lord and His saints that are venerated by the Orthodox faithful. The painted icons are understood to be windows to heaven whereby the honor paid to the icon translates directly to the person depicted therein, and ultimately to God, never to the object itself.

Incarnate/Incarnation—A word of Latin origin literally meaning *enfleshment*. The Incarnation proper is the coming of the Son of God into the world and taking on human flesh (Gk. *sarx*) through the conception and birthgiving of the Virgin Mary (Theotokos, Birthgiver of God). Incarnation is discussed in various contexts herein, reflecting the idea that the Christian is called to *incarnate* the qualities of the divine life, which have their origin in God, the Holy Trinity. In this volume the author also frequently uses the word to show the action of one language opening to receive the spirit, and in some sense taking on the flesh of another.

Jesus Prayer—The full prayer is "Lord Jesus Christ, Son of God, have mercy upon me, a sinner," but shorter forms are also used. In the Orthodox Church, this prayer is The Prayer, *par excellence*, with its centering in on the name of Jesus. The prayer may date to the Egyptian desert of the third or fourth century, but it is also alluded to in the Scriptures themselves (see Matt. 9:27). Certain methods are employed at times to facilitate the practice of the prayer such as posture, breathing technique, or the use of a prayer rope (woolen or beaded; *chotki* in Russian, *komboskini* in Greek), by which the prayer is repeated knot by knot. See also *Hesychia*.

Judgments (*krimata*)—Heb. מִשְׁפָּטִים (*mishpatim*). These are revelations of God in *judicial* terms: that is, as specific applications of His teaching in situations of human dispute or conflict, applications that divinely resolve human conflict. These "judgments" therefore involve a considerable dimension of *prophetic* functioning: i.e., direct revelation of God's will for us.

Kathisma/Kathismata—The Psalter is divided into twenty *kathismata* (pl.), each with three *stases*. See table in appendix for kathismata appointed to be read each day of the week.

Kenosis/Kenotic—Derived from the Greek verb *kenou*, which carries the meaning of draining something empty. In the Christian context, an act of *kenosis* carries the weight of extreme humility, epitomized in the self-emptying love of Jesus Christ seen in His Incarnation and His death on the Cross (see Phil. 2:6–7).

Lent/Lenten/Great Lent—Also known as the Great Fast, in the Eastern Orthodox Church Great Lent is a forty-day period preceding Holy Week, which culminates in the celebration of Holy Pascha (Easter). It begins with a communal rite of forgiveness on Forgiveness Sunday. The Lenten Fast exists not solely for the purpose of eating less food or abstaining from particular foods, but also as a time to practice abstinence from harmful speech and actions, and to strengthen one's repentance, prayer life, and almsgiving to the poor. The goal of the Fast is to reach, in purity of heart, the much-anticipated Pascha of the Lord so as to participate in His resurrection and be, with Him, quickened into Life. See also *Ascesis*.

Liturgy/Liturgical—Gk. *leitourgia*, which in a Christian context refers to an act of worship to God involving both clergy and laity. All of the worship in the Eastern Orthodox Church is done liturgically, as it always involves the mind of the Church Fathers and the inherited traditions of worship received from God Himself (i.e., Eucharistic Communion). Even private prayer in the homes of the faithful involves the liturgical influences of the larger church community. The Divine Liturgy proper, resurrectional and paschal in spirit, is the Eucharistic service composed by Saints John Chrysostom and Basil the Great that is celebrated on Sundays and special feast days (and daily in most monasteries) by the faithful gathered together.

Law (*nomos*)—Heb. תורה (*torah*). One of the "nine words" of Psalm 118 (see chapter 11). This is the manifestation of God that is *active in the present instant*—and is always (i.e., eternally) so active. *Nomos* is what the Apostles behold at the Transfiguration.

Logismos (-oi)—Thought(s). The word "(i) frequently signifies not thought in the ordinary sense but thought provoked by the demons, and therefore often qualified in translation by the adjective 'evil' or 'demonic'; it can also signify divinely inspired thought; (ii) a 'conceptual image', intermediate between fantasy and an abstract concept" (*Philokalia*, Glossary, "Thought"). This difference in meaning results from the fall of man, after which his *nous*, the faculty by which he is able to know God, became darkened and enslaved by "the passions, anxiety and the conditions of the environment" (Archimandrite Hierotheos Vlachos, *Orthodox Spirituality*, 42). The author defines the phenomenon as *intrusive thoughts* (chaotic feelings; endless terrors; swirls of mental busyness; profound tiredness).

LXX—The Roman numerals signifying *seventy*. This is a common abbreviation for the Septuagint text of the Old Testament, a translation carried out in the third century BC by seventy-two scholars (six from each of the Twelve Tribes of Israel). See *Septuagint*.

Masoretic Text (MT)—Refers to the extant Hebrew text of the Old Testament Scriptures, dating from around the ninth century AD. It differs in significant ways from the Hebrew original, of which much was lost in the destruction of Jerusalem in AD 70. Most English-language Bibles today are based on the Masoretic text. The Orthodox Church, however, prefers the Septuagint (LXX) as a more accurate witness to the original Hebrew, as the text quoted throughout the New Testament, and as a text more open (Prof. Sheehan says) to the incarnation of Jesus as the Messiah soon to come. For the reader who wants to pursue further the question of the dating of the Masoretic text, Fr. John Konkle offers this link: www.quora.com/Is-septuagint-older-than-masoretic-text

Matins—The morning office of the daily liturgical cycle. In Greek practice, Matins (Orthros) is celebrated in the morning preceding the Divine Liturgy. In Slavic churches, it is often customary to follow Vespers with the Matins service in the evening. The Matins service has many distinctive characteristics, one of which is the reading of the canon in honor of the saint or feast of the day.

Mind of Christ—Derives from Saint Paul, 1 Corinthians 2:16: "We have the mind of Christ." Prof. Sheehan has written that "we possess in ourselves the mind of Christ *solely because* God has given us this mind in order that we may know—in Saint Paul's own words—'the things freely given us by God' (1 Cor 2:12). Itself a gift, the mind of Christ in us is thus the mode wherein we know God's gifts" (Sheehan, *Psalms*, xxv). See Donald Sheehan, "The Mind of David and the Mind of Christ," Introduction to *The Psalms of David*.

Monk/Monasticism/Monastery—In Greek, *monos* means alone, corresponding to the Latin *solus*. The monastic life is characterized by various forms ranging from a community of persons (living within a coenobitic monastery) to the solitary eremitic life. The goal of monastic life is separation from the world in order to attain union with God. The goal in such separation is not to cut oneself off from the world utterly, but to be better able to love and pray for the world, having gained a spiritual state unaffected by the distractions and demands of worldly life through rigorous self-denial, volitional obedience, and the practice of inner prayer. Since the fourth century, monasticism and its spiritual witness have provided a crucial foundation and balance-point within the Orthodox Church.

Mother of God—See Theotokos; Dormition.

Mt. Athos/Athonite—A peninsula and mountain geographically located in the northeasternmost part of Greece, jutting out into the Aegean Sea. It is an autonomous polity of the Hellenic Republic. According to Orthodox tradition, the Virgin Mary was traveling with Saint John the Evangelist through the Aegean and, forced to land on the peninsula, was so moved by its beauty that she blessed it and asked that her Son give it to her to be her garden. His voice was heard to answer: "Let this place be your inheritance and your garden, a paradise and a haven of salvation for those seeking to be saved." Also called the Holy Mountain, it has existed as a monastic stronghold since the mid-tenth century, when Saint Athanasius founded the first monastic community known as the Great Lavra, which still exists today. The peninsula today is home to twenty monasteries as well as numerous sketes and hermitages. The term Athonite simply describes those monastics attached to a community on the Holy Mountain as well as those practices which have their origin there, and, in the author's experience, it implies a certain "savor."

Nine Words—In the LXX translation, nine Greek words are used for the various kinds of "law" mentioned in Psalms, especially in Psalms 18 and 118. They are *commandments, statutes, law, word, testimonies, teaching, judgments, way,* and *path.* The author pays a great deal of attention to these, especially in chapter 11; his brief definitions will be found in this glossary.

Nous/Noetic—Defined by the *Philokalia* as "the highest faculty in man, through which—provided it is purified—he knows God or the inner essences or principles of created things by means of direct apprehension or spiritual perception" (I:362). This faculty is distinguished from the reason or mind (*dianoia*), which works by sequences of logical connections. See also *Heart.*

Ontological—Derived from Gk. *ontos,* "being." Matters concerned with ontology have to do with the very being or essences of things. When the Orthodox Church Fathers speak of the ontology of God, they refer to God's uncreated essence or being, which is outside the realm of human understanding on *any* level. In reference to humans, ontology refers to the being or *is*ness of a person or what is often called personhood. To be affected on an ontological level is to be changed in a manner that is so fundamental as to change one's very being. See also *Hypostasis.*

Orthodox Church—The second largest Christian Church in the world, also called the Eastern Orthodox Church because of a division between the Eastern (centered in Constantinople) and Western (centered in Rome) halves of the Roman Empire that culminated in 1054 with mutual excommunication. The schism was based on growing differences of doctrine, politics, and practice (such as the Roman papal claim to primacy), leading finally to a change in the Nicene-Constantinopolitan Creed by Rome that was rejected by the East. Today approximately 300 million Christians worldwide follow the faith and practices that were defined by the first seven ecumenical councils. The councils that are recognized in the Eastern Orthodox Church are: Nicea I, 325; Constantinople I, 381; Ephesus, 431; Chalcedon, 451; Constantinople II, 553; Constantinople III, 680; and Nicea II, 787. The adherence to these particular councils is the full expression of what is understood to be the Orthodox Christian Faith.

The Orthodox Church found its way to North America with the arrival of Russian missionaries in Kodiak, Alaska, in 1794; and over the next centuries, through Greek, Slavic, Middle Eastern, and other Eastern Orthodox peoples' immigration to North America. Estimates of North American Orthodox today, both ethnic and converts, range from three to six million.

Path (*tribos*)—Heb. נְתִיבָה (*nethivah*). One of the "nine words" of Psalm 118. Largely synonymous in meaning with "way" (*hodos*), "path" differs in being a word of high literary antiquity—much the way the English word "abode" or "domicile" differs from "home" or "house."

Patristic—Those writings and teachings that were written by or refer to the Fathers of the Church. See *Church Fathers*.

Philokalia—An anthology of patristic writings on prayer first compiled by Saint Nicodemus of the Holy Mountain in the latter half of the eighteenth century. The title means "Love of the Beautiful," conveying the goal of the work, which is to guide the monastic in a life of purification from sin and attaining of the virtues. Translated into English in the 1980s, the work is read throughout the English-speaking Orthodox world today.

Pleonexia—Endless desiring. The author identifies *pleonexia* with the

Adamic fall. He writes: "The strength to master all things—especially the mastery over *pleonexia*—is a power arising solely from godliness. And godliness . . . occurs solely when all desire becomes an inclination of the heart to be rooted in God's testimonies."

Precepts—The orders that God gives concerning things He has given into our care (e.g., our family). This word (*piqqudim* in Hebrew) is absorbed in LXX Psalms into Greek *entolai*, "commandments," and *dikaiomata*, "statutes," signaling, the author says, a recognition of continuity between the divinely shaped statutes and certain historically actualized and human patterns of existence.

Repentance—Known as *metanoia* in Greek, it simply means a change of mind or purpose, a "turning around." John the Baptist, called the Forerunner, first sounded the call to "Repent, for the Kingdom of heaven is at hand!" (Matt. 3:2). One of Christ's first proclamations was to "Repent and believe in the gospel" (Mark 1:15). It is therefore with such primacy that the Orthodox Church regards repentance. While the act of repentance may have a simple inward movement behind it, it calls for the reorientation of one's whole life to God.

Saint Athanasius—Bishop of Alexandria and major theological writer in the fourth century. He wrote a treatise *On the Incarnation*, affirming that Jesus Christ was both God and man; participated in the first Council of Nicea in 325, which produced the Nicene (called by some the Athanasian) Creed; and he devoted much of his life, some of it in exile, to combatting the Arian heresy (which denied the divinity of the Son) and defending Nicene, Trinitarian Orthodoxy. See also *Hypostasis*; *Trinity*.

Saint Gregory of Nyssa—One of the great Cappadocian Fathers, Gregory of Nyssa (335–95) was the younger brother of Saint Basil the Great. He was instrumental in gaining victory for the Nicene doctrines promulgated at the Council of Constantinople in 381. Saint Gregory is also well-known as an apophatic theologian, utilizing negative terminology to describe divine concepts outside the realm of human understanding. This gained him a strong hand in battling the Arians, especially the heretic Eunomius, with whom he engaged in doctrinal battle in order to defend his departed brother Basil.

Saint Isaac the Syrian—Also known as Isaac of Nineveh, he was born in Kurdistan in the first half of the seventh century and resided as a monastic near modern-day Qatar. He was elected to the episcopacy in Nineveh, but sought to be released from this responsibility in order to pursue ascetic discipline. Having retired to the wilderness, he labored in fasting, prayer, and writing spiritual works, being so zealous in his labors that he lost his sight. He reposed in a monastery at the end of his life and is commemorated on January 28. His *Homilies* are considered "with the *Ladder* of Saint John Climacus, the indispensable guide for every Orthodox soul to journey safely towards God" (Hieromonk Makarios of Simonos Petra, *The Synaxarion: The Lives of the Saints of the Orthodox Church* [Ormylia (Chalkidike), Greece: Convent of the Annunciation of Our Lady, 2000], 3:337).

Saint John Climacus—Born in the latter part of the sixth century, he entered the Monastery of Saint Catherine on the Sinai Peninsula at the age of sixteen. Throughout his monastic life he advanced as a true example of asceticism to the point of becoming the Abbot of the Monastery. The name "Climacus" literally means "of the ladder" and refers to his most well-known written instruction entitled *The Ladder of Divine Ascent*.

Salvific—An adjective used to describe things pertaining to salvation; that is, those things which enact theosis in the life of an Orthodox Christian, transforming the entire being so that it may partake of the divine life of the Holy Trinity.

Septuagint/LXX—The Greek translation of the Hebrew Old Testament Scriptures. The title refers to the traditional understanding that seventy-two Hebrew scholars (six from each of the

Twelve Tribes) were called to Alexandria by the Pharaoh Ptol-
emy (reigned 285–46 BC) to translate the Hebrew Scriptures
into Greek, as knowledge of Hebrew was seen to be declining
in the Empire. The Septuagint represents a closer historical
link to the original writings of the Old Testament than any
other translation that exists today. For this reason, and because
of its use in the Hellenistic world during the spread of Christianity, it is held to be the authoritative text of the Old Testament in the Orthodox Church. See also *Masoretic Hebrew*.

Sin/Transgression—Sin (Gk. *hamartia*) literally means "to miss the
mark." In the Orthodox Christian understanding, sin is a
disease with which all humanity is afflicted, although we are
not utterly steeped in it from birth, as taught in the Western
Augustinian tradition (based, in the Orthodox view, on a
slight but crucial mistranslation into Latin of Romans 5:12).
Rather than inheriting the *guilt* of Adam's sin in the Garden
of Eden, humankind is afflicted with the *effects* of that sin,
especially death, under the shadow of which we are inclined,
over and over, to "miss the mark" of union with God. "Transgression" implies a deliberate trespass that results from the
condition of sin, though often the two are used synonymously.

Son of God—A title properly given to Jesus Christ, the Uncreated Son
of God, begotten of the Father before all time began. The title
denotes Christ's role within the Triune Godhead as well as
His fully divine nature, which He joined with human nature
in His single hypostasis (person) in the Incarnation. It also
denotes His birth from a virgin, as His Father is God.

Soteriological—Pertaining to salvation.

Spiritual Father—The tradition of spiritual fatherhood is ancient,
being expressed in the Bible as far back as Elijah and Elisha
(see 2 Kings 2:9–14) and continues in the Orthodox Church
today. The role of a spiritual father ranges from that of a priest
who is the consistent confessor for a person, to one who is a
spiritual guide in all aspects of life, down to the most practical

elements. The role of a spiritual father also differs depending on whether one lives within a monastic community or in the world, though many Orthodox who live in the world seek out spiritual fathers from within the monasteries.

Statutes (*dikaiomata*)—Heb. חֻקִּים (*huqqim*) and פִּקּוּדִים (*piqqudim*). One of the "nine words" of Psalm 118. The divine cuttings-into (or inscriptions) left by God in the creation to become the nourishment that powers our own true creativity; the divinely created acts whereby God formed the foundational patterns (better: the musical scores) of the entire creation, patterns within which all creation takes life and moves. They are, to us, incomprehensible and mysterious, for their roots are not in this world but in His infinite wisdom. The Greek *dikaiomata* also absorbs a number of instances of the Hebrew *piqqudim*, rendered "precepts" in translations based in the Masoretic Text.

Subdeacon/Subdiaconate—One of the minor clerical orders in the Orthodox Church. It follows the order of reader and precedes that of deacon. Modern-day subdeacons function primarily as attendants in the sanctuary (altar area) of the Church, especially in the presence of the bishop.

Teaching (*logion*)—Heb. אִמְרָה (*imrah*). One of the "nine words" of Psalm 118. (See chapter 11.) The expressed voice of God, the divine word (*logos*) become incarnate as a reality fully audible to human comprehension; hence, Scripture understood as the unceasingly living voice of Christ.

Testimonies (*martyriai*)—Heb. עֵדוּת (*eduth*). One of the "nine words" of Psalm 118. (See chapter 11.) The witnesses (especially the saints and *martyrs*) in actual human history of the divine *statutes*; that is, the *statutes* as active in the historical record.

Theoria—A Greek term referring to contemplation of God. True divine theoria does not refer to theory in the sense that the modern scientific community would frame it in. Far from being a matter subjected to human reason, divine theoria is suprarational and bestowed by the grace of God. Contemplation of

God occurs when a person has been cleansed from sin and the passions and can therefore begin to behold the Beauty of God by divine grace. Theoria is the second of three stages of the spiritual life described in the *Philokalia*, following catharsis (purification) and preceding theosis (deification).

Theosis—A condition of the soul in which "God fully bestows His glory upon man and thereby fully creates harmony between Himself and man *at the same moment* man remains fully distinct from God" (DS; see chapter 12). Theosis "literally means to become gods by Grace. The biblical words that are synonymous and descriptive of theosis are: adoption, redemption, inheritance, glorification, holiness, and perfection. Theosis is the acquisition of the Holy Spirit, whereby through Grace one becomes participant in the *Kingdom of God*. Theosis is an act of the uncreated and infinite love of God. It begins here in time and space, but it is not static or complete, and is an open-ended progression uninterrupted through all eternity" (Archimandrite George, *Theosis: The True Purpose of Human Life*, 86). See also *Deification*.

Theotokos—A Greek term meaning *Birthgiver of God* used in the Orthodox Church as a title of veneration for the Virgin Mary, the mother of Jesus Christ. The title was officially endorsed at the First Council of Ephesus in 431 and later ratified at Chalcedon in 451, in confirmation of the Orthodox understanding that the son to whom Mary gave birth was in very truth the Son of God, both wholly human and wholly divine. An often-used synonymous title is Mother of God. Greek Orthodox often use Panagia, meaning the All-Holy One. See also *Dormition*.

Tradition—Stemming from the Latin root *traditio* (Gk. *paradosis*), the word itself generally implies transmission, especially with regard to teaching and practice. In the Orthodox Church tradition can be understood in two aspects: Holy Tradition, which bears witness to the unchangeable doctrines of the Christian faith, such as the Virgin Birth, Jesus Christ being both God and man, etc.; and tradition that relates more to custom, i.e. those details of church life that are practiced especially with regard to various ethnicities and localities, and practices that come down to us through commonly accepted local historical witness. However, in the Orthodox view, these two aspects of Tradition are in no way separable but are part of a single all-encompassing reality of the life of the Church, continually inspired by the Holy Spirit in every age and in every place.

Transgression—See *Sin*.

Trinity/Holy Trinity—The Holy Trinity is the communion of the Father, Son, and Holy Spirit, which exists as God. While the three persons are distinct in personhood (hypostasis), they all share the same Uncreated Essence, incommunicable (except in its Energies) to human beings or to anything in the created world. While the Holy Trinity is a common doctrine of all traditional Christian confessions, its doctrine in the Orthodox Church is distinctive, beginning with reference to the three distinct Persons, as opposed to the One Essence that is emphasized in most Western confessions.

Way (*hodos*)—דֶּרֶךְ (*derekh*). One of the "nine words" of Psalm 118 (see chapter 11). This word signifies the human activity of moving toward union with God. The word's emphasis is on the actual practice of the movement; hence, it signifies ascetic practice. Psalm 118 opens, "Blessed are the blameless in the way, / Who walk in the law of the Lord."

Word (*logos*)—Heb. דָּבָר (*davar*). One of the "nine words" of Psalm 118 (see chapter 11). The *spoken* manifestation of God, the divine voice to which all creation responds because all creation arises from His *logos*. "Let there be light," says God in creating the world (Gen. 1:3): here is *logos*. And we hear the same divine Word speaking at the Transfiguration: "This is My beloved Son" (Matt. 17:5).

BIBLIOGRAPHY

Alter, Robert. *The Art of Biblical Narrative.* New York: Basic Books, 1981.

———, and Frank Kermode, eds. *The Literary Guide to the Bible.* Cambridge, MA: Belknap Press of Harvard University Press, 1990.

Athanasius (Saint), Patriarch of Alexandria. *St. Athanasius On the Incarnation: The Treatise* De Incarnatione. Verbi Dei. London, England: A. R. Mowbray & Co. 1970.

Biblia Hebraica Stuttgartensia: SESB Version. Electronic ed. Stuttgart, Germany: German Bible Society, 2003.

Braude, William G., translator. *The Midrash on Psalms.* New Haven, CT: Yale University Press, 1959.

Breck, John. *Scripture in Tradition: The Bible and Its Interpretation in the Orthodox Church.* Crestwood, NY: St. Vladimir's Seminary Press, 2001.

———. *The Shape of Biblical Language: Chiasmus in the Scriptures and Beyond.* Crestwood, NY: St Vladimir's Seminary Press, 1994.

Brenton, Lancelot C. L. *The Septuagint with Apocrypha: Greek and English.* Grand Rapids, MI: Zondervan, 1982.

Brown, Francis. *The New Brown–Driver–Briggs–Gesenius Hebrew and English Lexicon.* Peabody, MA: Hendrickson, 1979. Cited in notes as BDB, with the page (and sometimes volume) number of a combined 4-volume edition sequentially numbered.

Buber, Martin. *Good and Evil: Two Interpretations.* New York, NY: Charles Scribner's Sons, 1953.

———. *Right and Wrong: An Interpretation of Some Psalms.* Translated by Ronald Gregor Smith. Norwich, England: SCM Press, 1952.

Chariton (Igumen), ed. *The Art of Prayer: An Orthodox Anthology.* Revised edition. New York, NY: Farrar, Straus and Giroux, 1997.

Climacus, John (Saint). *The Ladder of Divine Ascent.* Boston, MA: Holy Transfiguration Monastery, 2001. The author also used the Classics of Western Spirituality edition. Mahwah, NJ: Paulist Press, 1982. Cited in text as *Ladder* with Step and Paragraph.

[Pseudo-]Dionysius. *Complete Works.* Classics of Western Spirituality. "The Mystical Theology" and "The Divine Names." Translated by Paul Rorem. Mahwah, NJ: Paulist Press, 1987.

Dostoevsky, Fyodor. *The Brothers Karamazov.* Translated and annotated by Richard Pevear and Larissa Volokhonsky. San Francisco, CA: North Point Press, 1990. Reprinted New York: Vintage, 1991. [Dr. Sheehan strongly recommended this translation, as made by Orthodox believers who understood and faithfully represented the Orthodox religion and culture about which Dostoevsky writes. —*Ed.*]

Florensky, Fr. Pavel. *The Pillar and Ground of the Truth.* Translated by Boris Jakim. Princeton, NJ: Princeton University Press, 1997.

Florovsky, G., to S. Sakharov. May 15, 1958. In: Archimandrit Sofronii [Sakharov], *Perepiska s Protoiereem Georgiem Florovskim.* Essex/Moscow: Svyato-Ioanno-Predtechenskii Monastyr'/Svyato-Troitskaya Sergieva Lavra, 2008. (Reference courtesy of †Fr. Matthew Baker).

George (Archimandrite). *Theosis: The True Purpose of Human Life.* Mount Athos, Greece: Holy Monastery of St. Gregorios, 2006. Also available online at http://orthodoxinfo.com/general/theosis-english.pdf.

Gesenius, H. F. W. *Gesenius' Hebrew Grammar.* Edited by E. Kautzsch and A. E. Cowley. Oxford, England: Oxford University Press. Edition unknown.

Groopman, Jerome. "A Model Patient: How Simulators are Changing the Way a Doctor Is Trained." *The New Yorker*, May 2, 2005.

Hartman, G. H., ed. *Midrash and Literature.* New Haven, CT: Yale University Press, 1986.

Hatch, Edwin, and Henry A. Redpath. *A Concordance to the Septuagint.* Second edition. Grand Rapids, MI: Baker Books, 1998. Cited in notes as HR.

Heil, Gunther, and A. M. Ritter. *Corpus Dionysiacum.* Berlin, Germany: DeGruyter, 1990. Penguin Classics, 2005. New edition.

Heine, Ronald E. *Gregory of Nyssa's Treatise on the Inscriptions of the Psalms.* New York, NY: Oxford University Press, 1995. Cited in notes as Heine, followed by Gregory's original part and paragraph numbers and the page number in this edition.

Herbert, George. *The Complete English Poems.* Edited by John Tobin. London, England: 2005.

Isaac the Syrian, Saint. *The Ascetical Homilies of St. Isaac the Syrian.* Boston, MA: Holy Transfiguration Monastery, 1984. This book has now been corrected and reprinted and is available in a revised second edition (Boston, MA: Holy Transfiguration Monastery, 2011), but with different pagination. Cited in notes by homily and the page number of the 1984 edition.

John Climacus (Saint). *The Ladder of Divine Ascent.* Boston, MA: Holy Transfiguration Monastery, 2001. Cited in notes as *Ladder*, followed by step and paragraph.

John of Damascus (Saint). *Writings. Fathers of the Church Patristic Series.* Translated by Frederic H. Chase, Jr. Catholic University Press of America, 1999.

Lampe, G. W. H. *A Patristic Greek Lexicon.* Oxford, England: Clarendon Press, 1969.

Lewis, C. S. *The Abolition of Man.* San Francisco, CA: HarperOne, 2001.

Lust, Johan, Erik Eynikel, Katrin Hauspie. *Greek English Lexicon of the Septuagint.* Part 2. Stuttgart, Germany: Deutsche Bibelgesellschaft, 1992 (Part 1) and 1996 (Part 2). Cited in notes as Lust.

Makarios (Hieromonk) of Simonos Petra. *The Synaxarion: The Lives of the Saints of the Orthodox Church.* Ormylia (Chalkidike), Greece: Convent of the Annunciation of Our Lady, 2000.

Maria, Mother [Lydia Gysi]. *Evil in the New Testament.* Toronto, Ontario: Peregrina, 2nd edition 1996.

————. *Orthodox Potential.* North Yorkshire, England: Greek Orthodox Monastery of the Assumption, 1973.

————. *The Psalms: An Exploratory Translation.* North Yorkshire, England: Greek Orthodox Monastery of the Assumption, 1973.

Mullins, Hilary. "The Transfiguration of Don Sheehan." *Numero Cinq Magazine*: http://numerocinqmagazine.com/2013/08/06/the-transfiguration-of-don-sheehan-essay-hilary-mullins/

Norris, Kathleen. *The Psalms.* New York, NY: Riverhead Books, 1997.

d'Olivet, Fabre. *The Hebraic Tongue Restored.* 1815. Translated by Nayán Louise Redfield. New York, NY: G. P. Putnam's Sons, 1921.

Orthodox Study Bible: Ancient Christianity Speaks to Today's World. Nashville, TN: Thomas Nelson, 2008.

Peterson, Eugene H. *Answering God: The Psalms as Tools for Prayer.* San Francisco, CA: HarperOne reprint edition, 1991.

_____. *Leap Over a Wall.* San Francisco, CA: HarperOne, 1998.

Philokalia. Compiled by St. Nikodimos of the Holy Mountain and St. Makarios of Corinth. Translated and edited by G. E. H. Palmer, Philip Sherrard, Kallistos Ware. Volumes 1, 2, and 4. London, Boston: Faber and Faber, 1981.

The Psalter According to the Seventy. Boston, MA: Holy Transfiguration Monastery, 1997.

Rahlfs, Alfred. *Septuaginta.* Stuttgart, Germany: Deutsche Bibelgesellschaft, 1979.

Saint Herman of Alaska Brotherhood. *Conquering Depression: Heavenly Wisdom from God Illumined Teachers.* Platina, CA: St. Herman Press, 1996.

Sheehan, Donald. *The Grace of Incorruption: The Selected Essays of Donald Sheehan on Orthodox Faith and Poetics.* Edited by Xenia Sheehan. Orleans, MA: Paraclete, 2015.

_____. *The Psalms of David: Translated from the Septuagint Greek by Donald Sheehan.* Edited by Xenia Sheehan and Hieromonk Herman Majkrzak. Eugene, OR: Wipf and Stock, 2013.

Sophrony [Sakharov] (Archimandrite; now Saint). *St. Silouan the Athonite.* Translated by Rosemary Edmonds. Crestwood, NY: St. Vladimir's Seminary Press, 1991.

———. *Wisdom from Mount Athos*. Crestwood, NY: St. Vladimir's Seminary Press, 2001.

Steiner, George. *After Babel: Aspects of Language and Translation*. Oxford, England: Oxford University Press, 2nd ed. 1998.

Taylor, Bernard A. *The Analytical Lexicon to the Septuagint*. Grand Rapids, MI: Zondervan, 1994.

Tehillim. Psalms: A New Translation with Commentary Anthologized from Talmudic, Midrashic, and Rabbinic Sources. English and Hebrew edition. Art Scroll, Mesorah Publications, 1986. Two volumes with continuous numbering.

Vlachos, Hierotheos (Archimandrite). *Orthodox Spirituality*. Levadia, Greece: Birth of the Theotokos Monastery, 1994.

Ware, Timothy (Metropolitan Kallistos). "The Debate about Palamism." *Eastern Churches Review* 9.1–2.

The Way of a Pilgrim and The Pilgrim Continues His Way. Translated from the Russian by R. M. French. Seabury Press, 1970. Most easily available today in this translation as a HarperOne edition published in 2010.

Wharton, E. R. *Etyma Graeca: An Etymological Lexicon of Classical Greek*. London, England: Percival and Co., 1890.

Zizioulas, John D. (Bishop). "The Contribution of Cappadocia to Christian Thought." *Sinasos in Cappadocia*. Edited by Frosso Pimenides, Stelios Roades. National Trust for Greece: Agra Publications, 1986.

SCRIPTURE INDEX

SUBJECT INDEX

A

Absalom, 89, 91, 93–94, 99, 109
abundant life, 1
actual, Psalms as, 6–7
Adam, 192, 226, 259
Adrian, Fr., of New Diveyevo, 216
affliction, 10, 183, 195, 197. *See also* brokenness; depression; humility
Akathist to the Mother of God, 26–27
Akel Dama (Field of Blood), xxviii–xxx
aleph, 205–6. See also *Aleph*-stanza under Psalm 118
Alexander, Christopher, 244, 251
aloe, 136
alphabetic sequence, Hebrew, 191–92
Alter, Robert, 16, 83–84, 94
alternating *(alloiōthēsomenōn/ shanah)*, 146–47
Amnon, 89, 91–92, 93
angels, 68, 71–72, 75, 87–88, 152
Ascension, xxvix
ascetic beauty, 146, 147–48, 238–39, 244, 257–58, 264
ascetic clarification, 137, 142–43, 144, 145–46, 147, 264
asceticism, 41–42, 55, 245, 260–61
asymmetricality, 174–75, 178–79, 182–83, 185–86, 187, 189
attentiveness, 15–16, 50

B

Babel narrative, 20
babies, murder of, 80
baptism, xxvix
Beatitudes, 116
beholding *(epiblepō)*, 202, 203, 204
beth, 205–6. See also *Beth*-stanza under Psalm 118
blessedness *(makarios)*, 76–77, 79–80, 113–14, 158, 178, 196, 197–98
blessing *(eulogia)*, 99–100
Body and Bride of Christ, 17, 134–35, 237, 261–62
bondage, 62–63, 260–61
boundless, Psalms as, 7
brokenness, 65, 84, 209. *See also* affliction; communion; depression
The Brown-Driver-Briggs-Gesenius Hebrew and English Lexicon (Brown), 8, 48, 193, 228
Buber, Martin, 148, 156
Buddhism, 11
burning bush, 35

C

cadential shape, 67–68, 72, 77–78, 241. *See also* chiastic structure
cassia, 136
ceaseless prayer, 14, 54, 87–88, 114
chanting, 58
chiastic structure
introduction, 69–70
chiastic center within Psalms, 158–59

ABOUT THE AUTHOR AND EDITOR

B orn in 1940, DONALD SHEEHAN received a Ph.D. in English from the University of Wisconsin–Madison, where he was also Managing Editor of Wisconsin Studies in Contemporary Literature. He taught at the University of Chicago, Franconia (NH) College, Plymouth (NH) State College, and Dartmouth College. He concurrently directed the Robert Frost Place Center for Poetry and the Arts in Franconia, NH (1978–2005), creating and directing a now internationally acclaimed poetry writing program. After becoming an Orthodox Christian in 1984, he spent the rest of his life revising all of his understanding and teaching to accord with his new faith. Along the way he taught himself Classical Greek, Biblical Hebrew, and LXX Greek.

His books include Fr. Pavel Florensky's *Iconostasis*, co-translated with Olga Andrejev (St. Vladimir's Seminary Press, 1996); *The Psalms of David, Translated from the LXX Greek by Donald Sheehan*, ed. Xenia Sheehan and Hieromonk Herman Majkrzak (Wipf & Stock, 2013); and *The Grace of Incorruption: The Selected Essays of Donald Sheehan on Orthodox Faith and Poetics*, ed. Xenia Sheehan

(Paraclete, 2015). He also published a number of articles and was involved in several books published by the Frost Place. He died in 2010 in Charleston, SC, and is buried at Panagia Proussiotissa Monastery in Troy, NC.

XENIA SHEEHAN, born in 1941, holds a BA in Philosophy (Antioch College, 1963) and an MA in Counseling (Norwich University); completed coursework towards an MA in English (UW–Madison), and studied theology at St. Vladimir's and St. Tikhon's Seminaries. She has raised two sons, created several alternative schools, built an off-grid house, worked as a counselor, and edited many books, beginning at the University of Wisconsin Press, then the University Press of New England, and finally freelancing. She has previously edited and published two posthumous volumes of her husband's work, as named above. Baptized in the Orthodox Church in 1989, she currently lives near the Holy Dormition Orthodox Monastery in Rives Junction, Michigan.

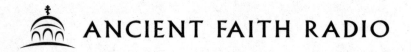